Exam Ref AZ-700 Designing and Implementing Microsoft Azure Networking Solutions

Charles Pluta

Exam Ref AZ-700 Designing and Implementing Microsoft Azure Networking Solutions

Published with the authorization of Microsoft Corporation by:
Pearson Education, Inc.

Copyright © 2022 by Pearson Education, Inc.

ISBN-13: 978-0-13-768277-5
ISBN-10: 0-13-768277-8

Library of Congress Control Number: 2022933634

1 2022

TRADEMARKS

WARNING AND DISCLAIMER

SPECIAL SALES

For information about buying this title in bulk quantities, or for special sales opportunities (which may include electronic versions; custom cover designs; and content particular to your business, training goals, marketing focus, or branding interests), please contact our corporate sales department at corpsales@pearsoned.com or (800) 382-3419.

For government sales inquiries, please contact governmentsales@pearsoned.com.

For questions about sales outside the U.S., please contact intlcs@pearson.com.

CREDITS

EDITOR-IN-CHIEF
Brett Bartow

EXECUTIVE EDITOR
Loretta Yates

SPONSORING EDITOR
Charvi Arora

DEVELOPMENT EDITOR
Songlin Qiu

MANAGING EDITOR
Sandra Schroeder

SENIOR PROJECT EDITOR
Tracey Croom

COPY EDITOR
Scout Festa

INDEXER
Timothy Wright

PROOFREADER
Gill Editorial Services

TECHNICAL EDITOR
Thomas Palathra

EDITORIAL ASSISTANT
Cindy Teeters

COVER DESIGNER
Twist Creative, Seattle

COMPOSITOR
codeMantra

Pearson's Commitment to Diversity, Equity, and Inclusion

Pearson is dedicated to creating bias-free content that reflects the diversity of all learners. We embrace the many dimensions of diversity, including but not limited to race, ethnicity, gender, socioeconomic status, ability, age, sexual orientation, and religious or political beliefs.

Education is a powerful force for equity and change in our world. It has the potential to deliver opportunities that improve lives and enable economic mobility. As we work with authors to create content for every product and service, we acknowledge our responsibility to demonstrate inclusivity and incorporate diverse scholarship so that everyone can achieve their potential through learning. As the world's leading learning company, we have a duty to help drive change and live up to our purpose to help more people create a better life for themselves and to create a better world.

Our ambition is to purposefully contribute to a world where:

- Everyone has an equitable and lifelong opportunity to succeed through learning.
- Our educational products and services are inclusive and represent the rich diversity of learners.
- Our educational content accurately reflects the histories and experiences of the learners we serve.
- Our educational content prompts deeper discussions with learners and motivates them to expand their own learning (and worldview).

While we work hard to present unbiased content, we want to hear from you about any concerns or needs with this Pearson product so that we can investigate and address them.

- Please contact us with concerns about any potential bias at https://www.pearson.com/report-bias.html.

Contents at a glance

Contents

Chapter 4   Secure and monitor networks   159

Acknowledgments

I would like to thank my wife, Jennifer, for being supportive and putting up with the odd hours getting this book finished. To Elias Mereb and Brian Svidergol, thank you for the years of friendship, conferences, dinners, and everything else. And to my friends and colleagues Ed Gale, Joshua Waddell, and Aaron Lines, thank you for your friendship, mentorship, and advice the last couple of years. To all the cloud professionals and readers of this book, thank you for taking the time to read, explore, learn, test, and "play around" with these technologies while you are learning. Keep it up, and good luck!

About the Author

CHARLES PLUTA is a technical consultant and Microsoft Certified Trainer who has authored several certification exams, lab guides, and learner guides for various technology vendors. As a technical consultant, Charles has assisted small, medium, and large organizations in deploying and maintaining their IT infrastructure. He is also a speaker, staff member, or trainer at several large industry conferences every year. Charles has a degree in Computer Networking and holds over 25 industry certifications. He makes a point to leave the United States to travel to a different country once every year. When not working on training or traveling, he plays pool in Augusta, Georgia.

Introduction

This book takes a high-level approach to the list of topics and skills measured on the Designing and Implementing Microsoft Azure Networking Solutions (AZ-700) exam, which is required to obtain the Microsoft Certified: Azure Network Engineer Associate certification. This exam focuses on networking topics in Microsoft Azure, but it does require additional knowledge of the Azure Portal and related services such as virtual machines, storage accounts, monitoring tools, and more. If you are not already familiar with general Azure services, I suggest that you begin with Azure Fundamentals (AZ-900) or Azure Administrator (AZ-104) before focusing on this exam.

This book provides step-by-step examples of configuring the Azure services that are outlined in the topic list using the Azure Portal. However, the certification exam could also ask you questions about PowerShell or CLI commands that perform the same actions as those in the portal. You should use this book as a supplement to your learning journey and practice other methods of configuring these services in addition to what is outlined in the book.

This book covers every major topic area found on the exam, but it does not cover every exam question. Only the Microsoft exam team has access to the exam questions, and Microsoft regularly adds new questions to the exam, making it impossible to cover specific questions. You should consider this book a supplement to your relevant real-world experience and other study materials. If you encounter a topic in this book that you do not feel completely comfortable with, use the "Need more review?" links you'll find in the text to find more information, and take the time to research and study the topic. Great information is available on MSDN, on TechNet, and in blogs and forums.

Organization of this book

This book is organized by the "Skills measured" list published for the exam. The "Skills measured" list is available for each exam on the Microsoft Learn website: *http://aka.ms/examlist*. Each chapter in this book corresponds to a major topic area in the list, and the technical tasks in each topic area determine a chapter's organization. If an exam covers six major topic areas, for example, the book will contain six chapters.

Microsoft certifications

Microsoft certifications distinguish you by proving your command of a broad set of skills and experience with current Microsoft products and technologies. The exams and corresponding certifications are developed to validate your mastery of critical competencies as you design and develop, or implement and support, solutions with Microsoft products and technologies both on-premises and in the cloud. Certification brings a variety of benefits to the individual and to employers and organizations.

> **NEED MORE REVIEW?**   **ALL MICROSOFT CERTIFICATIONS**
>
> For information about Microsoft certifications, including a full list of available certifications, go to *http://www.microsoft.com/learn*.

Check back often to see what is new!

Errata, updates, and book support

We've made every effort to ensure the accuracy of this book and its companion content. You can access updates to this book—in the form of a list of submitted errata and their related corrections—at:

MicrosoftPressStore.com/ExamRefAZ700/errata

If you discover an error that is not already listed, please submit it to us at the same page.

For additional book support and information, please visit

MicrosoftPressStore.com/Support

Please note that product support for Microsoft software and hardware is not offered through the previous addresses. For help with Microsoft software or hardware, go to *http://support.microsoft.com*.

Stay in touch

Let's keep the conversation going! We're on Twitter: *http://twitter.com/MicrosoftPress*.

CHAPTER 1

Design, implement, and manage hybrid networking

In this chapter the resources and tools that you can use to implement hybrid networking with Azure are introduced. This primarily revolves around virtual network gateways for site-to-site and point-to-site VPNs, and ExpressRoute for private and dedicated connectivity from your on-premises location to an Azure region.

Skills in this chapter:

- Skill 1.1: Design, implement, and manage a site-to-site VPN connection
- Skill 1.2: Design, implement, and manage a point-to-site VPN connection
- Skill 1.3: Design, implement, and manage Azure ExpressRoute

Skill 1.1: Design, implement, and manage a site-to-site VPN connection

Virtual private networks (VPNs) have long been a way to provide secure connectivity over the internet between two locations. Hybrid connectivity using a VPN can be accomplished by using a virtual network gateway in your Azure subscription. Using a virtual network gateway also requires you to configure a local network gateway. The various connection types and configuration of these gateways are discussed in this skill section.

This skill covers how to:

- Design a site-to-site VPN connection for high availability
- Select an appropriate virtual network gateway SKU
- Identify when to use policy-based VPN versus route-based VPN
- Create and configure a local network gateway
- Create and configure a virtual network gateway
- Create and configure an IPsec/IKE policy
- Diagnose and resolve VPN gateway connectivity issues

Design a site-to-site VPN connection for high availability

By default, when you deploy one Azure VPN gateway, there are two instances of the gateway configured in an active/standby configuration. This standby instance provides some redundancy but is not quite highly available, as it might takes a few minutes for the second instance to come online and reconnect to the destination of the VPN. For this lower level of redundancy, you can choose whether the VPN is regionally redundant or zone-redundant. If you choose to use a *Basic* public IP address, then the VPN that you configure can only be regionally redundant. If you have a need for a zone-redundant configuration, then you must use a *Standard* public IP address with the VPN gateway. Figure 1-1 displays a simple deployment with a single Azure VPN gateway deployed, resulting in a standby instance in the same region.

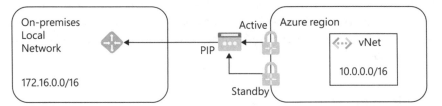

FIGURE 1-1 One VPN gateway connected to an on-premises gateway device

If you would rather have the VPN gateway in the Azure region be zone-redundant, then when you configure it with a Standard public IP address, you'll also have the option of choosing the zone(s) that you wish to deploy the instance to. Figure 1-2 displays the design of a zone-redundant configuration. Alternatively, you can also choose to deploy both instances in the same zone for a zonal (single zone) gateway configuration.

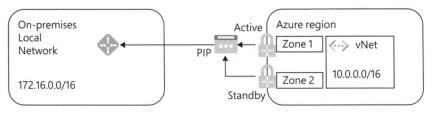

FIGURE 1-2 One zone-redundant VPN gateway connected to an on-premises gateway device

While the above scenarios might provide some redundancy, they wouldn't be considered highly available. There would be some amount of downtime in minutes for the Azure VPN gateways to fail over between the active and standby instances. There is also a single point of failure with the single on-premises gateway devices for that side of the connection. Figure 1-3 enhances this configuration by adding two gateway devices for the on-premises network. However, the Azure side still only has redundancy instead of high availability.

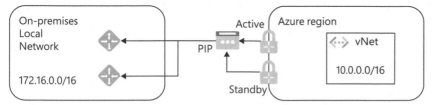

FIGURE 1-3 One VPN gateway connected to two on-premises gateway devices

> *NOTE* **PRESENTED SCENARIOS**
>
> The scenarios and step-by-steps that focus on on-premises as the target destination in this chapter are not the only ways to configure a VPN. A VPN can be used to connect two VNets, a VNet to on-premises, a VNet to another public cloud, or a vendor/partner organization.

In this configuration, network traffic is through both active connections simultaneously. While the primary benefit is redundancy, you might also see a small performance increase by creating an additional tunnel for traffic to transverse. By introducing two active connections, there are other considerations and requirements that must be met for this to be deployed correctly. These requirements include:

- The Azure VPN gateway must have two independent connections defined as part of the configuration using the same local network gateway that represents the on-premises network. Local network gateways will be discussed in more detail later in this skill section.

- The local network gateways associated with the Azure VPN gateways must have unique public IP addresses for the *GatewayIpAddress* property, as well as a unique BGP peer IP address for the *BgpPeerIpAddress* property.

- The routes that are advertised by the BGP peers should use the same address prefixes for the on-premises networks, with traffic forwarded through each tunnel simultaneously.

- The routing method between sites must be configured as equal-cost multi-path (ECMP).

- Each connection defined in the Azure VPN gateway counts toward the maximum number of tunnels supported by the SKU that you select. VPN gateway SKUs are discussed in the next topic of this skill section.

The best of both worlds would be to configure redundancy on both sides of the VPN. In this case, that would be deploying two gateway devices on-premises, as well as two Azure VPN gateway instances in your Azure region. The above requirements also apply for this configuration. With two active instances each with two connections, there will be four total VPN tunnels between the sites. Because ECMP is required, network traffic will be distributed across all four active connections. Figure 1-4 displays this active/active configuration. When combined as a zone-redundant configuration, this results in the best highly available configuration for a single Azure region.

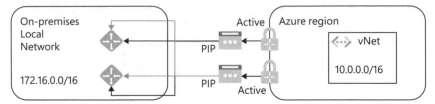

FIGURE 1-4 Two VPN gateways connected to two on-premises gateway devices

---

NEED MORE REVIEW? **HIGHLY AVAILABLE VPNS**

For more information on deploying highly available VPNs, visit *https://docs.microsoft.com/ en-us/azure/vpn-gateway/vpn-gateway-highlyavailable*.

Select an appropriate virtual network gateway SKU

When you deploy an Azure VPN gateway, one of the required options is to select the SKU of the gateway. This SKU determines the maximum number of tunnels, connections, network throughput, and whether BGP and zone-redundancy are supported. Depending on whether you select an active/standby or active/active configuration, that can limit which SKUs you can deploy to implement that configuration. Table 1-1 lists the various SKUs among VPN generations with the relevant supported metrics as of the time of this writing.

TABLE 1-1 Virtual network gateway SKUs

Generation	SKU	Maximum site-to-site tunnels	Throughput benchmark	BGP support	Zone-redundant deployment
Generation1	Basic	10	100 Mbps	No	No
Generation1	VpnGw1	30	650 Mbps	Yes	No
Generation1	VpnGw2	30	1 Gbps	Yes	No
Generation1	VpnGw3	30	1.25 Gbps	Yes	No
Generation1	VpnGw1AZ	30	650 Mbps	Yes	Yes
Generation1	VpnGw2AZ	30	1 Gbps	Yes	Yes
Generation1	VpnGw3AZ	30	1.25 Gbps	Yes	Yes
Generation2	VpnGw2	30	1.25 Gbps	Yes	No
Generation2	VpnGw3	30	2.5 Gbps	Yes	No
Generation2	VpnGw4	30	5 Gbps	Yes	No
Generation2	VpnGw5	30	10 Gbps	Yes	No

Generation	SKU	Maximum site-to-site tunnels	Throughput benchmark	BGP support	Zone-redundant deployment
Generation2	VpnGw2AZ	30	1.25 Gbps	Yes	Yes
Generation2	VpnGw3AZ	30	2.5 Gbps	Yes	Yes
Generation2	VpnGw4AZ	30	5 Gbps	Yes	Yes
Generation2	VpnGw5AZ	30	10 Gbps	Yes	Yes

EXAM TIP

Exam questions do not generally test on memorization or comparison between SKUs. However, core differences between generations or supported minimums and maximums can be frequent exam questions.

Note that in general, the difference between generations is that Generation1 has a maximum of 1.25 Gbps throughput, and Generation2 offers at least 1.25 Gbps of throughput. BGP is supported for every SKU except Basic. The maximum number of connections per VPN gateway is limited to 30. If you need to configure more than 30 separate connections, then you must use Virtual WAN. Virtual WAN is discussed in more detail in skill section 2.4. Finally, you can resize to a different SKU, as long as it is within the same generation.

NEED MORE REVIEW?   VPN SKUS

For more information on each VPN gateway SKU, visit *https://docs.microsoft.com/en-us/azure/vpn-gateway/vpn-gateway-highlyavailable*.

Identify when to use policy-based VPN versus route-based VPN

The main point of consideration for choosing policy-based versus route-based is simply the vendor, device type, and operating system version of the remote device that you plan to connect to the Azure VPN gateway.

The basic difference between the two configuration types is that policy-based uses static routes based on address prefixes. Therefore, each subnet must be included in the VPN configuration. Route-based VPNs use a route table to direct network packets to the appropriate tunnel connection. The individual interface then performs encryption or decryption using wildcards as the traffic selector.

NEED MORE REVIEW?   VALIDATED VPN DEVICES

For more information on deploying highly available VPNs, visit *https://docs.microsoft.com/en-us/azure/vpn-gateway/vpn-gateway-about-vpn-devices*.

Create and configure a local network gateway

A local network gateway can be confusing based on the name. Because you are making the configuration from Azure, it might seem like the local network gateway represents your Azure network in some way. However, the local network gateway is a resource that you create in Azure but is a logical object that represents the on-premises network that you are connecting.

To create a local network gateway in your Azure subscription, follow these steps:

1. Sign in to the Azure portal at *https://portal.azure.com*.

2. In the search bar, search for local network gateways, then select the **Local network gateways** result.

3. On the local network gateways page, click **Create**.

4. In the Name field, provide a display name for the VPN gateway, such as **onprem_network**.

5. For the endpoint toggle, select whether you will specify an IP address or a fully qualified domain name (FQDN) for the on-premises connection. This will represent the public IP or name of your on-premises device. For this example, we will leave the default endpoint selected, **IP address**.

6. In the IP address field, enter the public IP address of the on-premises device that you plan to connect to.

7. In the Address space field, enter the address range(s) that represents the internal IP address scheme of the on-premises environment.

8. If necessary, select **Configure BGP settings** and provide the BGP peer ID. This is required if you plan to implement a highly available deployment with multiple VPN gateways. For this example, we will leave the default of **cleared**.

9. In the Subscription dropdown, select the subscription that the resource will be associated with.

10. In the Resource group dropdown, select or create a resource group for the local network gateway to be assigned to.

11. In the Location dropdown, select the Azure region to associate the local network gateway with. A best practice recommendation is to place this in the same region as your virtual network and VPN gateway, but this is not required. For this example, select **East US**.

12. Click **Create**.

Figure 1-5 displays the completed configuration of the local network gateway. If you choose FQDN over using an IP address, Azure currently requires that the name resolve to an IPv4 address; IPv6 is not supported. Additionally, if multiple IP addresses are returned by DNS, the Azure VPN gateway will attempt to connect only to the first IP address that is returned. You cannot create a redundant connection to multiple IP addresses by using DNS.

FIGURE 1-5 Local network gateway configuration

Create and configure a virtual network gateway

The virtual network gateway is the primary Azure resource that you create to communicate with the target. The gateway resource uses the local network gateway from the previous section and gets associated with a virtual network in Azure. Combined with the IPsec/IKE policy discussed in the next section, this defines the characteristics of the VPN.

As part of creating the virtual network gateway, you must select a virtual network to associate the gateway with. This virtual network must have available address space to create an additional and dedicated subnet specifically for the gateway, named *GatewaySubnet*.

To create a virtual network gateway resource, follow these steps:

1. Sign in to the Azure portal at *https://portal.azure.com*.

2. In the search bar, search for virtual network gateways, then select the **Virtual network gateways** result.

3. On the local network gateways page, click **Create**.

4. In the Subscription dropdown, select the subscription to associate the gateway with.

5. In the Name field, enter a display name for the gateway resource, such as **vpn_to_onprem**.

6. In the Region dropdown, select the same region as your virtual network. For this example, select **East US**.

7. For Gateway type, select **VPN**.

8. For VPN type, select **Route-based**.

9. For SKU, select an appropriate SKU for your scenario. In this example, select **VpnGw2**.

10. For Generation, select **Generation2**.

11. For Virtual network, select a virtual network that is defined in your Azure subscription, or create a new one.

12. For the gateway subnet address range, enter an address range in CIDR notation that is available from the virtual network that you selected or created. For example, enter **10.0.255.0/24**. This range will be used to create the *GatewaySubnet* in the virtual network.

13. For the public IP address, select **Create new**, and then enter a name such as **vpn_pip** for the name.

14. If you plan to use active/active mode and/or BGP, enable them here. For this example, accept the default of **Disabled**.

15. Click **Review + create**, and then click **Create**. Figure 1-6 displays a completed create screen based on the settings used in these steps.

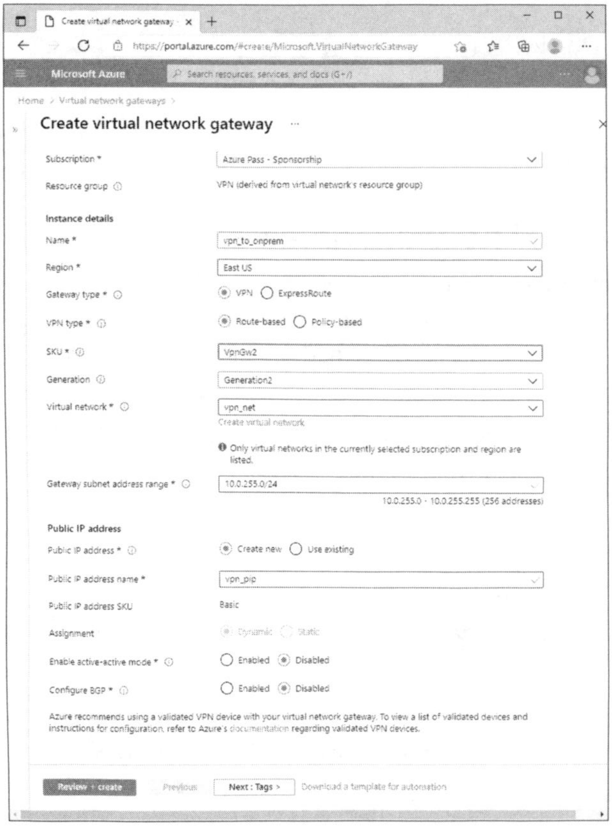

FIGURE 1-6 Virtual network gateway configuration

Creating the gateway resource itself is not the only step required to create the VPN connection to the on-premises environment. After the gateway has been deployed, you must also configure a connection that is associated with the local network gateway.

To create a connection, follow these steps:

1. If necessary, sign in to the Azure portal at *https://portal.azure.com* and navigate to the gateway resource that you deployed.

2. On the virtual network gateway, click the **Connections** blade.

3. From the Connections page, click **Add**.

4. In the Name field, provide a name for the connection. For this example, use **azure_to_onprem**.

5. In the Connection type dropdown menu, select **Site-to-site (IPsec)**.

6. For Virtual network gateway, select the gateway that you previously configured. By following these steps, and if you only have one gateway, the selection will be automatically made.

7. For Local network gateway, click the field and then select the **vpn_to_onprem** local network gateway that was configured in the previous section. Figure 1-7 displays the previously created local network gateway.

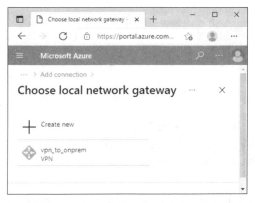

FIGURE 1-7 Selecting the local network gateway

8. In the Shared key (PSK) field, enter a character string to secure the tunnel with. Both endpoints of the VPN tunnel must use the same key. For this example, use **abcd1234**.

9. Leave the default of **cleared** for both Use Azure Private IP address and Enable BGP.

10. For the IKE Protocol, leave the default of **IKEv2**.

11. Click **OK** to create the connection. Figure 1-8 displays the completed connection configuration.

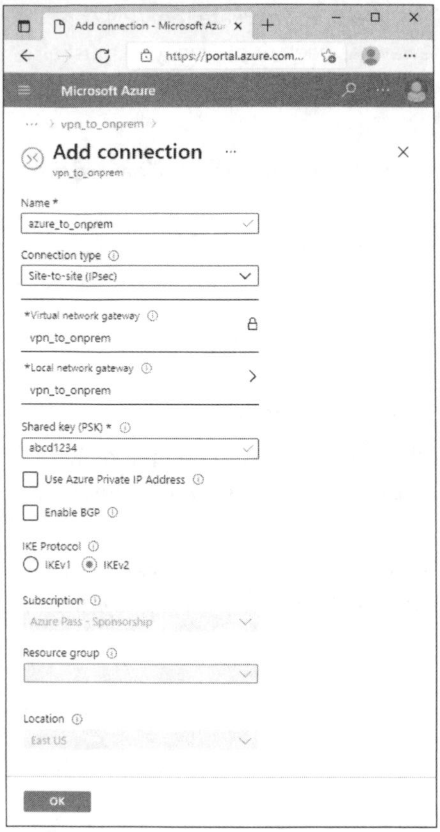

FIGURE 1-8 Configuring the gateway connection

Initially, the connection might show a status of Not connected until you either configure the destination side of the VPN or customize the policy that is used to complete the tunnel. Both of these topics are covered in the next sections of this skill section. Figure 1-9 shows the configured, but not connected, VPN gateway.

Note that when you are configuring the connection, there is a Connection type dropdown menu that has three options for configuring a connection:

- VNet-to-VNet
- Site-to-site (IPsec)
- ExpressRoute

The same virtual network gateway can be used to create multiple connection types, including point-to-site. Point-to-site is covered in detail in skill section 1.2.

A VNet-to-VNet gateway is used when network peering is not possible, or not desired for encryption requirements. The same virtual network gateway is also used to configure an ExpressRoute circuit, which provides a dedicated connection to an on-premises environment. ExpressRoute is covered in skill section 1.3.

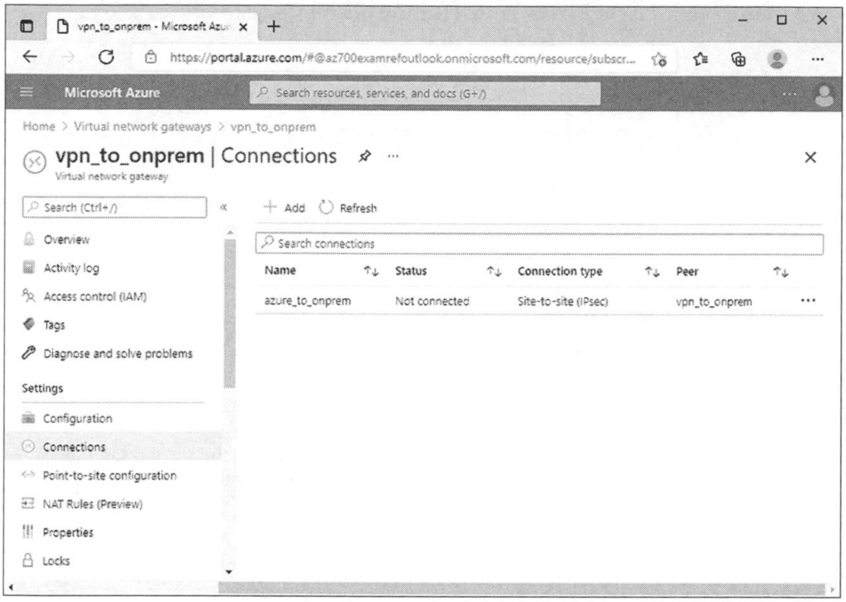

FIGURE 1-9 Configured VPN connections

Create and configure an IPsec/IKE policy

If you have completed the steps to configure a local network gateway, a virtual network gateway, and a connection, then you might have expected to need to configure the IKE parameters as part of the VPN tunnel connect. However, Azure uses a default set of IKE parameters, depending on whether you configured a policy-based or route-based type of gateway. Table 1-2 contains the default Phase 1 parameters for the IKE handshake.

TABLE 1-2 IKE Phase 1 default parameters

Property	Policy-based	Route-based
IKE version	IKEv1	IKEv1 or IKEv2
Diffie-Hellman (DH) Group	Group 2 (1024 bit)	Group 2 (1024 bit)
Authentication method	Pre-shared key	Pre-shared key
Encryption & Hashing algorithms	<ul><li>AES256, SHA256</li><li>AES256, SHA1</li><li>AES128, SHA1</li><li>3DES, SHA1</li></ul>	<ul><li>AES256, SHA1</li><li>AES256, SHA256</li><li>AES128, SHA1</li><li>AES128, SHA256</li><li>3DES, SHA1</li><li>3DES, SHA256</li></ul>
Security Association (SA) lifetime	28,800 seconds	28,800 seconds

Table 1-3 contains the default Phase 2 parameters for the IKE handshake.

TABLE 1-3 IKE Phase 2 default parameters

Property	Policy-based	Route-based
IKE version	IKEv1	IKEv1 or IKEv2
Encryption & Hashing algorithms	■ AES256, SHA256 ■ AES256, SHA1 ■ AES128, SHA1 ■ 3DES, SHA1	Varies depending on if the Azure gateway is the initiator or the responder
SA Lifetime (Time)	3,600 seconds	27,000 seconds
SA Lifetime (Bytes)	102,400,000 KB	102,400,000 KB
Perfect Forward Secrecy (PFS)	No	Only if Azure gateway is the responder; then varies on encryption method
Dead Peer Detection (DPD)	No	Yes

If you need to customize any of these settings for the IKE handshake, then you must create a custom IKE policy. Table 1-4 contains the supported parameters for configuring the IKE policy of the VPN.

TABLE 1-4 Supported parameters for IKE policy

Parameter	Supported options
IKE encryption	AES256, AES192, AES128, 3DES, DES
IKE integrity	SHA384, SHA256, SHA1, MD5
DH Group	DHGroup24, ECP384, ECP256, DHGroup14, DHGroup2048, DHGroup2, DHGroup1, None
IPsec encryption	GCMAES256*, GCMAES192*, GCMAES128*, AES256, AES192, AES128, 3DES, DES, None
IPsec Integrity	GCMASE256, GCMAES192, GCMAES128, SHA256, SHA1, MD5
PFS Group	PFS24, ECP384, ECP256, PFS2048, PFS2, PFS1, None
QM SA Lifetime	Optional: default values are used if not specified Seconds minimum 300, default 27000 KBytes minimum 1024, default 102400000
Traffic Selector	True/False False is default if not specified
DPD timeout	Seconds, 9-3600, default 45

* If you select GCMAES for the IPsec encryption, then you must select the same GMCAES algorithm and key length for IPsec integrity.

A custom IKE policy can be created for each connection that you define for a virtual network gateway. To create a custom policy, follow these steps:

1. If necessary, sign in to the Azure portal at *https://portal.azure.com* and navigate to the gateway resource that you deployed.

2. On the virtual network gateway, click the **Connections** blade.

3. Click the name of the connection that was previously created. For example, click **azure_to_onprem**.

4. From the connection, click the **Configuration** blade.

5. Under IPsec/IKE policy, toggle the button to **Custom**.

6. Use the dropdown and input fields to complete the custom policy, selecting the supported options that are in Table 1-4, and then click **Save**.

Figure 1-10 displays a custom configuration of the IKE policy.

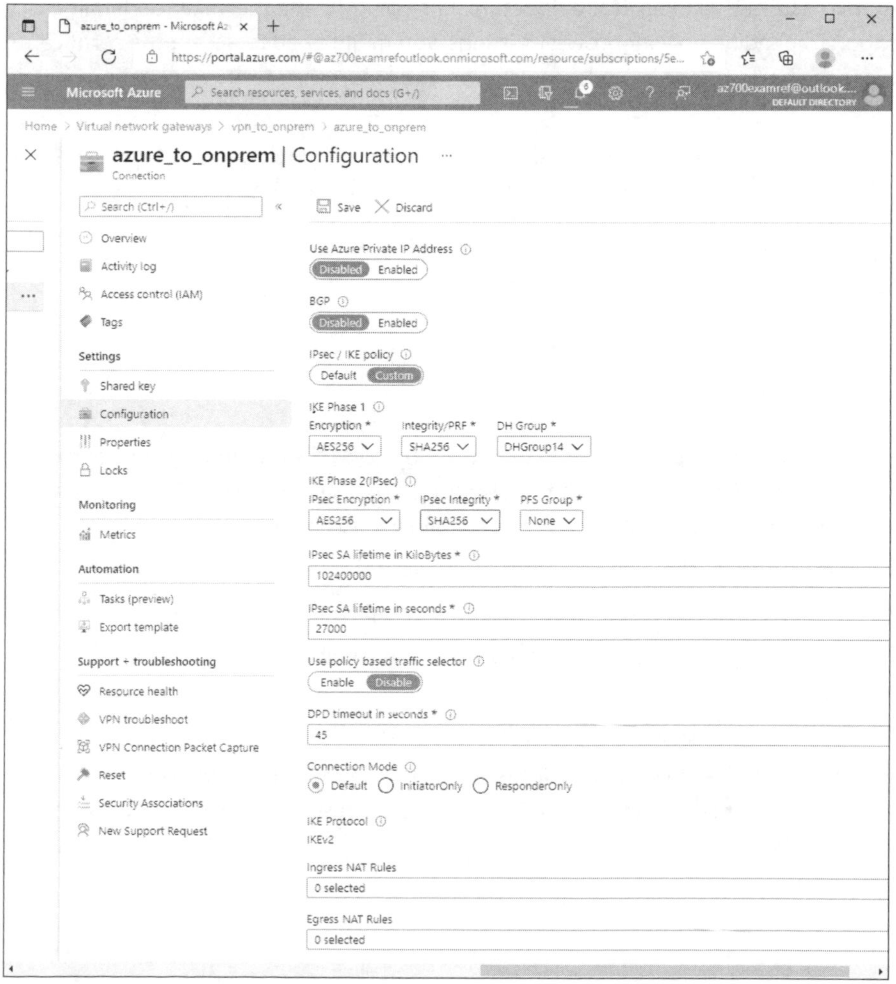

FIGURE 1-10 Custom IKE policy

Diagnose and resolve VPN gateway connectivity issues

When you are troubleshooting connectivity issues, the first steps are to verify the existing configuration and ensure that it matches the configuration of the on-premises or target device. The most common mismatches could be:

- Pre-shared key
- Peer IP addresses
- Subnets match, if using policy-based
- IKE policy

In addition to the configuration settings, you should verify that the Azure virtual network gateway instance is up and running. The easiest way to verify this is by checking the health probe of the virtual network gateway. To check the health probe, navigate to *https://<VirtualNetworkGatewayPublicIP>:8081/healthprobe*.

If the instance is up and running, it should return a line of XML with the instance details and version number. Depending on your browser settings, you might need to accept the certificate warning before the health probe is displayed. Figure 1-11 displays the results of a healthy virtual network gateway.

FIGURE 1-11 Virtual network gateway health probe

You can also troubleshoot the status of a connection by using the logging features of the virtual network gateway. This requires that the *Microsoft.Insights* resource provider be registered with the subscription. To register the provider, follow these steps:

1. If necessary, sign in to the Azure portal at *https://portal.azure.com*.

2. In the search bar, search for subscriptions, and then select the **Subscriptions** result.

3. On the Subscriptions page, select the subscription that you want to register the provider on.

4. On the individual subscription page, click the **Resource Providers** blade.

5. Locate and select the **Microsoft.Insights** provider, and then click **Register**. This might take 5–10 minutes to complete. Figure 1-12 displays the result before you click Register.

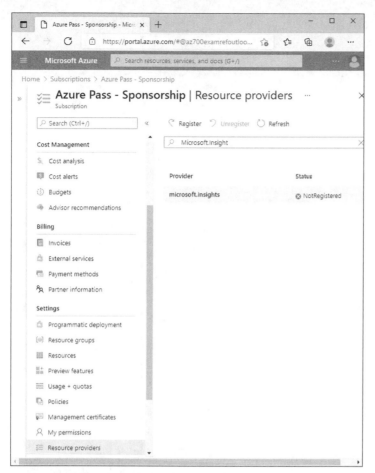

FIGURE 1-12 Microsoft.Insights resource provider

After the provider has been registered, you'll need a log analytics workspace to use the built-in querying tools to search through the logs. To create a log analytics workspace, follow these steps:

1. If necessary, sign in to the Azure portal at *https://portal.azure.com*.

2. In the search bar, search for **Log Analytics workspace**, and then select the **Log Analytics Workspaces** result.

3. On the Log Analytics workspaces page, click **Create**.

4. Select the appropriate subscription and resource group to create the resource in.

5. For the Name field, enter a name for the resource, such as **LA-workspace01**.

6. Select the desired region, ideally the same as the other resources that you have deployed. For this example, select **East US**.

7. Click **Review + Create**, and then click **Create**. Figure 1-13 displays the review screen with the configured settings.

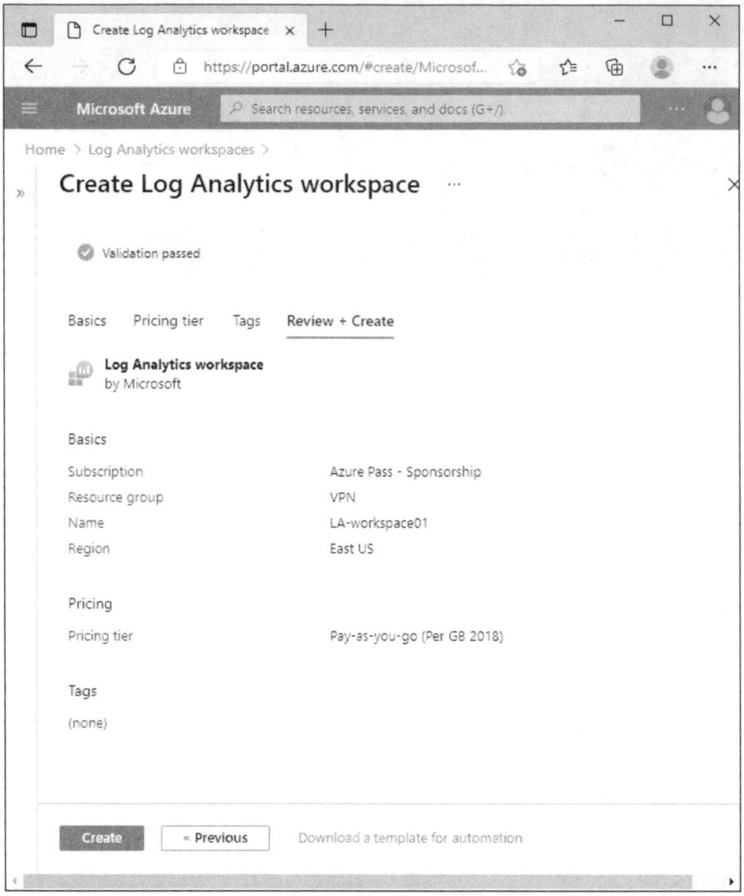

FIGURE 1-13 Log Analytics workspace deployment

After Log Analytics has been deployed, you can use the querying feature to search through the virtual network gateway diagnostic logs. The diagnostic log data is captured and stored in the Log Analytics workspace as a repository and then is queried using the Kusto Query Language (KQL). To enable diagnostic logging and use the KQL querying tool, follow these steps:

1. If necessary, sign in to the Azure portal at *https://portal.azure.com* and navigate to the gateway resource that you deployed.

2. On the virtual network gateway, click the **Activity log** blade.

3. On the Activity log page, click **Diagnostics settings**, as shown in Figure 1-14.

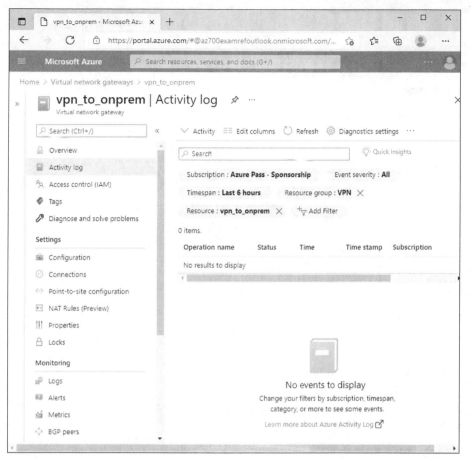

FIGURE 1-14 Virtual network gateway activity log

4. From the Diagnostic settings page, click **Add diagnostic setting**.

5. Provide a name for the diagnostic settings, such as **LogCapture**.

6. To select the desired categories to capture for logging, select the checkbox next to the category name, such as **ServiceHealth**, **Alert**, **Policy**, and **ResourceHealth**.

7. Select the checkbox next to **Send to Log Analytics workspace**, and then select the workspace that you previously deployed. Figure 1-15 displays the completed configuration.

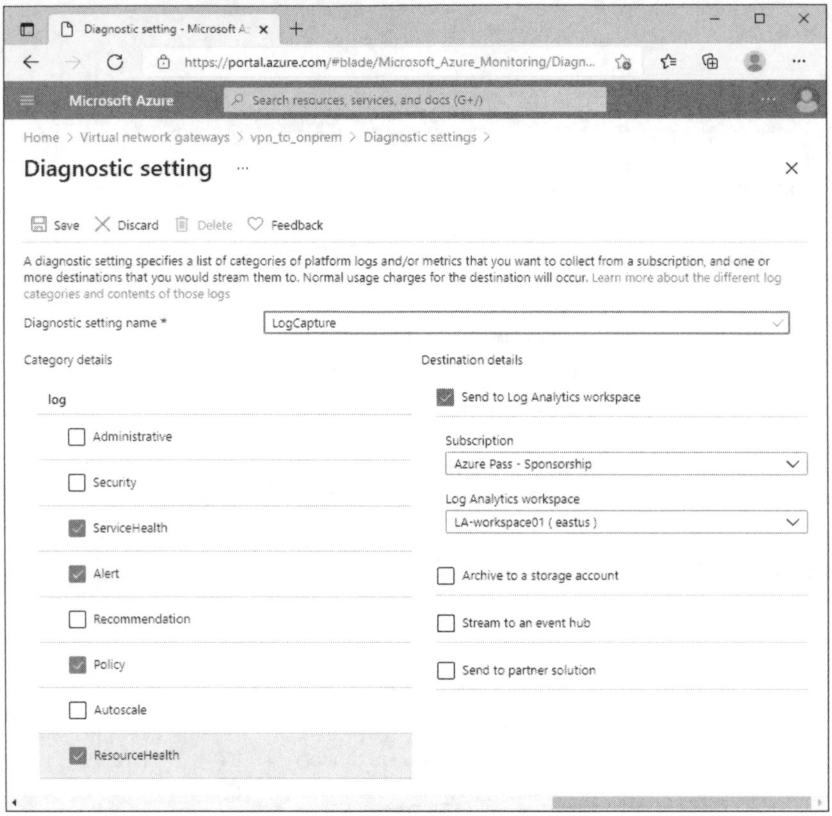

FIGURE 1-15 Virtual network gateway diagnostic

8. Click **Save**.

9. Navigate back to the virtual network gateway, and then select the **Logs** blade.

10. In the query selector, locate a desired KQL query to run against the collected diagnostic data. For example, under VPN Gateway, select **Load to Editor** for the S2S tunnel connect/disconnect events.

11. The following KQL will prepopulate into the editor. If you've successfully connected a VPN, click **Run**.

```
AzureDiagnostics
where TimeGenerated > ago(24h)
where Category == "TunnelDiagnosticLog" and (status_s == "Connected" or status_s == "Disconnected")
project TimeGenerated, Resource , status_s, remoteIP_s, stateChangeReason_s
```

Another way to troubleshoot the connectivity of a VPN is to use the VPN troubleshoot tool of Network Watcher. This requires a storage account to be created to hold the logs as the troubleshooter runs. To configure and use the VPN troubleshoot tool, follow these steps:

1. If necessary, sign in to the Azure portal at *https://portal.azure.com* and navigate to the gateway resource that you deployed.

2. On the virtual network gateway, click the **VPN troubleshoot** blade.

3. On the VPN troubleshoot page, click **Select storage account**.

4. Select an existing storage account, or use the **+ Storage account** button to create a new one.

5. On the storage account, create or select an existing blob container to store the trouble-shooting data in.

6. After selecting the storage account and container, select the checkbox next to the connection that you need to troubleshoot, and then click **Start troubleshooting**. Figure 1-16 displays the desired configuration. (This process might take a few minutes to run to collect the relevant data from the connection.)

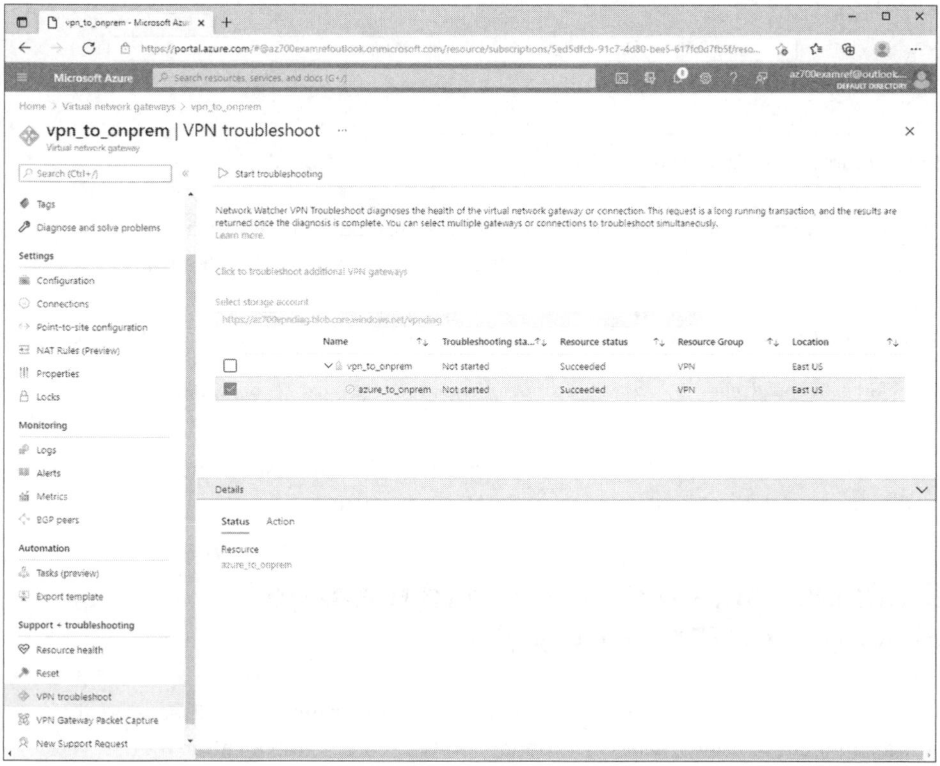

FIGURE 1-16 VPN troubleshooting

7. From the Azure portal, navigate to the storage account that you selected for the troubleshooting data.

8. From the storage account, click **Storage Explorer (preview)**.

9. From Storage Explorer, expand Blob Containers, then expand the name of the container that you selected.

10. When the troubleshooting tool has completed, a compressed ZIP file will be available through the folder structure to download from the blob container. Select the file, and then click **Download** and click the download arrow. See Figure 1-17.

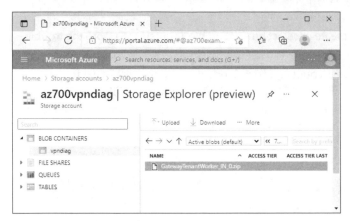

FIGURE 1-17 Troubleshoot file download

11. Open the ConnectionStats.txt file within the compressed folder to see an overview of the status. The following is an excerpt of the file that shows the overall error.

```
Connectivity State : NotConnected
Ingress Packets Dropped due to Traffic Selector Mismatch (since last connected) : 0
Packets
Egress Packets Dropped due to Traffic Selector Mismatch (since last connected) : 0
Packets
```

12. The error message "dropped due to traffic selector mismatch" would indicate a configuration mismatch on at least one side of the VPN connection.

Skill 1.2: Design, implement, and manage a point-to-site VPN connection

Virtual network gateways can be used to connect site-to-site locations with IPsec, as well as distributed connections using a variety of connection types and authentication methods. These distributed connections are point-to-site connections that allow various client devices to securely access Azure resources through a VPN. In this skill section, we discuss the various options for connection types and authentication methods that are available with virtual network gateways and point-to-site configurations.

This skill covers how to:

- Select an appropriate virtual network gateway SKU
- Plan and configure RADIUS authentication
- Plan and configure certificate-based authentication
- Plan and configure Azure Active Directory (Azure AD) authentication
- Implement a VPN client configuration file
- Diagnose and resolve client-side and authentication issues

NOTE **OBJECTIVE LIST**

The objective domain for the exam also mentions "Plan and configure OpenVPN authentication." However, OpenVPN is a connection type, not an authentication method. The examples in this chapter use OpenVPN. However, be aware of other connection types and authentication methods defined in the list of objectives.

Select an appropriate virtual network gateway SKU

When you are planning to deploy an Azure VPN gateway for point-to-site connections, you use the same virtual network gateway that is deployed when planning a site-to-site VPN. Table 1-5 looks very similar to Table 1-1 earlier in this chapter but focuses on the point-to-site connection maximums. Note that the throughput benchmark is a combined amount in the scenario that you use both point-to-site and site-to-site connection methods with the same virtual network gateway.

TABLE 1-5 Virtual network gateway maximums

Generation	SKU	Maximum P2S SSTP connections	Maximum P2S IKEv2/OpenVPN connections	Throughput benchmark
Generation1	Basic	128	Not supported	100 Mbps
Generation1	VpnGw1	128	250	650 Mbps
Generation1	VpnGw2	128	500	1 Gbps
Generation1	VpnGw3	128	1,000	1.25 Gbps
Generation1	VpnGw1AZ	128	250	650 Mbps
Generation1	VpnGw2AZ	128	500	1 Gbps
Generation1	VpnGw3AZ	128	1,000	1.25 Gbps

Generation	SKU	Maximum P2S SSTP connections	Maximum P2S IKEv2/OpenVPN connections	Throughput benchmark
Generation2	VpnGw2	128	500	1.25 Gbps
Generation2	VpnGw3	128	1,000	2.5 Gbps
Generation2	VpnGw4	128	5,000	5 Gbps
Generation2	VpnGw5	128	10,000	10 Gbps
Generation2	VpnGw2AZ	128	500	1.25 Gbps
Generation2	VpnGw3AZ	128	1,000	2.5 Gbps
Generation2	VpnGw4AZ	128	5,000	5 Gbps
Generation2	VpnGw5AZ	128	10,000	10 Gbps

The zone-redundancy column has purposely been excluded from this table and is identical to the options found in Table 1-1 earlier in the chapter. The headers of the table display the three supported connection types for point-to-site VPNs:

- Secure Socket Tunneling Protocol (SSTP)
- OpenVPN
- IKEv2

SSTP is a VPN tunnel that uses TLS 1.2 and is supported only with Windows operating system clients. However, as Table 1-5 shows, the scalability is limited at 128 connections per gateway. OpenVPN also uses TLS, but it has more connection support, depending on the gateway SKU, and broader operating system support including:

- Android
- Apple iOS
- Windows
- Linux
- macOS 10.13 and above

The point-to-site IKEv2 VPN uses an IPsec VPN and supports macOS 10.11 and higher operating system devices. The next sections discuss the various authentication types that you can use with gateways.

Plan and configure RADIUS authentication

If you plan to use a RADIUS server for authentication, you can choose whether the RADIUS server is deployed on-premises or in an Azure virtual network. If the RADIUS server is located on-premises, then the existing connection must be an IPsec site-to-site VPN. Using ExpressRoute with a RADIUS point-to-site VPN is not supported. Figure 1-18 displays a sample design of an on-premises RADIUS deployment.

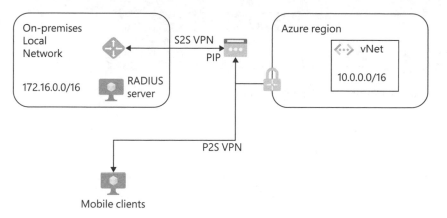

FIGURE 1-18 On-premises RADIUS deployment

Adding a point-to-site connection can be configured after you deploy a virtual network gateway. If you need to deploy the gateway, follow the steps in the *Create and configure a virtual network gateway* topic in skill section 1.1. To configure the point-to-site with RADIUS, follow these steps:

1. If necessary, sign in to the Azure portal at *https://portal.azure.com* and navigate to the gateway resource that you deployed.

2. On the virtual network gateway, click the **Point-to-site configuration** blade.

3. On the Point-to-site configuration page, click **Configure now**.

4. In the address pool field, provide an IP address range for the client VPN connections, such as **192.168.1.0/24**.

5. In the Tunnel type, select the desired connection type(s) to use with the tunnel. Select **OpenVPN (SSL)**, but other available options include:

   - OpenVPN (SSL)

   - SSTP (SSL)

   - IKEv2

   - IKEv2 and OpenVPN (SSL)

   - IKEv2 and SSTP (SSL)

6. From the Authentication type dropdown menu, select **RADIUS authentication**.

7. In the Primary Server IP address field, enter the IP address of the RADIUS server. For example, enter **172.16.1.5**.

8. In the Primary Server secret field, enter the shared secret that has also been configured on the RADIUS server. For example, enter **a1b2c3**.

9. Click **Save**. Figure 1-19 displays the sample configuration.

10. After clicking Save, click the **Download VPN client** button to assist with client configuration.

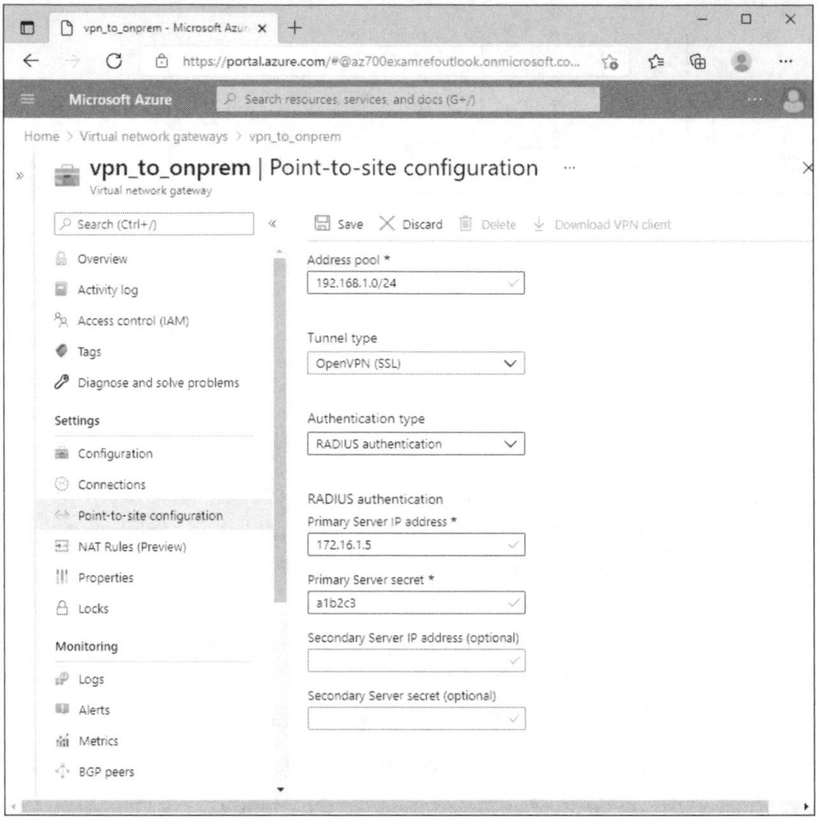

FIGURE 1-19 Point-to-site with RADIUS authentication

> **NEED MORE REVIEW?** **POINT-TO-SITE WITH RADIUS AUTHENTICATION**
>
> For more information on point-to-site VPNs with RADIUS authentication, visit *https://docs.microsoft.com/en-us/azure/vpn-gateway/point-to-site-how-to-radius-ps*.

Plan and configure certificate-based authentication

Another authentication option for point-to-site VPNs is to use certification-based authentication. To use certification authentication, you will need the public key (.CER file) for the root certificate. As part of the configuration process, you will need to specify the public key. After uploading the root certificate, the gateway will generate a client certificate that is used with the VPN client configuration.

To create a point-to-site VPN configuration using certificate-based authentication, follow these steps:

1. If necessary, sign in to the Azure portal at *https://portal.azure.com* and navigate to the gateway resource that you deployed.

2. On the virtual network gateway, click the **Point-to-site configuration** blade.

3. On the Point-to-site configuration page, click **Configure now**.

4. In the address pool field, provide an IP address range for the client VPN connections. For example, enter **192.168.1.0/24**.

5. From the Tunnel type dropdown, select the desired tunnel. For this example, select **OpenVPN (SSL)**.

6. From the Authentication type dropdown, select **Azure certificate**.

7. In the Root certificates Name field, provide a name for the certificate, such as **RootCert**.

8. In the Root certificates Public certificate data field, paste in the value of the public certificate.

9. Click **Save**. Figure 1-20 shows a completed configuration.

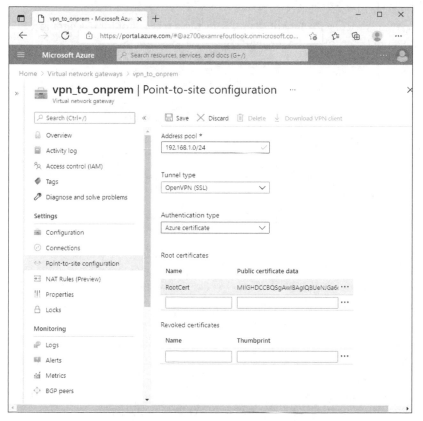

FIGURE 1-20 Point-to-site with certificate authentication

Plan and configure Azure Active Directory (Azure AD) authentication

If you plan to use Azure AD as the authentication method with a point-to-site VPN, then you must use the OpenVPN connection type. This configuration also requires using the Azure VPN client and does not support built-in operating system or third-party VPN clients.

To configure Azure AD authentication, follow these steps:

1. If necessary, sign in to the Azure portal as a global administrator at *https://portal.azure.com.*
2. From the Azure portal, search for and select **Azure Active Directory**.
3. From Azure AD, click the **Properties** blade.
4. In the Overview blade, copy the tenant ID and save it to a text editor for use later in these steps. Figure 1-21 displays the tenant ID of our sample directory.

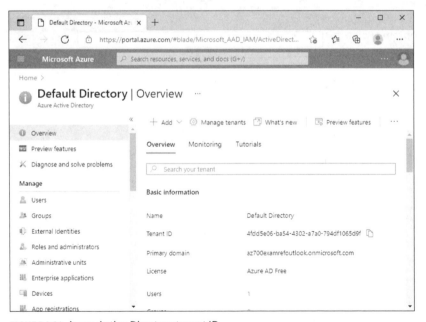

FIGURE 1-21 Azure Active Directory tenant ID

5. Navigate to the virtual network gateway that you have previously deployed.
6. From the gateway, click the **Point-to-site configuration** blade.

7. In the Address pool field, enter an address range in CIDR notation for the client connections. For example, enter **192.168.1.0/24**.

8. In the Tunnel type dropdown menu, select **OpenVPN (SSL)**.

9. In the Authentication type dropdown menu, select **Azure Active Directory**.

10. In the Azure AD Tenant field, enter the following URL, replacing tenantID with the tenant ID you copied earlier in these steps: *https://login.microsoftonline.com/tenantID/*

11. In the Audience field, enter one of the following strings, depending on the Azure cloud you are using:

    - Enter **41b23e61-6c1e-4545-b367-cd054e0ed4b4** for Azure Public

    - Enter **51bb15d4-3a4f-4ebf-9dca-40096fe32426** for Azure Government

    - Enter **538ee9e6-310a-468d-afef-ea97365856a9** for Azure Germany

    - Enter **49f817b6-84ae-4cc0-928c-73f27289b3aa** for Azure China 21Vianet

12. In the Issuer field, enter the following URL, replacing *tenantID* with the ID that you copied earlier: *https://sts.windows.net/tenantID/*

13. Click **Save**. Figure 1-22 displays the completed configuration.

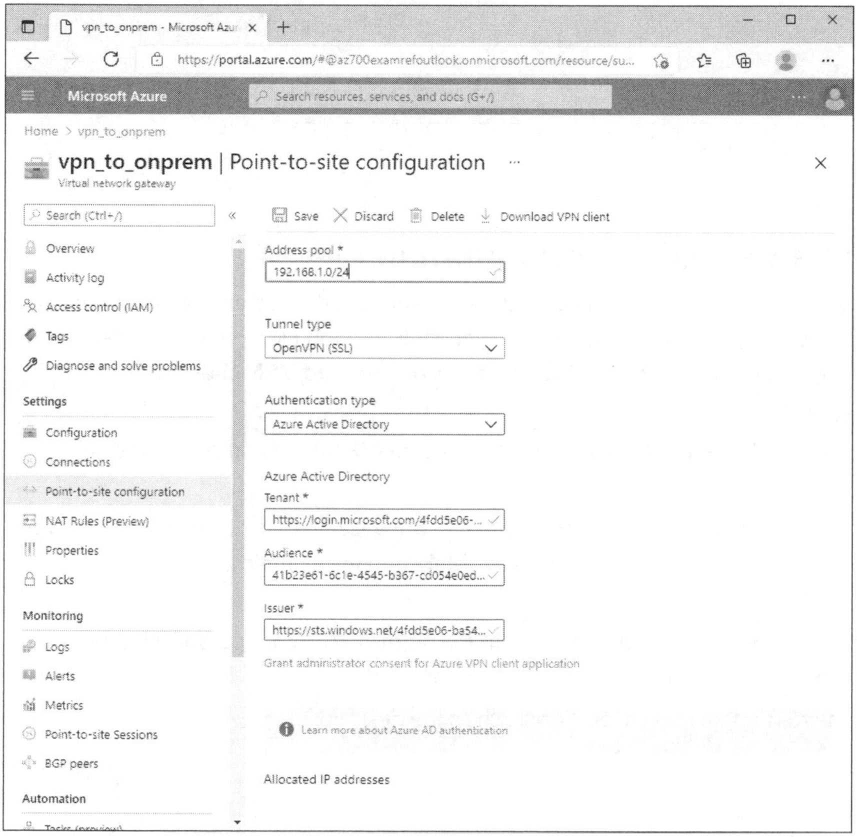

FIGURE 1-22 Azure Active Directory P2S authentication

14. After you save the configuration, a link will appear to **Grant administrator consent for Azure VPN client application** below your configuration details. Click this link, and then sign in using the global administrator account of your tenant.

15. Select the checkbox next to **Consent on behalf of your organization**, and then click **Accept,** as shown in Figure 1-23.

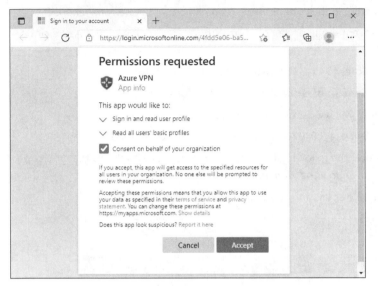

FIGURE 1-23 Granting VPN permission

Implement a VPN client configuration file

After you have configured a point-to-site configuration with the desired connection type and authentication method, you can download the client configuration file from the point-to-site configuration page. Refer back to Figure 1-22 to see the **Download VPN client** button that is available on the page.

To use the Azure VPN client, which is required for Azure AD authentication, follow these steps:

1. Download the Azure VPN client from the Microsoft website at *https://go.microsoft.com/ fwlink/?linkid=2117554*. Follow the steps to obtain and install the client from the Microsoft store.

2. Download the VPN client information from the point-to-site configuration blade. The downloaded file will be a .ZIP compressed folder.

3. Extract the folder to a known location, such as the desktop.

4. Launch the Azure VPN client. On the main page, click the + icon, and then click ← **Import** to add a connection, as shown in Figure 1-24.

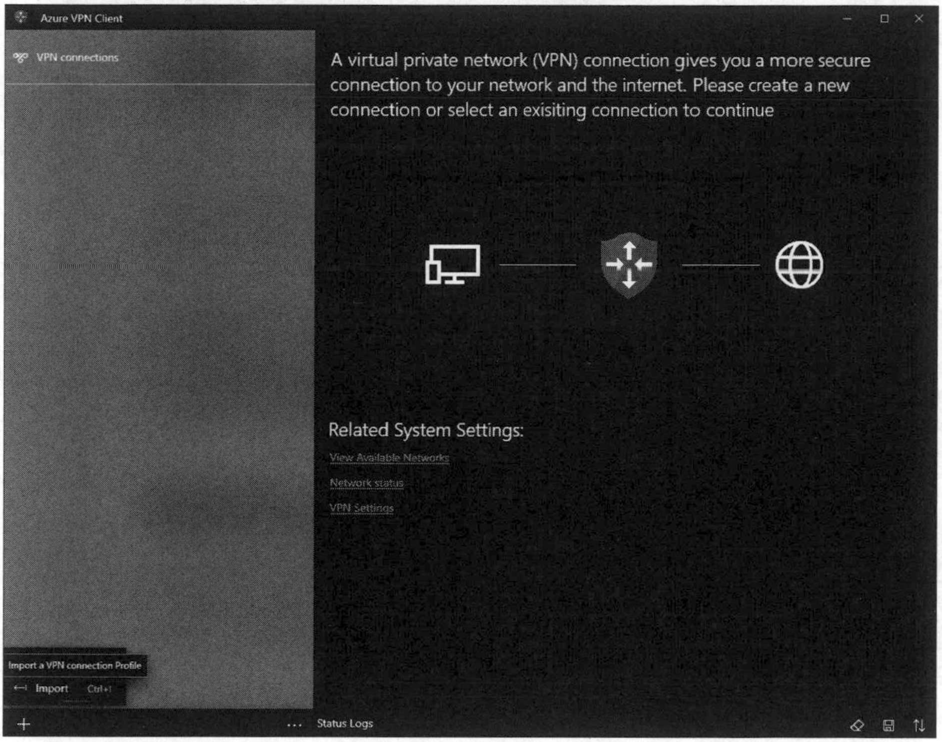

FIGURE 1-24 Azure VPN client – import configuration

5. Browse to the location of the extracted VPN client files, open the **AzureVPN** folder, and then select the **azurevpnconfig.xml** file.

    The Azure VPN client will read and display the configuration information that is defined in the file, as shown in Figure 1-25.

6. Set the Authentication Type dropdown menu to Username/Password. Specify a valid username and password in the Azure tenant.

7. Click **Save**.

8. To connect to the VPN, click **Connect**.

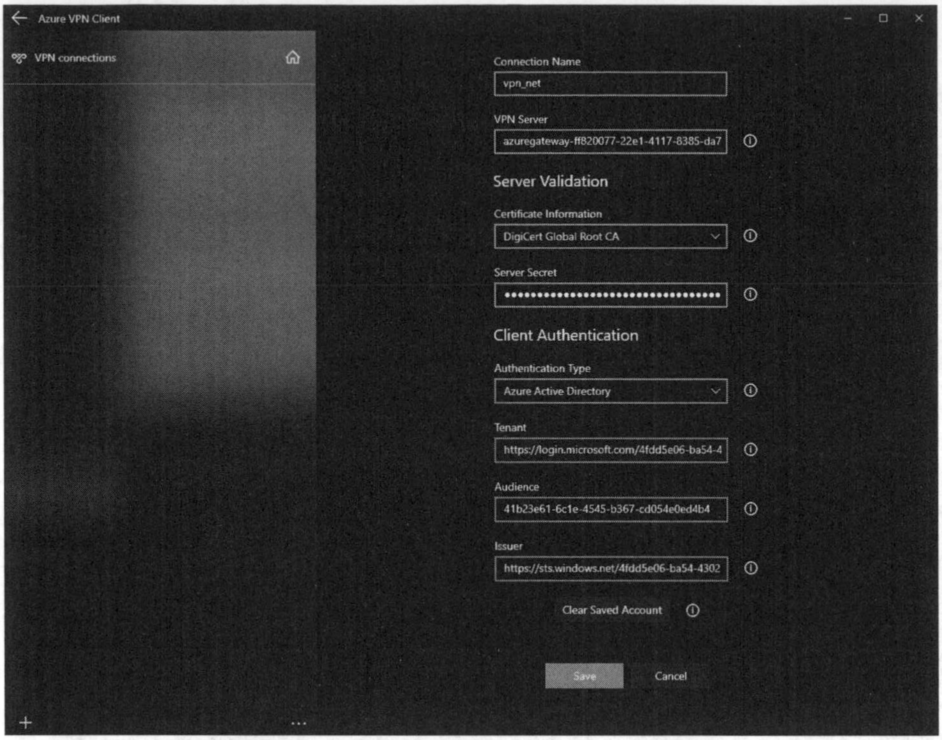

FIGURE 1-25 Azure VPN client – imported configuration

Diagnose and resolve client-side and authentication issues

A majority of the client-side issues that you might need to troubleshoot will depend on the type of authentication method that you have configured. For example, if you plan to use certificate-based authentication with the Azure VPN client, then the AzureClient.pfx and AzureRoot.cer certificate files must be imported into the correct location on the client device. Table 1-6 displays the correct location for each file.

TABLE 1-6 Certificate file paths

Certificate	Location path
AzureClient.pfx	Current User\Personal\Certificates
AzureRoot.cer	Local Computer\Trusted Root Certification Authorities
AzureGateway-GUID.cloudapp.net	Local Computer\Trusted Root Certification Authorities
Azuregateway-GUID.cloudapp.net	Current User\Trusted Root Certification Authorities

If you plan to use an IKEv2 connection type with Windows 10 or Server 2016, you might need to also install an update and set a registry value to use IKEv2 specifically. Table 1-7 displays the operating system version and knowledgebase update to install.

TABLE 1-7 IKEv2 updates

OS version	Knowledgebase article
Windows Server 2016	KB4057142
Windows 10, version 1607	KB4057142
Windows 10, version 1703	KB4057144
Windows 10, version 1709	KB4089848

In addition to the corresponding update, you need to set the following REG_DWORD key in the registry to **1**.

```
HKEY_LOCAL_MACHINE\SYSTEM\CurrentControlSet\Services\RasMan\ IKEv2\DisableCertReqPayload
```

> **NEED MORE REVIEW?** **POINT-TO-SITE TROUBLESHOOTING**
>
> For more information on troubleshooting point-to-site VPNs, visit *https://docs.microsoft.com/en-us/azure/vpn-gateway/vpn-gateway-troubleshoot-vpn-point-to-site-connection-problems*.

Skill 1.3: Design, implement, and manage Azure ExpressRoute

Azure ExpressRoute provides a hybrid connectivity across your on-premises environment and an Azure region by using a dedicated circuit through a third-party telecommunications provider. ExpressRoute circuits are commonly compared to MPLS circuits, although they function slightly differently. However, the general concept is the same: a telecom provider terminates connectivity—typically fiber but could be Ethernet—at your on-premises location. After configuring the software-defined connection in your Azure subscription, you have a dedicated, private circuit from the virtual network that you associate with the configuration and your on-premises network.

ExpressRoute relies on the telecommunications provider for the physical connectivity between your on-premises location and the Azure region that you plan to connect to. Therefore, different Azure regions support different telecommunication vendors and vary by Azure region and geography.

This skill covers how to:

- Choose between provider and direct model (ExpressRoute Direct)
- Design and implement Azure cross-region connectivity between multiple ExpressRoute locations
- Select an appropriate ExpressRoute SKU and tier
- Design and implement ExpressRoute Global Reach
- Design and implement ExpressRoute FastPath
- Choose between private peering only, Microsoft peering only, or both
- Configure private peering
- Configure Microsoft peering
- Create and configure an ExpressRoute gateway
- Connect a virtual network to an ExpressRoute circuit
- Recommend a route advertisement configuration
- Configure encryption over ExpressRoute
- Implement Bidirectional Forwarding Detection
- Diagnose and resolve ExpressRoute connection issues

Choose between provider and direct model (ExpressRoute Direct)

Choosing between a "regular" ExpressRoute circuit and an ExpressRoute Direct circuit is primarily based on two decision points:

- Do you have a bandwidth requirement of more than 10 Gbps?
- If yes, do you have, or can you acquire, the required hardware to use an ExpressRoute Direct circuit?

To compare the ExpressRoute options, a regular circuit provides up to 10 Gbps of connectivity through the service provider and can be terminated on-premises with Ethernet or MPLS connection options. An ExpressRoute Direct circuit can provide up to 100 Gbps connectivity but requires single-mode fiber terminations with a router-pair at the on-premises location. The full ExpressRoute Direct requirements for the routing hardware include:

- Dual 10 Gigabit or 100-Gigabit Ethernet ports only across router pair
- Single-mode Long Reach (LR) fiber connectivity
- IPv4 and IPv6
- Transmission size of 1500 bytes

There are requirements at the switching layer, including:

- One 802.1Q tag or two Tag 802.1Q (QinQ) tag encapsulation
  - If using QinQ, you must be able to configure a Microsoft-specified VLAN ID tag
- Ethertype must be 0x8100
- Must support multiple BGP sessions (VLANs) per port and device
- IPv4 and IPv6 connectivity
  - For IPv6, no extra subinterface will be created. An IPv6 address will be added to the existing subinterface.

Optionally, you can also configure Bidirectional Forwarding Detection (BFD) support, which is configured by default on all Private Peerings on ExpressRoute circuits. We discuss BFD later in this skill section.

Another consideration between the two options would be pricing. Using the Azure Pricing Calculator (*https://aka.ms/pricing*), a regular ExpressRoute premium circuit in the United States at 10 Gbps and 100 TB of data transfer per month would be approximately $9,000 per month. Upgrading the circuit to ExpressRoute Direct with 100 Gbps connectivity increases the price to over $55,000 per month. Note that these cost estimates are examples and vary by geography, subscription type, and actual data usage.

Design and implement Azure cross-region connectivity between multiple ExpressRoute locations

Designing cross-region connectivity with ExpressRoute sounds like it could be a complex and difficult process. However, it's easy because an ExpressRoute circuit can be associated and connected to multiple virtual networks, depending on the ExpressRoute SKU that you deploy, even if the virtual networks are in two different regions or subscriptions. Figure 1-26 shows the desired connectivity state.

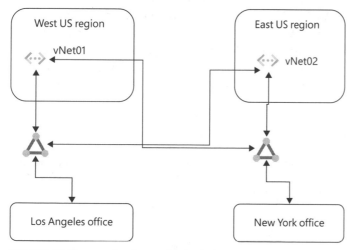

FIGURE 1-26 Cross-region ExpressRoute design

The challenge that this scenario introduces is around network routing. Each ExpressRoute connection has a routing weight configuration, which specifies the logical cost of using the route. Customize the connection weight to enforce specific routing paths between the offices and the Azure regions. Additionally, you can advertise the available networks through the same BGP Autonomous System (AS) numbers.

Select an appropriate ExpressRoute SKU and tier

Determining which ExpressRoute SKU to use depends on the workload and goals of the design. The following SKUs are available for ExpressRoute gateways:

- Standard
- High performance
- Ultra performance
- ERGW1AZ
- ERGW2AZ
- ERGW3AZ

Table 1-8 shows the feature support for the various SKU types.

TABLE 1-8 ExpressRoute gateway SKU support

SKU	FastPath support	Maximum number of circuit connections
Standard / ERGW1AZ	No	4
High performance / ERGW2AZ	No	8
Ultra performance / ERGW3AZ	Yes	16

Notice that in Table 1-8, there is no feature difference for FastPath or circuit connection support for Standard SKU and ERGW1AZ SKU. The difference between these two SKUs is that the AZ SKU supports Availability Zones if the region you deploy the gateway to also supports Availability Zones. If you need support for FastPath, which is discussed later in this skill section, your only options are the Ultra performance or ERGW3AZ SKUs. Otherwise, your selection from the remaining four will depend on the desired performance. Table 1-9 displays the tested performance for each SKU.

TABLE 1-9 ExpressRoute SKU performance

SKU	Connections per second	Mb/s	Packets per second	Supported number of VMs in the vNet
Standard / ERGW1AZ	7,000	1,000	100,000	2,000
High performance / ERGW2AZ	14,000	2,000	250,000	4,500
Ultra performance / ERGW3AZ	16,000	10,000	1,000,000	11,000

Design and implement ExpressRoute FastPath

ExpressRoute FastPath is a performance-enhancing feature that is available only on the top-tier SKUs: Ultra performance and ERGW3AZ. Additionally, if you plan to use IPv6, then you can only use the ERGW3AZ SKU.

In all ExpressRoute configurations, the circuit is terminated to a virtual network gateway in the Azure subscription. This additional hop does add to the latency of any network traffic to virtual machines that are on a virtual network. ExpressRoute FastPath optimizes the network routing so that traffic destined to virtual machines is delivered directly and bypasses the virtual network gateway, lowering the overall latency.

To configure ExpressRoute FastPath, you link a virtual network to an ExpressRoute circuit. Standard circuits support up to 10 virtual network links, regardless of SKU. Premium circuits depend on the size of the circuit in Mbps. Refer back to Table 1-10 earlier in this skill section for specific limits.

To enable FastPath on an existing ExpressRoute circuit, follow these steps:

1. Sign in to the Azure portal at *https://portal.azure.com*.
2. In the search bar, search for ExpressRoute, then select the **ExpressRoute circuits** result.
3. Select a circuit that you have already configured and want to enable FastPath on.
4. Click the **Connections** blade, and then click the existing connection.
5. On the specific connection, click the **Configuration** blade.
6. Select the checkbox next to **FastPath**, and then click **Save**. Figure 1-29 displays the location of the FastPath checkbox.

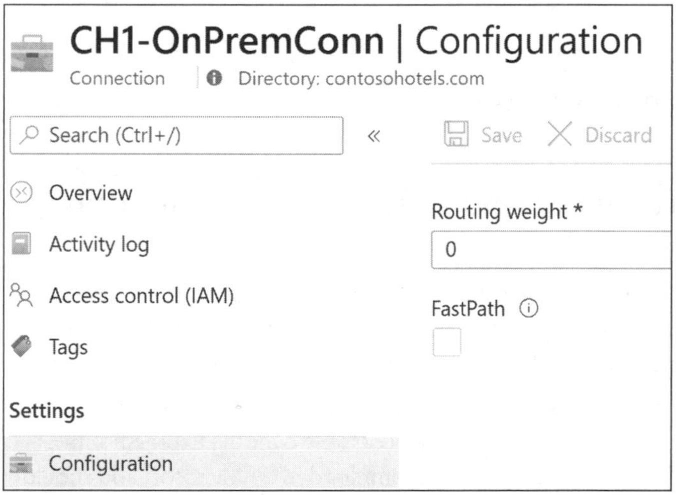

FIGURE 1-29 ExpressRoute FastPath configuration

You can also enable FastPath when adding a connection from the virtual network gateway. Figure 1-30 displays the **Add connection** options of the gateway, including the option to enable FastPath. For the detailed steps of adding a connection, refer back to skill section 1.1.

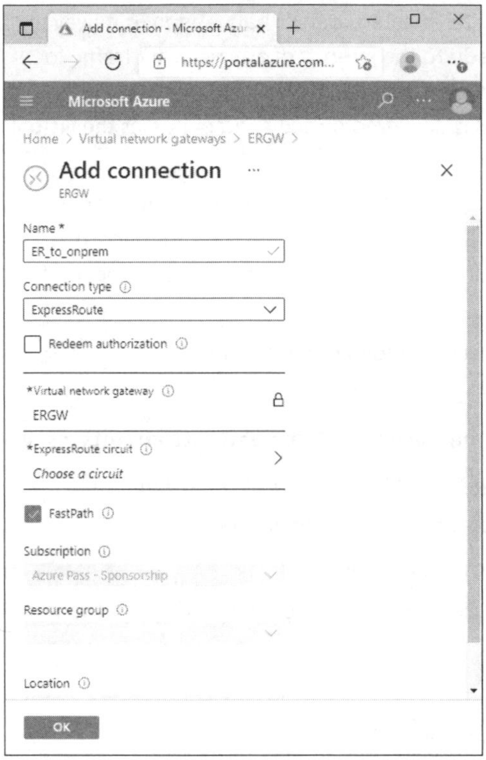

FIGURE 1-30 Add connection from a virtual network gateway

Choose between private peering only, Microsoft peering only, or both

As part of the ExpressRoute configuration, you have the option of configuring Azure private peering, Microsoft peering, or both. Azure private peering provides connectivity from your on-premises environment to the Azure subscriptions and resources that you link the circuit to.

In rare circumstances, you might also want Microsoft 365 services, such as Microsoft Exchange Online and Microsoft SharePoint Online, to be accessible over the ExpressRoute circuit. This scenario uses Microsoft peering, but it is not recommended by Microsoft and should be used only if your organization has strict requirements for network traffic. Microsoft 365 was designed to be securely accessed over the public internet, and still requires public internet access for certain services even if Microsoft peering over ExpressRoute is configured. Table 1-11 compares the technical requirements for configuring both Azure private peering and Microsoft peering.

TABLE 1-11 Peering comparison

	Azure private peering	**Microsoft peering**
Maximum supported address prefixes	Standard: 4,000 Premium: 10,000	200
IP address ranges supported	Any valid IP address	Public IP addresses only
AS Number requirements	Private and public AS numbers	Private and public AS numbers
IP protocols supported	IPv4 IPv6 (preview, as of this writing)	IPv4 and IPv6
Routing interface IP addresses	Private or public IP addresses	Public IP addresses only
MD5 Hash support	Yes	Yes

If you choose to use both Azure private and Microsoft peering, each peering type requires separate BGP to provide high availability across both connections.

Configure private peering

To configure Azure private peering, the provider status of the ExpressRoute circuit must display **Provisioned**. As part of this provisioning, some ExpressRoute providers will manage the routing as part of the circuit, and these steps would not be necessary. If the provider does not manage the routing, then you'll need to follow these steps:

1. Sign in to the Azure portal at *https://portal.azure.com*.
2. In the search bar, search for ExpressRoute, then select the **ExpressRoute circuits** result.
3. Select a circuit that you have already configured and want to configure private peering for.
4. Click the **Peerings** blade, and then click **Azure private**.
5. On the Private peering page, configure the Peer ASN, protocol, subnets, and VLAN ID. An example configuration is shown in Figure 1-31.
6. Click **Save**.

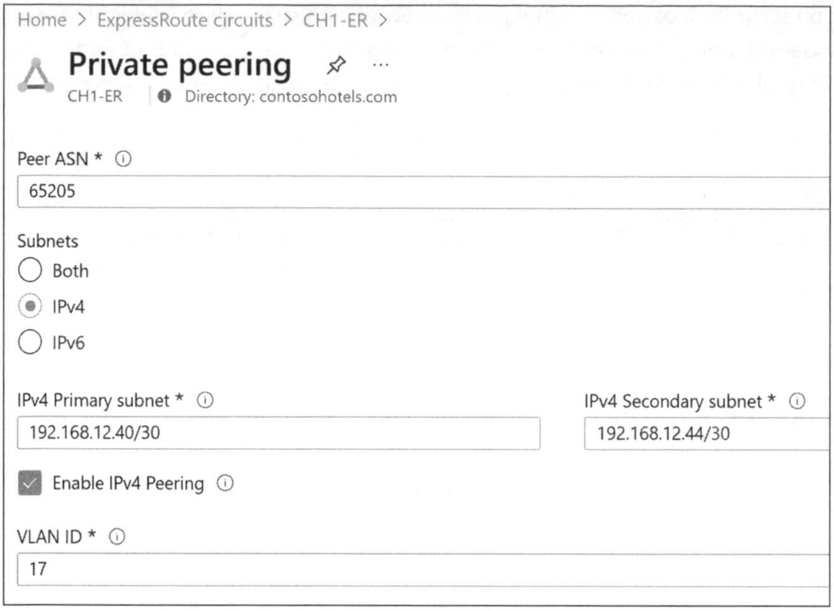

FIGURE 1-31 Private peering configuration

Configure Microsoft peering

To configure Microsoft peering, the provider status of the ExpressRoute circuit must display **Provisioned**. Note that Microsoft peering requires the use of public IP addresses but can use either public or private AS numbers. To configure Microsoft peering, follow these steps:

1. Sign in to the Azure portal at *https://portal.azure.com*.

2. In the search bar, search for ExpressRoute, then select the **ExpressRoute circuits** result.

3. Select a circuit that you have already configured and want to configure private peering for.

4. Click the **Peerings** blade, and then click **Microsoft peering**.

5. On the Microsoft peering page, configure the Peer ASN, protocol, subnets, advertised prefixes, and VLAN ID. An example configuration is shown in Figure 1-32.

Microsoft peering ⚲ ⋯
CH1-ER   ⓘ Directory: contosohotels.com

ⓘ To receive route advertisements on Microsoft peering, attach route filters to the circuit after creating Microsoft Peering. Learn more ☐

Peer ASN * ⓘ

| 394749 |

Subnets
- ⚪ Both
- ⦿ IPv4
- ⚪ IPv6

IPv4 Primary subnet * ⓘ

| 64.191.192.240/30 |

IPv4 Secondary subnet * ⓘ

| 64.191.192.240/30 |

IPv4 Advertised public prefixes * ⓘ

| 64.191.192.224/28 |

☑ Enable IPv4 Peering ⓘ

VLAN ID * ⓘ

| 152 |

FIGURE 1-32 Microsoft peering configuration

Create and configure an ExpressRoute gateway

An ExpressRoute gateway is still a virtual network gateway, only with different options selected. To create a virtual network gateway for ExpressRoute, follow these steps:

1. Sign in to the Azure portal at *https://portal.azure.com*.
2. In the search bar, search for virtual network gateways, then select the **Virtual network gateways** result.
3. On the local network gateways page, click **Create**.
4. In the subscription dropdown, select the subscription to associate the gateway with.
5. In the Name field, enter a display name for the gateway resource. For example, enter **ER_to_onprem.**
6. In the Region dropdown, select the same region as your virtual network. For this example, select **East US**.
7. For Gateway type, select **ExpressRoute**.
8. In the SKU dropdown field, select the desired SKU. For this example, select **Standard**.
9. In the Virtual network dropdown menu, select the vNet that includes a subnet named **GatewaySubnet** to use with ExpressRoute.
10. In the Public IP address name field, enter **ERPIP**. Figure 1-33 displays the final completed configuration.
11. Click **Review + create**, and then click **Create**.

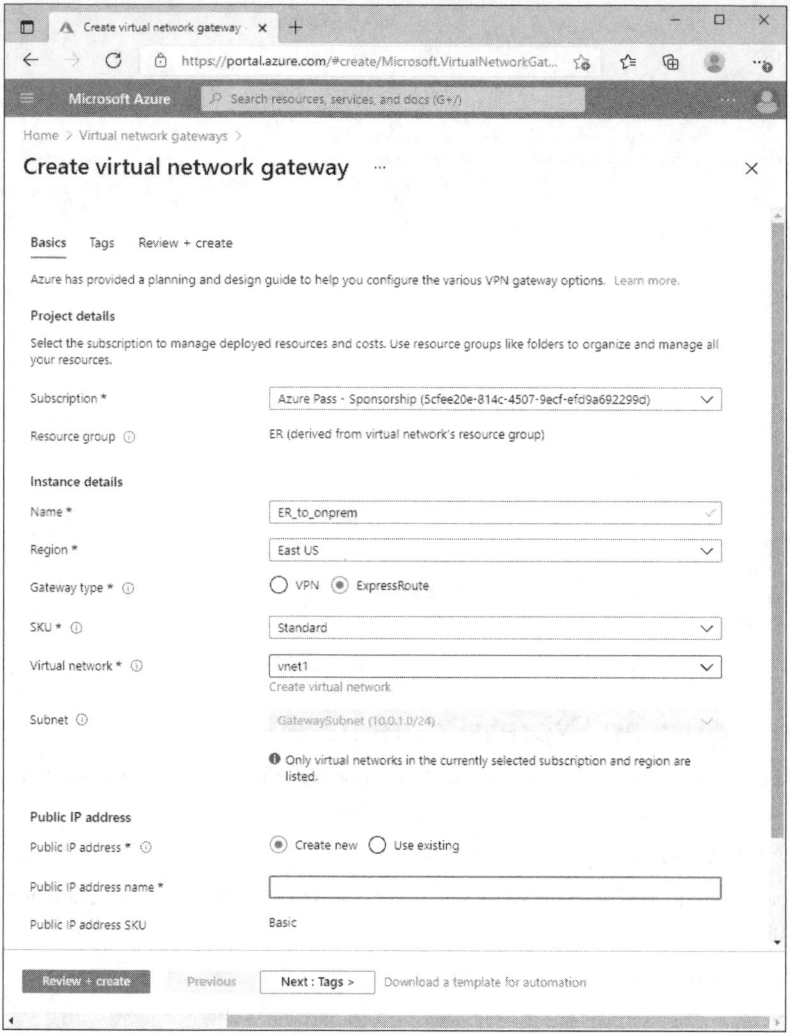

FIGURE 1-33 ExpressRoute virtual network gateway

Connect a virtual network to an ExpressRoute circuit

Similar to creating a VPN, creating the virtual network gateway as an ExpressRoute gateway does not create the connection for the ExpressRoute circuit. After you create the gateway, you must also create a connection to link the circuit to a virtual network.

To create a connection on an existing ExpressRoute circuit, follow these steps:

1. Sign in to the Azure portal at *https://portal.azure.com*.

2. In the search bar, search for ExpressRoute, then select the **ExpressRoute circuits** result.

3. Select a circuit that you have already created.

4. Click the **Connections** blade, and then click **Add**.

5. In the Name field, provide a name for the connection, such as **L3_onprem**.

6. In the Connection type dropdown menu, select **ExpressRoute**.

7. Select **ExpressRoute circuit**, and select the configured circuit. Figure 1-34 displays a partial configuration of the connection.

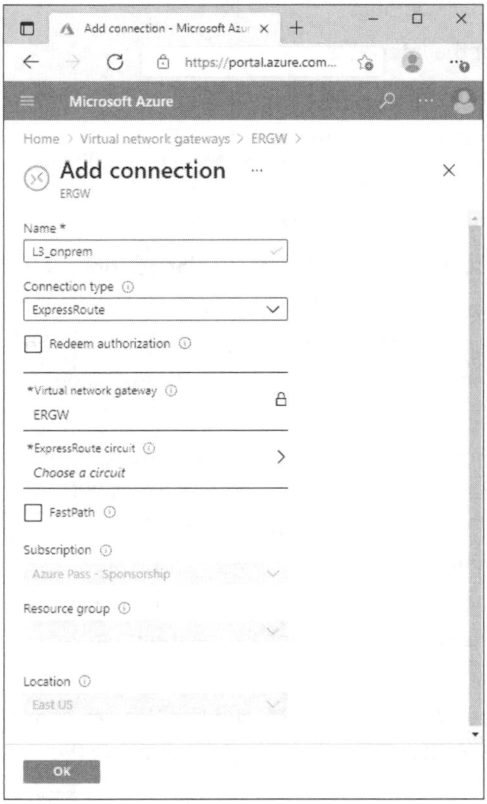

FIGURE 1-34 ExpressRoute Add connection

8. Click **OK** to create the connection.

Recommend a route advertisement configuration

Some telecommunication companies that offer ExpressRoute services also offer a managed routing service as part of the deployment. If this is the case, then you don't need to do anything additional to configure route advertisements. However, if you need or plan to configure the route advertisement manually, then you need to meet the following requirements. For IPv4, the requirements include:

- A single /29 or two /30 subnets for the interfaces
  - If you use a /29, it is separated into a /30 anyway
  - The first /30 is for the primary link

- The second /30 is for the secondary link
- The first available IP address must be used on your hardware
- The second available IP address will be used by Azure

- For Azure private peering, the addresses used can be public or private
- These ranges must not conflict with any virtual network in Azure you plan to connect to

Similar requirements exist if you plan to use IPv6, including:

- A single /125 subnet or two /126 subnets for the interfaces
  - If you use a /125, it is split into two /126 subnets
  - The first available IP address must be used on your hardware
  - The second available IP address will be used by Azure
- For Azure private peering, the addresses used can be public or private
- These ranges must not conflict with any virtual network in Azure you plan to connect to

If you plan to use Microsoft peering, then you must use public IP addresses, which is required for BGP sessions. You must also be able to verify ownership of the addresses through the Internet Routing Registry. The same requirements above apply to Microsoft peering but are only supported with public IP addresses.

After you determine which peering type and protocol that you will use, you can plan route aggregation and default routes. Azure ExpressRoute private peering supports up to 4,000 individual IPv6 prefixes, and 100 IPv6 prefixes that will be advertised. If you enable the premium SKU, then you can increase the IPv4 limit up to 10,000 prefixes.

You can also configure the ExpressRoute circuit to be the default route for Azure virtual networks. This will ensure that all traffic from Azure then flows through ExpressRoute to your on-premises hardware before being routed to the internet.

For BGP and AS numbers, Microsoft uses AS number 12076 for its AS number. You can connect to individual communities for various services within the region that you configure the ExpressRoute circuit in.

> **NEED MORE REVIEW?** **BGP COMMUNITIES**
>
> For more information on the available BGP communities for Azure regions, visit *https://docs.microsoft.com/en-us/azure/expressroute/expressroute-routing#bgp*.

Configure encryption over ExpressRoute

ExpressRoute on its own is a private, dedicated connection through your selected telecommunication provider to an Azure region. However, that does not mean that the traffic is encrypted. You have two options for configuring encryption over ExpressRoute:

- A site-to-site VPN using a virtual network gateway
- A site-to-site VPN using Azure Virtual WAN

The configuration of the site-to-site VPN using a virtual network gateway is no different from the configuration that was discussed in skill section 1.1. If you plan to use a virtual network gateway, it must be deployed as a zone-redundant gateway. Azure Virtual WAN is discussed in a later chapter.

Implement Bidirectional Forwarding Detection

Bidirectional Forwarding Detection (BFD) is useful to accelerate the realization that one of the ExpressRoute links has failed. The BGP keep-alive time is typically configured at 60 seconds, and the hold-time configured at 180 seconds. This means it can take up to three minutes for the service to realize that one of the ExpressRoute links has failed. With BFD, you can lower the keep-alive times as low as 300 milliseconds, allowing failovers to occur in under a second.

BFD is configured by default for all new ExpressRoute private peer connections. After making the configuration change on the on-premises hardware, you only need to reset the ExpressRoute private peer connection to renegotiate the connection with BFD. To reset an existing connection, follow these steps.

1. Sign in to the Azure portal at *https://portal.azure.com*.

2. In the search bar, search for ExpressRoute, then select the **ExpressRoute circuits** result.

3. Select a circuit that you have already configured and want to configure private peering for.

4. Click the **Peerings** blade, and then click **Azure private**.

5. On the Private peering page, clear the checkbox next to **Enable IPv4 Peering**, as shown in Figure 1-35.

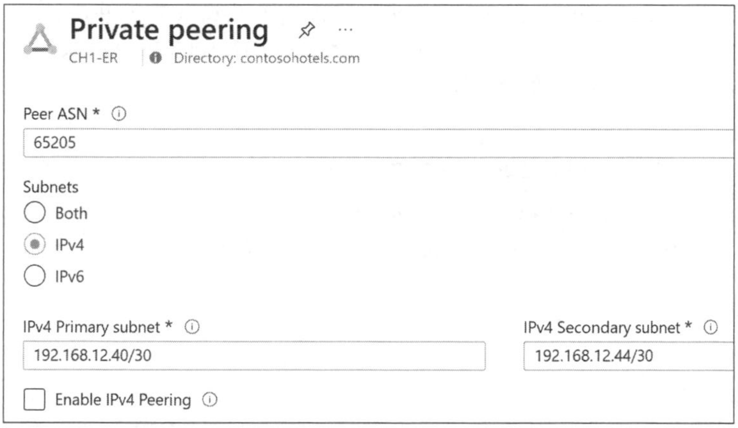

FIGURE 1-35 Reset private peering connection

6. Click **Save**.

7. Select the checkbox next to **Enable IPv4 peering**, and then click **Save**.

Diagnose and resolve ExpressRoute connection issues

Troubleshooting an ExpressRoute connection can be time-consuming because of the number of factors involved across your network, the telecommunication provider network, and the Azure configuration. The first place to begin troubleshooting is the Overview page of the ExpressRoute circuit. As shown in Figure 1-36, the circuit status should display Enabled, and the Provider status should display Provisioned. Anything other than these status indicators might require additional assistance from the provider.

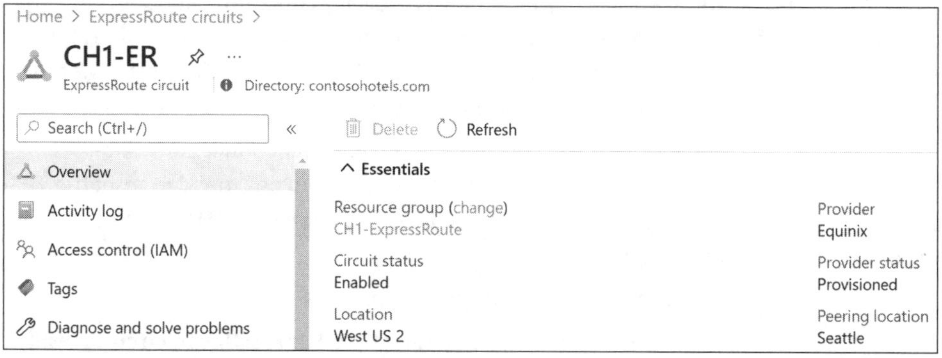

FIGURE 1-36 ExpressRoute overview

If the status labels show Enabled and Provisioned, a common problem with ExpressRoute is routing. Verify that you have the correct address prefixes defined on both sides of the configuration, and test the routing by using a tool such as *tracert*.

If the problems that you are encountering are performance or latency related, you can use the Azure Connectivity Toolkit (AzureCT) to assist with troubleshooting. AzureCT is a PowerShell tool that tests basic network connectivity between two hosts. The AzureCT PowerShell module is available to download at *https://aka.ms/AzureCT*.

> **NEED MORE REVIEW?** **EXPRESSROUTE TROUBLESHOOTING**
>
> For more information on troubleshooting ExpressRoute, visit *https://docs.microsoft.com/en-us/azure/expressroute/expressroute-troubleshooting-network-performance*.

Chapter summary

- Virtual network gateways can be deployed in either zone-redundant or zonal configurations.
- For zone-redundant virtual network gateways, you must use a Standard SKU public IP address.
- The virtual network gateway SKU determines the throughput and maximum number of site-to-site tunnels.

- Policy-based VPNs use static routes based on address range prefixes.
- Route-based VPNs use a route table to direct packets.
- When configuring a virtual network gateway, the virtual network must have a subnet named *GatewaySubnet*.
- A local network gateway is an Azure resource that represents the destination address range.
- Point-to-site VPNs support SSTP, OpenVPN, or IKEv2 connection types.
- The virtual network gateway SKU determines the throughput and maximum number of point-to-site connections.
- Point-to-site VPN tunnels can use RADIUS, certificate, or Azure AD for authentication.
- When using Azure AD for authentication, you must use the Azure VPN client.
- ExpressRoute provides a private, direct connection from your on-premises environment to Azure.
- The ExpressRoute SKU determines the bandwidth and connection limit for the circuit.
- ExpressRoute Global Reach requires the Premium add-on and provides connectivity to multiple Azure regions through one ExpressRoute circuit and is configured on the Private peer.
- ExpressRoute FastPath bypasses the virtual network gateway and communicates directly with virtual machines and is configured on the circuit connection.
- Private peering provides access from your on-premises network to Azure.
- Microsoft peering provides access from your on-premises network to Microsoft 365 services, but it is not recommended.
- ExpressRoute route advertisement is configured by using BGP.

Thought experiment

In this thought experiment, demonstrate your skills and knowledge of the topics covered in this chapter. You can find the answers in the section that follows.

Contoso Mortgage is a financial services company that has two primary datacenters in Chicago and New York. The datacenters have a redundant 5 Gbps connection between them. The company also has smaller branch offices with site-to-site VPN tunnels from the branch office to each datacenter. The IT and executive staff have software-defined VPNs on mobile devices for remote connectivity to each datacenter.

Contoso plans to move their primary application from the on-premises datacenters to the Azure cloud. The network must support the migration and on-going connectivity similarly to the current on-premises design. In the event that one region or connectivity provider has a severe outage, the on-premises datacenter must still be able to communicate with Azure. Figure 1-37 depicts the existing on-premises design.

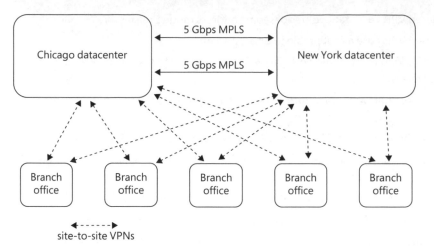

FIGURE 1-37 Contoso Mortgage existing network design

Your goal is to design the network infrastructure for the new Azure environment. For each goal, identify the Azure service to use and incorporate it into the existing architecture.

1. What should you use to provide hybrid connectivity to each datacenter?

2. What should you use to provide hybrid connectivity to each branch office?

3. How should the services be deployed to ensure highly available connectivity?

4. What should the IT and executive staff use to connect to Azure remotely?

Thought experiment answers

This section contains the solution to the thought experiment. Each answer explains why the answer choice is correct.

The desired design based on the requirements of Contoso Mortgage would include ExpressRoute connections from both on-premises datacenters to two Azure regions for the desired redundancy. In this scenario, we can select East US 2 and Central US as the target regions. Because of the requirement to communicate across regions through either of the ExpressRoute circuits, Global Reach must be configured on the circuits. This also means that the circuits have to be ExpressRoute with the Premium add-on. Finally, to address any possible severe outages across providers, the ExpressRoute circuits should be two different connectivity providers for each region.

The branch offices can continue to connect to the on-premises datacenters using site-to-site VPNs. You can configure additional VPNs for each branch office if or when they need the connectivity to Azure.

1. What should you use to provide hybrid connectivity to each datacenter?

   Each datacenter should have an Azure ExpressRoute circuit with Global Reach to meet the design requirements.

2. What should you use to provide hybrid connectivity to each branch office?

Each branch office should have a site-to-site VPN defined to each Azure region.

3. How should the services be deployed to ensure highly available connectivity?

Each branch office should have an independent site-to-site VPN to each Azure region. Each ExpressRoute circuit should have Global Reach enabled for cross-region connectivity.

4. What should the IT and executive staff use to connect to Azure remotely?

The Azure regions should have a virtual network gateway with point-to-site connectivity configured for the IT and executive staff to connect remotely with their mobile devices.

Figure 1-38 shows the final intended design.

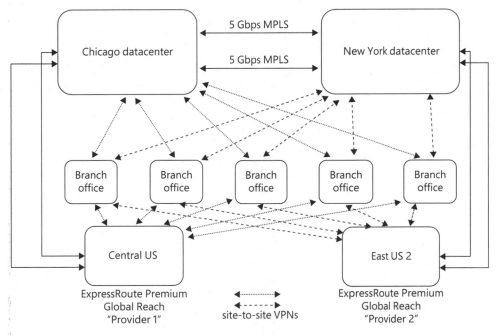

FIGURE 1-38 Contoso Mortgage proposed network design

CHAPTER 2

Design and implement core networking infrastructure

In this chapter we discuss the primary components of a network infrastructure in Azure, which starts with virtual networks. The virtual network provides the connectivity to virtual machines that are deployed in each Azure region, as well as private connectivity through service and private endpoints. Most applications (and people) prefer to use names instead of IP addresses, so the ability to resolve names to IP addresses becomes a critical component of the core network. As the environment grows with additional virtual networks, the need to facilitate communication between networks becomes important and can be addressed with peering. Finally, for a managed hybrid solution, you can use Virtual WAN to have cross-site transitive connectivity through a cloud service.

Skills in this chapter:

- Skill 2.1: Design and implement private IP addressing for virtual networks
- Skill 2.2: Design and implement name resolution
- Skill 2.3: Design and implement cross-VNet connectivity
- Skill 2.4: Design and implement an Azure Virtual WAN architecture

Skill 2.1: Design and implement private IP addressing for virtual networks

The core networking infrastructure in Azure revolves around virtual networks. Virtual networks define the address space for both IPv4 and IPv6 networks that you will use with your Azure services. Virtual networks are required for virtual machines, firewalls, application gateways, virtual network gateways, and more. This skill section focuses on the private connectivity provided by virtual networks and how to integrate the network with other Azure services.

Create a virtual network

A virtual network is one of the foundational services that is deployed in a subscription to facilitate communication for virtual machines, hybrid connectivity, and private communication to Platform as a Service (PaaS) resources. When you create a virtual network, you must specify the Azure region in which to deploy the virtual network. Individual virtual networks span only the single region you deploy them in. If you plan to have a highly available deployment across multiple regions, you will need to deploy at least one virtual network in each region. For larger-scale deployments, you might even deploy multiple virtual networks in a single region for hub-and-spoke type design models.

The process of creating a virtual network is relatively easy. However, the planning and design leading into its creation is much more complex. Some Azure services, such as virtual network gateways and Azure Bastion, require dedicated subnets. We'll discuss subnetting for specific services in the next section.

When you create a virtual network, the two primary planning pieces that the create wizard will ask for are the address space and the first subnet. The address space is at least one IPv4 range and can also include multiple IPv6 ranges. The address ranges that you specify can then be used to create subnets within the virtual network. A best practice is not to overlap address spaces when you plan to deploy multiple virtual networks, even across other subscriptions. Virtual networks that have overlapping IP address spaces *cannot* be peered.

The second component of a virtual network that is defined when you create it is the first subnet.

To create a virtual network, follow these steps:

1. Sign in to the Azure portal at *https://portal.azure.com*.
2. In the search bar, search for and select **Virtual networks**.
3. On the Virtual networks page, click **Create**.
4. In the Subscription dropdown menu, select the subscription that the virtual network should be created in.
5. In the Resource group dropdown menu, create a new, or select an existing, resource group for the virtual network.

6. In the Name field, provide a name for the network, such as **hub-vnet-eus-01**.

7. In the Region dropdown menu, select the region where the virtual network will be used with other resources. For this example, select **East US**.

8. Click **Next: IP Addresses**.

9. Note that the IPv4 address space is already populated with a default address space of 10.0.0.0/16. You can modify or add address spaces if necessary for the virtual network. There is also a subnet named "default" using the first /24 address space. Accept the default, as shown in Figure 2-1, and then click **Next: Security**.

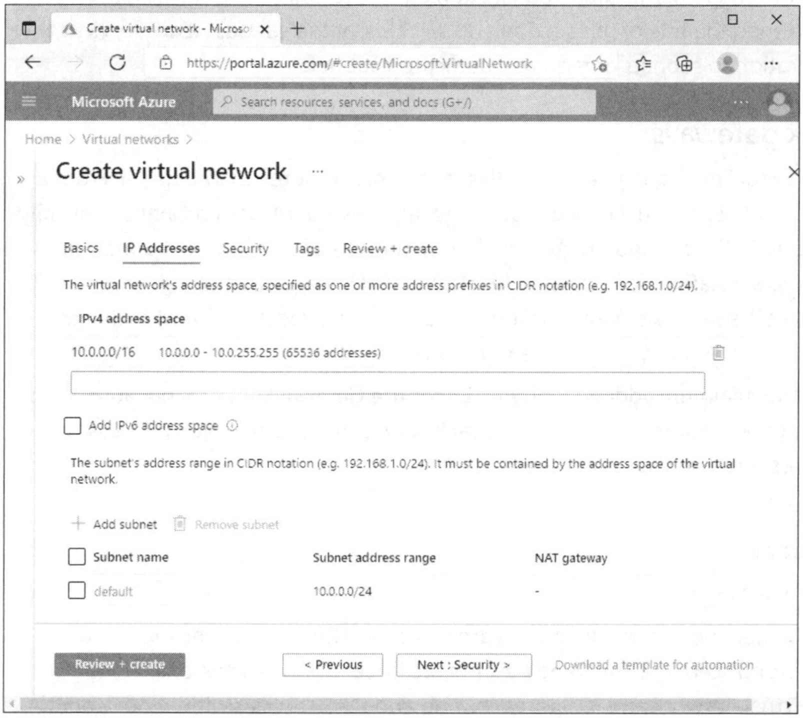

FIGURE 2-1 Virtual network IP addresses

EXAM TIP

This Exam Ref and the exam assume that you are already familiar with networking fundamentals, including subnetting, CIDR notation, TCP/IP, and more. If these are new concepts, you should spend additional time preparing with the *Fundamentals of computer networking* module on Microsoft Learn at *https://docs.microsoft.com/en-us/learn/modules/network-fundamentals/*.

---

10. The Security tab of the Create virtual network page displays the available security services that you can deploy and configure at the same time as the virtual network: BastionHost, DDoS Protection Standard, and Firewall. These are all set to **Disable** by default and can be configured after the virtual network is created. Access the defaults and click **Review + Create**.

Plan and configure subnetting for services

The full name of the objective in the skill is P*lan and configure subnetting for services, including VNet gateways, private endpoints, firewalls, application gateways, and VNet-integrated platform services*. We've shortened the title of this section and will look at the various Azure services that either require integration to subnets or require a dedicated subnet.

Virtual network gateways

Chapter 1 discusses virtual network gateways, VPNs, and ExpressRoute in more detail. From a virtual network perspective, a virtual network gateway requires a dedicated subnet specifically named *GatewaySubnet* to be configured. At a minimum, the size of the GatewaySubnet must be at least a /29 in CIDR notation, for example, 10.0.100.0/29. However, a small subnet like /29 is useful only for a single site-to-site VPN. For future planning, it is recommended to assign a larger address space, such as a /27, to the GatewaySubnet.

The reason that the minimum address range is /29 for the GatewaySubnet is because of how virtual networks allocate IP addresses per subnet. Each subnet has five reserved addresses that cannot be used by resources in your subscription:

- Network identifier
- Broadcast address
- Three Azure-specific services

The network identifier and broadcast address are standard TCP/IP functions that occur in any type of subnetting scenario. The three Azure-specific services are what enables the software-defined virtual network and facilitates routing and DNS services within the subnet.

Using the same 10.0.100.0/29 example earlier, this would result in only three usable addresses:

- 10.0.100.0 – Network identifier, not usable
- 10.0.100.1 – 10.0.100.3 – Azure-specific services, not usable
- 10.0.100.4 – 10.0.100.6 – Usable IP addresses
- 10.0.100.7 – Broadcast address, not usable

When you click + Gateway Subnet from the virtual network, the subnet Name field prepopulates with the name GatewaySubnet and cannot be changed. Figure 2-2 displays the gateway subnet with the example configuration.

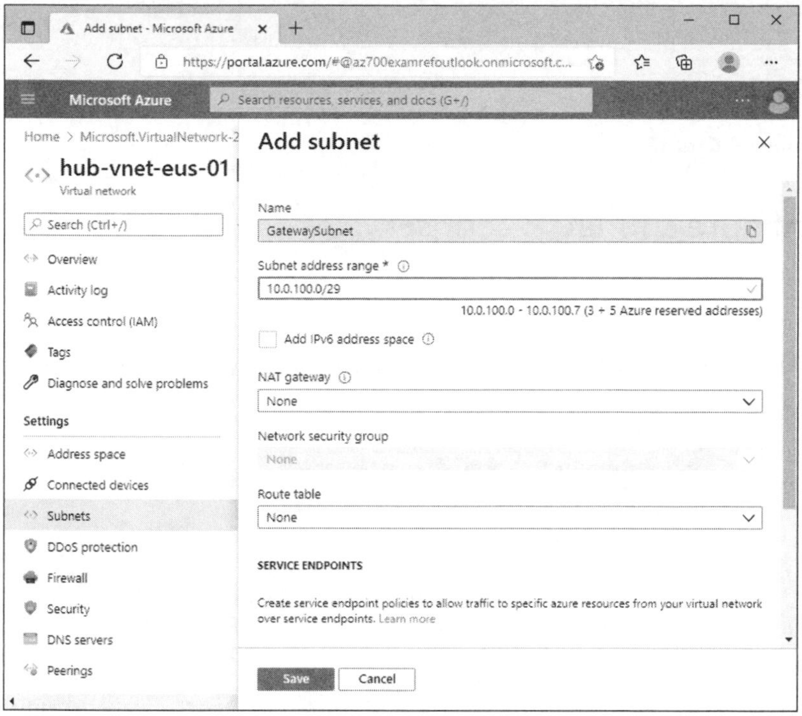

FIGURE 2-2 GatewaySubnet configuration

Firewalls

Azure Firewalls are managed PaaS firewalls that you can associate with a virtual network to protect the resources in the network. The Azure Firewall service is discussed in more detail in Chapter 4, but it is another service that requires a dedicated subnet, specifically named *AzureFirewallSubnet*.

The recommended size of the AzureFirewallSubnet is a /26 in CIDR notation. Azure Firewalls can be set to auto-scale based on CPU percentage or throughput, and each instance requires an additional internal IP address in the AzureFirewallSubnet. A /26 ensures that there are enough IP addresses in the subnet for any possible scaling actions that are taken by the service.

If you try to create a firewall using an existing virtual network, the Azure portal will require that the AzureFirewallSubnet be created before you can create the firewall. Figure 2-3 displays the Create a firewall screen with an error indicating that the existing virtual network must have a subnet named AzureFirewallSubnet.

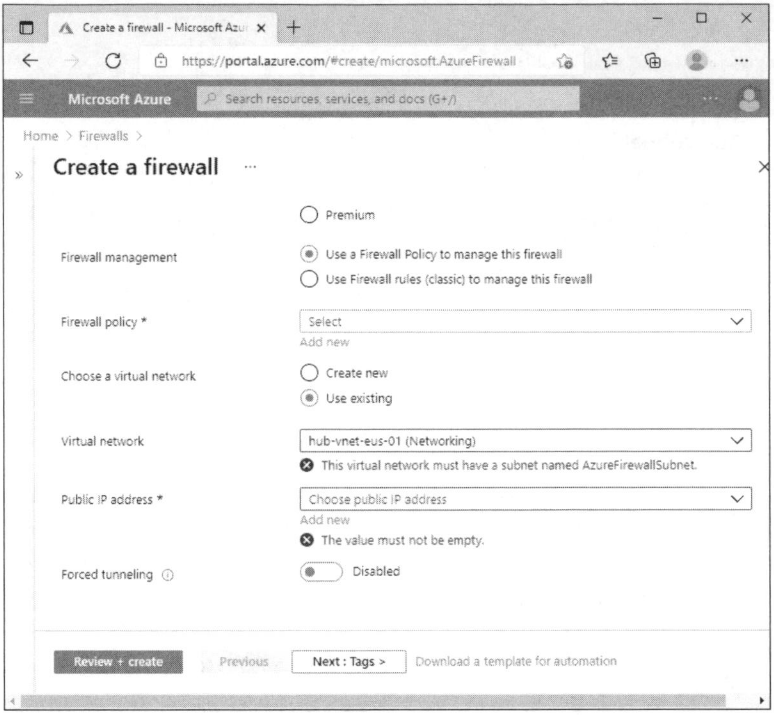

FIGURE 2-3 Azure Firewall missing subnet

Additionally, if you create the AzureFirewallSubnet with a subnet size smaller than /26, you will receive an error. Figure 2-4 shows using an existing virtual network that contains a subnet named AzureFirewallSubnet, but the subnet is not a sufficient size. The error can be confusing, as it says the prefix must be smaller than or equal to 26; meaning the actual integer used for the prefix must be lower—for example a /25, resulting in a larger subnet.

Application gateways

Azure Application Gateway is another PaaS resource that is associated with your virtual networks to protect resources, and is discussed more in Chapter 3. Application gateways require a dedicated subnet within the virtual network, but the subnet does not need to have a specific name. However, the subnet must be empty and not contain any virtual machines or other Azure resources. The recommended size of the subnet depends on the SKU of the application gateway that you use.

Application gateways come in two versions of SKUs—for example, *Standard* and *Standard_v2*. First-generation application gateways can scale up to 32 instances; therefore, a /26 is the recommended subnet size. Application gateways with the v2 SKU can scale up to 125 instances, so a minimum subnet size of /24 is recommended. Unlike with Azure Firewalls, the Azure portal will not give you an error if you happen to create a smaller subnet than recommended. This would then prevent the service from scaling beyond the available IP addresses in the subnet.

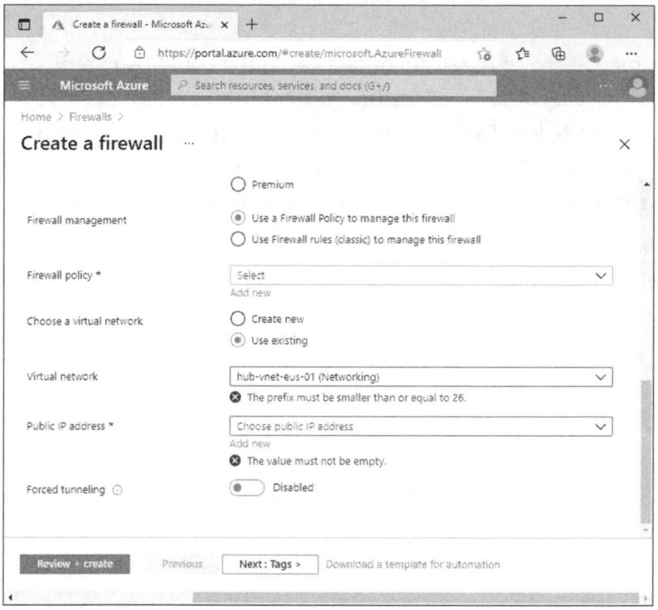

FIGURE 2-4 Azure Firewall incorrect subnet size

You can reuse the same subnet for additional application gateways. However, the gateways in the subnet must be the same version of SKU. For example, you can have two different application gateway deployments using the Standard_v2 SKU. But you cannot have two application gateways in the same subnet: one with Standard and the other at Standard_v2. Figure 2-5 shows the Create application gateway screen with an existing virtual network and subnet selected.

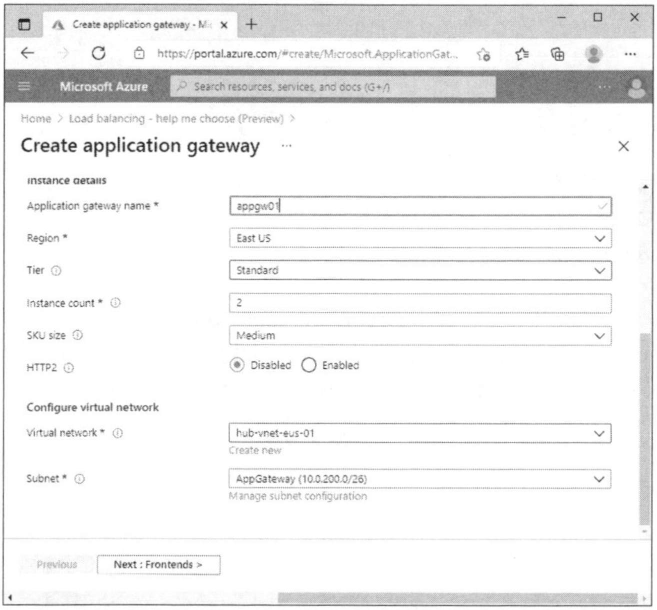

FIGURE 2-5 Application gateway with existing network selected

Bastion

Azure Bastion is not specifically named in any of the exam objectives, but it could be categorized as a "virtual network integrated platform service." Bastion is a PaaS service that provides secure management connectivity, either RDP or SSH, to virtual machines on a virtual network. This secure access is provided by opening HTTPS port 443 to the Bastion service, but it does not require any ports or IP addresses opened to the internet from individual virtual machines.

Bastion requires a dedicated subnet on the virtual network with the specific name of *AzureBastionSubnet*, with a subnet prefix of at least /27. Figure 2-6 displays the error from the Azure portal if you attempt to use an existing virtual network that does not have the subnet predefined.

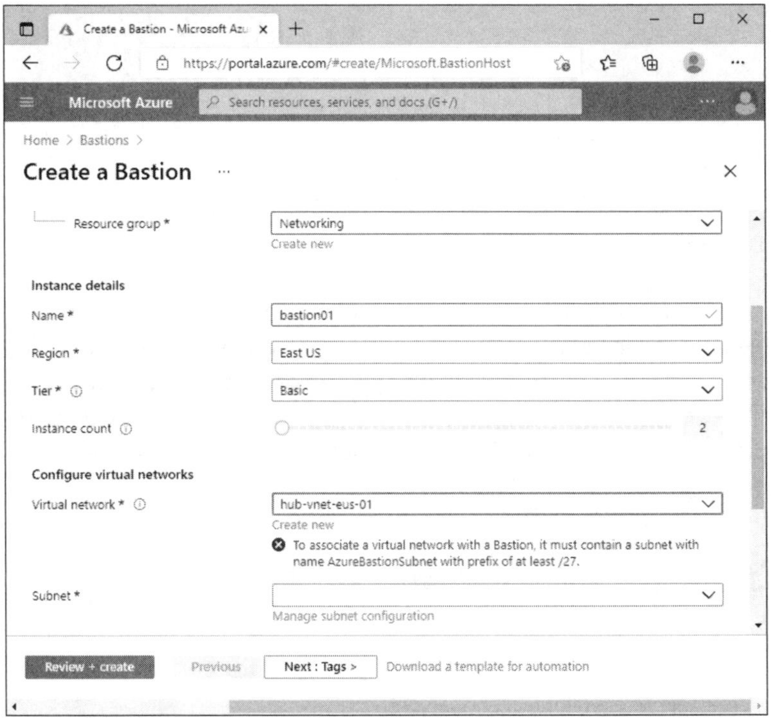

FIGURE 2-6 Bastion service without AzureBastionSubnet

As with Azure Firewalls, if you create the AzureBastionSubnet manually with an address range that is too small, the Azure portal will give you an error indicating that the prefix must be at least /27. Figure 2-7 displays the error message from the portal when the AzureBastionSubnet exists but is misconfigured.

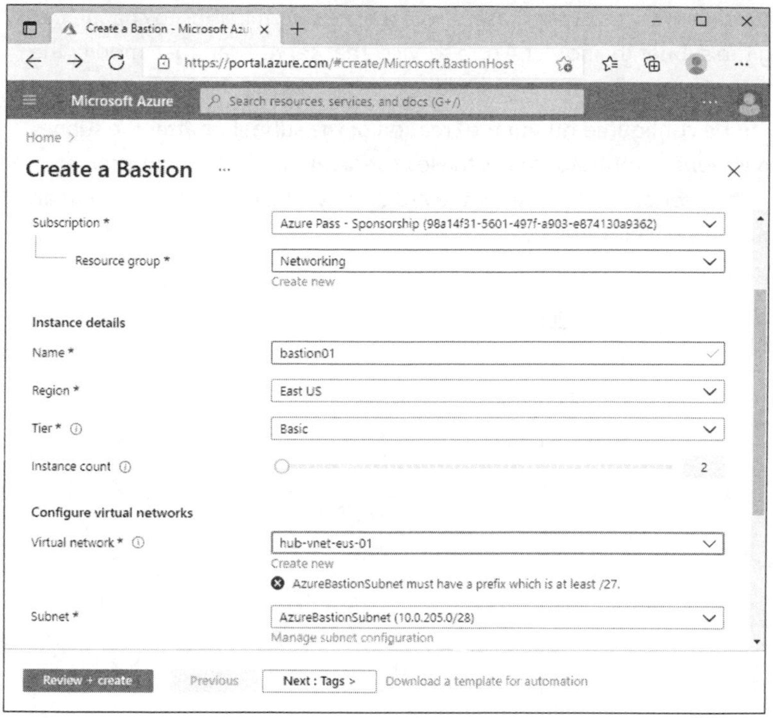

FIGURE 2-7 Bastion service with too small a subnet

Private endpoints

Private endpoints offer a method of using Azure PaaS services, which are typically public end-points, and assigning that service a private IP address on a subnet within a virtual network. For example, in a default configuration, if a virtual machine connects to an Azure storage account for a blob file, the virtual machine would contact storageaccount.blob.core.windows.net, with the DNS name resolving to a public IP address.

If you configure a private endpoint with the storage account, you can then associate that storage account with a subnet. Then, virtual machines on the same virtual network would resolve and connect to the storage account using the assigned private IP address. Virtual machines or services outside the virtual network would still resolve and connect to the public IP address. Private and service endpoints are discussed in more detail in Chapter 5.

Plan and configure subnet delegation

Azure resources, including virtual networks, are managed by using role-based access control (RBAC). As a resource owner, if you need to allow other administrators to perform manage-ment actions on the resource, you must assign a role to the user or group. If you need to assign permissions to the resource to another Azure service, you can delegate that management, enabling the integration of Azure services with a subnet.

Delegating a subnet is similar to assigning a user a role that has permissions to change the resource. By delegating the subnet to another Azure service, that service can then modify the configuration of the subnet to provide a managed and recommended configuration.

Subnet delegation can be configured during the creation of the subnet or after the subnet has been created. The Network Contributor role is the lowest-level role that has appropriate permissions to delegate the subnet to a service. Figure 2-8 displays the Delegate subnet to a service dropdown menu of an existing subnet.

FIGURE 2-8 Subnet delegation

Plan and configure subnetting for Azure Route Server

Azure Route Server is a service that simplifies the routing for hybrid connectivity. From a virtual network perspective, it is similar to the other services discussed in this skill section in that it requires a dedicated subnet with a specific name: *RouteServerSubnet*. Additionally, the minimum size of the subnet is /27. The virtual network that contains this subnet must be in the same Azure region as the route server that you plan to deploy.

Skill 2.2: Design and implement name resolution

Name resolution is a critical part of any infrastructure design, and maybe more so in a cloud environment. In an on-premises environment, names are prevalent and commonly used, but they map to static IP addresses a lot of times, and thus don't change often. However, in the cloud, more and more addresses and services use dynamic IP addresses, making DNS that much more important. Azure has two primary DNS solutions—public and private DNS zones—which are discussed in this skill section.

> **This skill covers how to:**
> - Design public DNS zones
> - Design private DNS zones
> - Design name resolution inside a virtual network
> - Configure a public or private DNS zone
> - Link a private DNS zone to a virtual network

Design public DNS zones

Azure DNS is a PaaS service that provides an authoritative DNS service for a domain name in your environment. The domain name should be a public domain that you have the ability to configure the name servers for. After you create the public DNS zone, you must change the name servers with the domain registrar so that the records that you create will work properly. This will have an impact on any existing DNS configuration.

To create a public DNS zone, follow these steps:

1. Sign in to the Azure portal at *https://portal.azure.com*.
2. In the search bar, search for and select **DNS zones**.
3. On the DNS zones page, click **Create**.
4. In the Subscription dropdown menu, select the subscription to create the zone in.
5. In the Resource group dropdown menu, create or select a resource group to logically organize the resource in.
6. In the Name field, provide a valid domain name that you own, for example **az700examref.com**.
7. Click **Review + Create**, and then click **Create**. Figure 2-9 displays the completed configuration.

After creating the DNS zone, take note of the name servers provided by the Azure service. These name servers must be configured with the domain so that the records that you create resolve correctly. Each registrar has its own steps and methods of updating the name servers for their domain names. Figure 2-10 displays the name servers assigned to the new az700examref.com zone.

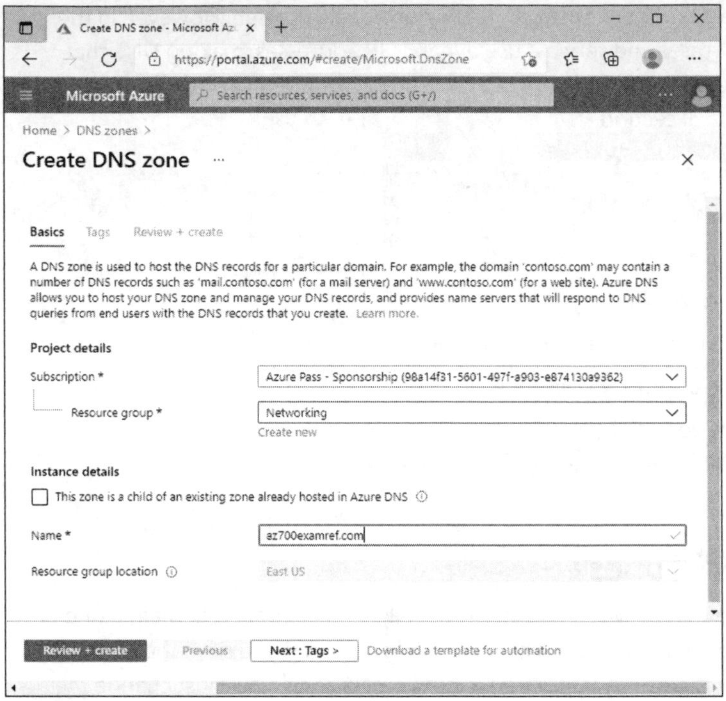

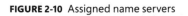

FIGURE 2-9 Create DNS zone

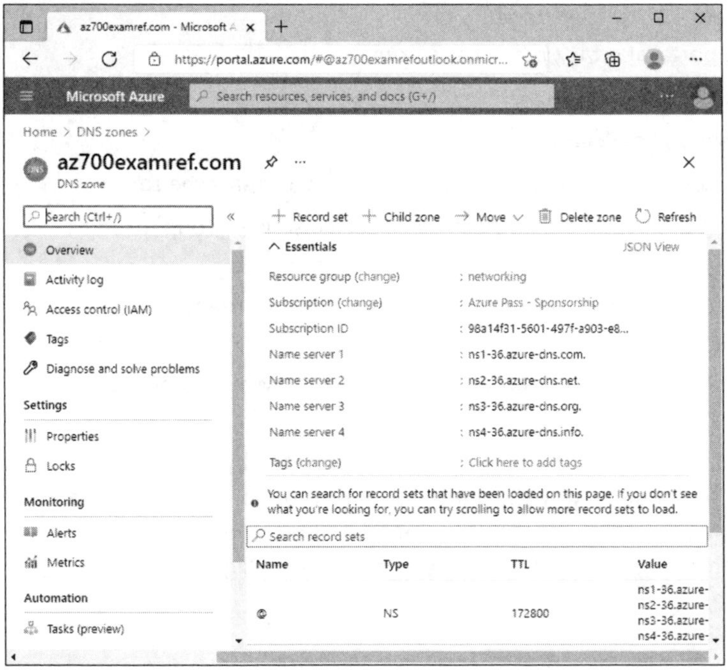

FIGURE 2-10 Assigned name servers

After you have made the name server change with the domain registrar, you can verify that the change is accurately propagated on the internet by using *nslookup*. Figure 2-11 shows the nslookup utility being used to query the name servers for the az700examref.com domain.

```
C:\Windows\system32\cmd.exe - nslookup                        —   □    ×

C:\>nslookup
Default Server:  UnKnown
Address:  192.168.1.1

> set type=ns
> az700examref.com
Server:  UnKnown
Address:  192.168.1.1

Non-authoritative answer:
az700examref.com          nameserver = ns2-36.azure-dns.net
az700examref.com          nameserver = ns3-36.azure-dns.org
az700examref.com          nameserver = ns4-36.azure-dns.info
az700examref.com          nameserver = ns1-36.azure-dns.com

ns1-36.azure-dns.com    internet address = 150.171.10.36
ns1-36.azure-dns.com    AAAA IPv6 address = 2603:1061:0:10::24
ns2-36.azure-dns.net    internet address = 150.171.16.36
ns2-36.azure-dns.net    AAAA IPv6 address = 2620:1ec:8ec:10::24
ns3-36.azure-dns.org    internet address = 13.107.222.36
ns3-36.azure-dns.org    AAAA IPv6 address = 2a01:111:4000:10::24
ns4-36.azure-dns.info   internet address = 13.107.206.36
ns4-36.azure-dns.info   AAAA IPv6 address = 2620:1ec:bda:10::24
> _
```

FIGURE 2-11 nslookup utility

Design private DNS zones

Private DNS zones are similar to public zones in that they still contain records for resources and can even be public domain names. However, with a private zone, you do not need to modify the public name servers. Instead, you link the private DNS zone to the virtual networks where you would like name resolution to work. Resolution will then only occur from within the virtual network, and not externally or publicly. This means that the domain name does not even need to be a valid or routable domain.

To create a private DNS zone, follow these steps:

1. Sign in to the Azure portal at *https://portal.azure.com*.

2. In the search bar, search for and select **Private DNS zones**.

3. On the Private DNS zones page, click **Create**.

4. In the Subscription dropdown menu, select the subscription to create the zone in.

5. In the Resource group dropdown menu, create or select a resource group to logically organize the resource in.

6. In the Name field, provide a valid domain name that you own, for example **az700examref.private**.

7. Click **Review + Create**, and then click **Create**. Figure 2-12 displays the completed configuration.

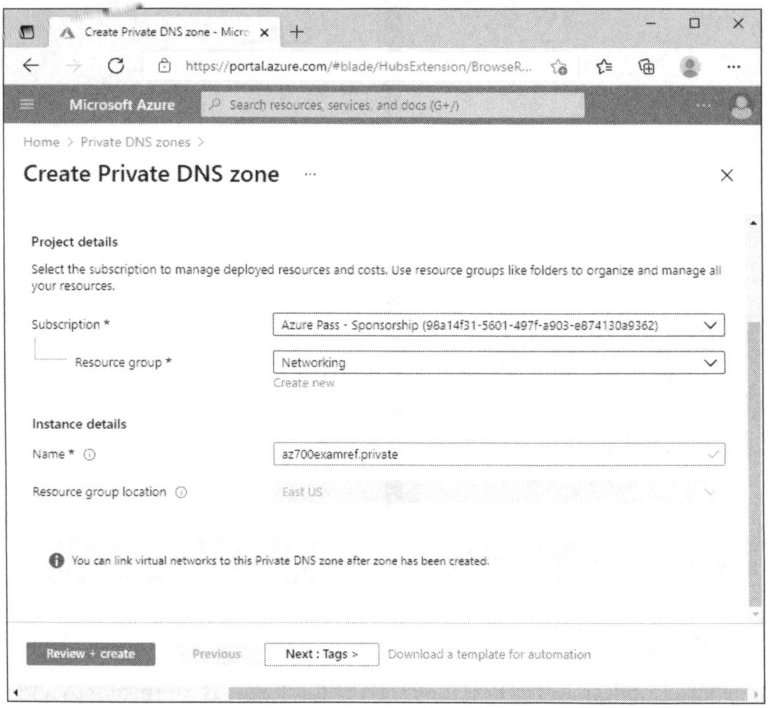

FIGURE 2-12 Private DNS zone creation

> **NOTE USING ALTERNATE TOP-LEVEL DOMAINS**
>
> Although we are using a *.private* top-level domain (TLD) name in this scenario to show that the service supports it, it is not recommended to use alternate TLDs because not all operating systems support them.

After a private DNS zone is created and linked to a virtual network, the name resolution occurs within the virtual network. The diagram in Figure 2-13 displays the three steps for VM1 resolving the IP address of VM2:

1. VM1 wants to connect to VM2.az700examref.private but does not know the IP address and requests it from the virtual network's DNS server.

2. The private DNS zone has a record for VM2 and responds to the DNS request with an IP address of 10.0.0.4.

3. VM then connects directly to VM2 using the 10.0.0.4 IP address.

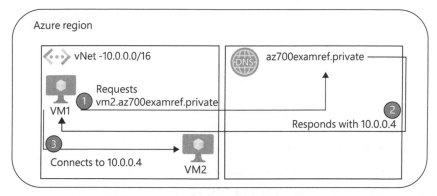

FIGURE 2-13 Private DNS steps

Design name resolution inside a virtual network

Determining whether to use public DNS zones, private DNS zones, or a combination of the two is the primary factor for designing how name resolution works in the environment. Private zones give you the flexibility to use a desired naming solution within your virtual network without modifying external, public DNS records. Private zones also give you the ability to configure "split-horizon" DNS where the same fully qualified name, such as app1.contoso.com, resolves to one service internally and another service externally. Other benefits of using private zones include:

- Automatic hostname management
- Hostname resolution between virtual networks
- Reverse DNS lookups, but only within the virtual network

Private DNS zones also have limitations. When using automatic registration of hostnames, then the virtual network can only be linked to one private DNS zone. The DNS zone can still have multiple virtual networks linked. Another limitation is that conditional forwarding does not have native support and requires additional configuration to resolve on-premises names.

Both public and private DNS zones in Azure use the same dedicated IP address for DNS queries: 168.63.129.16. This is a static IP address, and it does not change per zone, subscription, or tenant.

Configure a public or private DNS zone

Both public and private DNS zones support the common DNS record types:

- A
- AAAA
- CNAME
- MX
- PTR
- SRV
- TXT

To create a new record, follow these steps:

1. Sign in to the Azure portal at *https://portal.azure.com*.
2. In the search bar, search for and select **Private DNS zones**.
3. Click the name of the private zone you have previously created.
4. In the private zone, click **+ Record set**.
5. In the Name field, provide a name for the record as part of the fully qualified domain name, such as **app1**.
6. In the Type dropdown menu, select the desired type of record. In this example, select **CNAME**.
7. Leave the TTL value default, which is the amount of time the DNS record will be cached before being looked up again.
8. Provide an alias for the CNAME record, which is where DNS will redirect the connection request to. In this example, use **www.microsoft.com**.
9. Click **OK**. Figure 2-14 displays the completed configuration.

The process for creating a record set for a public DNS zone is the same. With public DNS zones, you also have the ability to create CAA and NS record types. Otherwise, the steps are similar to add a record in either a public or a private DNS zone.

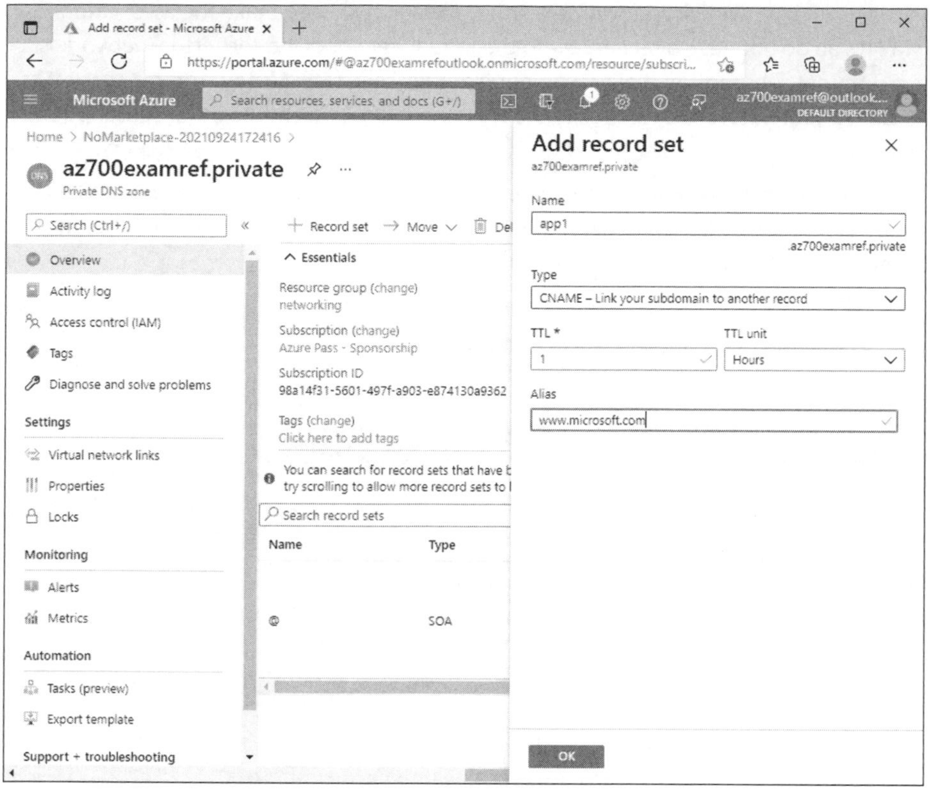

FIGURE 2-14 Add record set

Link a private DNS zone to a virtual network

For a private DNS zone to return queries, it must be linked to a virtual network. Creating a private DNS zone and adding record entries does not make the association with a virtual network. To link a private DNS zone to a virtual network, follow these steps:

1. Sign in to the Azure portal at *https://portal.azure.com*.

2. In the search bar, search for and select **Private DNS zones**.

3. Click the name of the private zone you have previously created.

4. Click the **Virtual network links** blade.

5. Click **+ Add**.

6. Provide a name for the association because the private DNS zone can be linked with multiple virtual networks. In this example, use **eus-vnet01**.

7. In the Subscription dropdown, select the subscription where the virtual network is located.

8. In the Virtual network dropdown, select the virtual network to make the association with. If you do not have direct access to the virtual network, and the virtual network is in a different subscription that you do not manage, select the **I know the resource ID of the virtual network** checkbox and obtain the full path from the other subscription owner.

9. If you want auto-registration of resources in the virtual network with the private DNS zone, select the checkbox. However, this will prevent the virtual network from being linked to any other private DNS zone.

10. Click **OK**. Figure 2-15 displays the completed configuration.

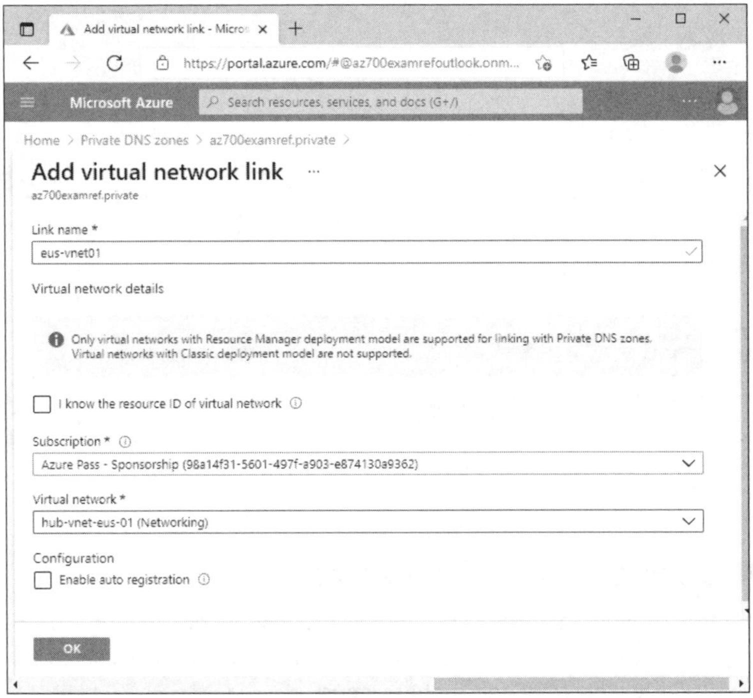

FIGURE 2-15 Add virtual network link

Skill 2.3: Design and implement cross-VNet connectivity

When you are designing a mid-size or enterprise-scale landing zone, you will most likely have multiple subscriptions, and thus multiple networks. However, just because applications are segmented by subscription, that does not mean that two applications will never communicate. Additionally, when you have hybrid resources with VPN or ExpressRoute connectivity in a shared subscription, the application might need to use these connections. This skill section focuses on connecting networks using both virtual network peering and virtual network gateways.

This skill covers how to:

- Implement virtual network peering
- Design service chaining, including gateway transit
- Design VPN connectivity between virtual networks

Implement virtual network peering

While a single network is scalable and can support thousands of virtual machines and services, it is not recommended to have only one virtual network. The reference architecture for an enterprise-scale landing zone, and even for mid-size deployments, includes a hub-and-spoke architecture. We create this architecture in Azure by using one virtual network as the hub network, which might contain other connectivity resources such as VPNs and ExpressRoute (discussed in Chapter 1). Then each application could be represented by a spoke network but would be a separate virtual network that could even be in a different subscription.

> **NEED MORE REVIEW?** **ENTERPRISE-SCALE LANDING ZONE**
>
> For more information on an enterprise-scale landing zone, visit *https://docs.microsoft.com/en-us/azure/cloud-adoption-framework/ready/enterprise-scale/architecture*.

The hub network contains not only the additional connectivity, but probably other monitoring or compliance resources. The next step is to then determine how the spoke network can communicate with the hub network. The easiest method of facilitating this connectivity is to use virtual network peering. The primary requirement to use virtual network peering is that the two virtual network address spaces cannot overlap.

Configuring peering between two virtual networks essentially extends the network using the Azure network backbone. The network communication is private connectivity between the two networks. Figure 2-16 shows a sample configuration of a peering connection between the East US and UK South Azure regions.

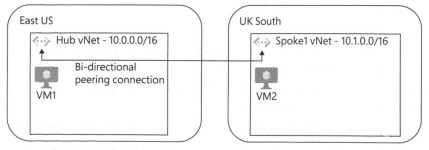

FIGURE 2-16 Virtual network peering

The diagram in Figure 2-16 also implies a couple of other things to know about virtual network peering:

- Supports both uni-directional and bi-directional.
- Virtual networks can be in the same or different Azure regions.
- Virtual networks can be in the same or different subscriptions.

In this scenario, VM1 and VM2 would be able to communicate with each other over any port and protocol across the virtual networks without any additional configuration. When you create a peering connection from the portal, it provides the options for a bi-directional connection. Each option is presented twice in the interface: once for *this* virtual network to the remote. Then, the reverse: from the remote virtual network to *this* network. *This* network being the network that you are performing the configuration from. Table 2-1 outlines the configuration options that are available when configuring peering.

TABLE 2-1 Virtual network peering options

Setting	This virtual network	Remote virtual network
Peering link name	Display name	Display name
Traffic to remote virtual network	Allow (default) Block	Allow (default) Block
Traffic forwarded from remote virtual network	Allow (default) Block	Allow (default) Block
Virtual network gateway or Route Server	Use this network's gateway Use the remote gateway None (default)	Use this network's gateway Use the remote gateway None (default)

To create a peering connection using two virtual networks that were already created, follow these steps:

1. Sign in to the Azure portal at *https://portal.azure.com*.
2. In the search bar, search for and select **Virtual networks**.
3. Click the name of one of the virtual networks that you want to configure peering on. In this example, we will configure from the spoke network to the hub network.
4. Click the **Peerings** blade.
5. Click **+ Add**.
6. In the Peering link name field for this virtual network, provide a name for the connection. For example, enter **spoke-to-hub**, since we are configuring *from* the spoke.
7. For the *Traffic to remote virtual network* and *traffic forwarded from remote virtual network* settings, accept the default, **Allow**.
8. In the Virtual network gateway or Route Server setting, accept the default of **None**.
9. In the Peering link name field for the remote virtual network, provide a name such as **hub-to-spoke**.

10. If the virtual network is in the same subscription, select the appropriate subscription and virtual network from each dropdown list. If you do not have access to the subscription, select the **I know my resource ID** checkbox and obtain the ID from the remote subscription owner.

11. For the *Traffic to remote virtual network* and *traffic forwarded from remote virtual network* settings, accept the default, **Allow**.

12. In the Virtual network gateway or Route Server setting, accept the default of **None**.

13. Click **Add**. Figure 2-17 displays a portion of the completed configuration.

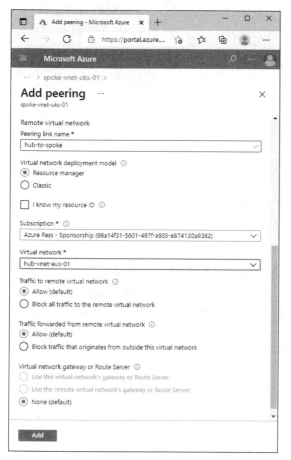

FIGURE 2-17 Add peering

After you complete the peering connection, the peer with the status will be displayed on the Peerings blade of both virtual networks and should have a status of **Connected**. Figure 2-18 displays the Peerings blade after a successful connection.

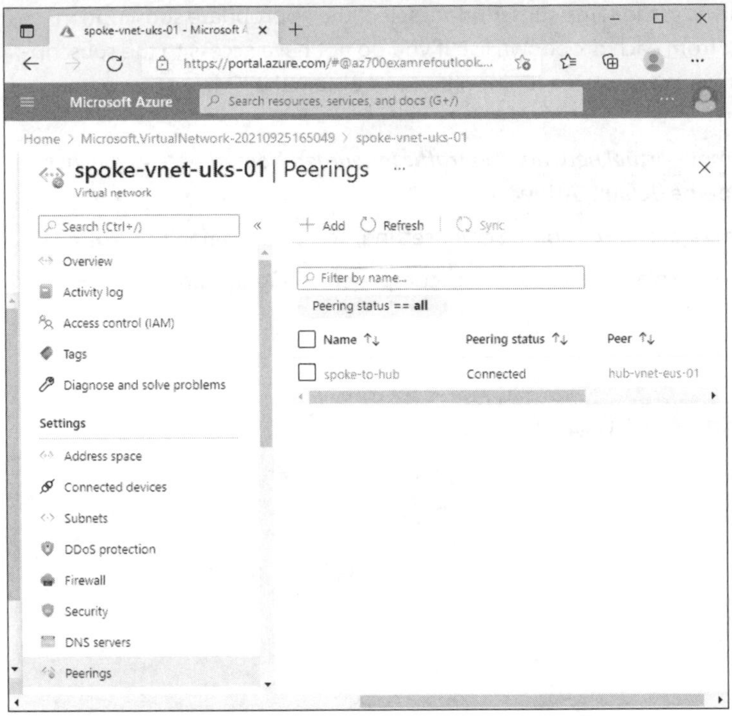

FIGURE 2-18 Connected peer

Design service chaining, including gateway transit

When you connect two virtual networks with peering, by default there is full communication between the two networks. A way to think about this connection is that it is essentially a static route from the address space of one network to the address space of the second network. Then, for the purposes of routing, these static routes are *not* advertised to any other virtual network.

Because this route is not advertised, when you have two (or more) spoke networks connected to a hub, it does not mean that the spokes can then communicate with each other. For example, in Figure 2-19, there are two spoke networks, Spoke1 and Spoke2, connected with peering to a hub network.

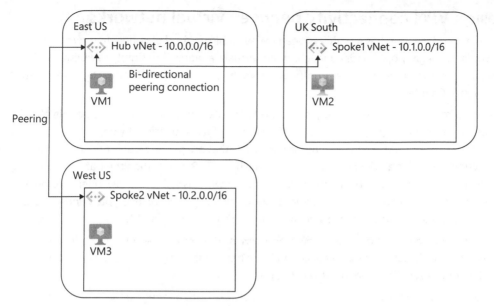

FIGURE 2-19 Peering with multiple spokes

In the scenario presented in Figure 2-19, although both spoke networks are connected with peering to the hub, the two spoke networks cannot communicate by default. The connection is there, but because of the lack of route advertisements, the 10.2.0.0 network in Spoke2 does not know how or where to send traffic that might be destined for the 10.1.0.0 network in Spoke1.

There are two options for facilitating this communication:

- Routing table
- Virtual network gateway (or other route server)

The most simple and rudimentary of these options is a route table. You can create a route table, associate it with the subnets in the Spoke2 virtual network, and list a next hop IP address in the hub network that can then route the traffic to Spoke1. While this is a valid configuration, the administrative overhead can grow to be unmanageable as you scale. Route tables are discussed in more detail in Chapter 3.

The scalable solution is to use a virtual network gateway, or other route server, to facilitate the routing. Referring back to Figure 2-17, when you create a peering connection, you have the option to use a gateway in one or both of the virtual networks. This association then allows the peered virtual network to communicate with another peer or on-premises environment through a VPN or ExpressRoute that is defined as part of the virtual network gateway.

Design VPN connectivity between virtual networks

Virtual network peering has not always been the available method of connecting two virtual networks. The legacy option for connecting two virtual networks is to simply establish a VPN connection between them. This is no different from the site-to-site VPN connections that were discussed in Chapter 1.

While it might be considered a legacy method of implementation, there are a couple of scenarios where you might prefer to use a VPN instead of using peering. By default, peering allows full communication between the two networks that are peering but is not an encrypted connection. If you use an unencrypted protocol such as HTTP or FTP, then the traffic between virtual networks, although private on the Microsoft network, is still technically unencrypted. If you have use cases or compliance scenarios in which all traffic must be encrypted and you are forced to use unencrypted protocols, then you must consider using a VPN.

The possible downside of using a VPN is that this introduces another public IP address to manage on the virtual network gateway, and it has bandwidth limitations based on gateway SKU that you select, discussed in detail in Chapter 1.

The mostly likely scenario is that you will probably use both peering and VPNs in your design. For applications that require additional levels of encryption, compliance, or connections to third-party vendors, VPNs might be more suitable. For internal connections that already use TLS connections, peering might be more suitable.

Skill 2.4: Design and implement an Azure Virtual WAN architecture

In this section, we introduce and discuss Azure Virtual WAN, which provides a managed cloud service that facilitates transitive cross-site connectivity through VPNs, ExpressRoute, and virtual networks. In the scenario that multiple on-premises locations exist, and each requires a VPN plus individual client connections using point-to-site VPNs, the hybrid connectivity can continue to increase management overhead. Virtual WAN simplifies the configuration by bringing all services to one location, and then it gives the ability for the various connections to communicate with each other through the hub in the Virtual WAN.

> **This skill covers how to:**
> - Design an Azure Virtual WAN architecture, including selecting SKUs and services
> - Create a hub in Virtual WAN
> - Connect a virtual network gateway to Azure Virtual WAN
> - Create a network virtual appliance in a virtual hub
> - Configure virtual hub routing

Design an Azure Virtual WAN architecture, including selecting SKUs and services

Through Chapter 1 and 2 so far, we've discussed methods of hybrid connectivity with VPNs and ExpressRoute, and native Azure connectivity with virtual networks. In an environment where there might be several point-to-site and site-to-site VPN connections, ExpressRoute, and virtual-network-to-virtual-network connections, managing the various connection types can become an administrative burden. Azure Virtual WAN is a management and connectivity solution to bring these connections together. There are two SKUs of Virtual WAN:

- Basic
- Standard

The Basic SKU type can only support site-to-site VPN connections. The Standard SKU can support multiple connection types:

- Site-to-site VPN
- Point-to-site VPN
- ExpressRoute
- Inter-hub connectivity
- Azure Firewall
- Network Virtual Appliances

The Virtual WAN acts as a central hub for these various connection types in a hub-and-spoke model. You use Virtual WAN to centralize these connections to provide transitive connectivity across the different types of connections. Figure 2-20 shows a single-region deployment of Virtual WAN with various connection types.

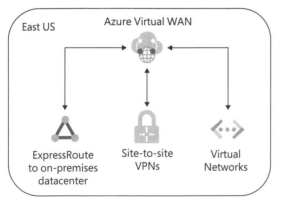

FIGURE 2-20 Single-region Virtual WAN

To create an Azure Virtual WAN, follow these steps:

1. Sign in to the Azure portal at *https://portal.azure.com*.
2. In the search bar, search for and select **Virtual WANs**.
3. On the Virtual WANs page, click **Create**.

4. In the Subscription dropdown menu, select the desired subscription to add the Virtual WAN to.

5. In the Resource group dropdown menu, select a resource group to organize the resource in. For this example, create or select a group named **Networking**.

6. In the Resource group location, select the location where the resource should be deployed. For this example, select **East US**.

7. In the Name field, provide a name for the resource, such as **VWAN-EUS**.

8. In the Type dropdown menu, select the desired SKU of the Virtual WAN, such as **Standard**. Figure 2-21 shows the completed fields.

9. Click **Review + Create**, and then click **Create**.

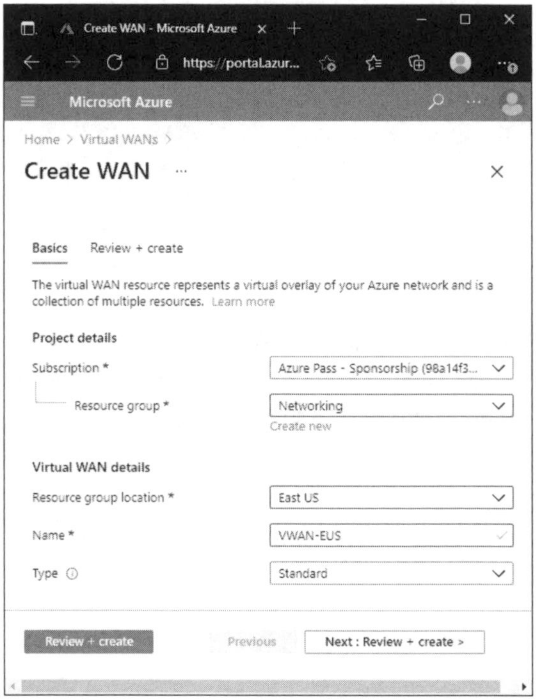

FIGURE 2-21 Create a Virtual WAN

As you plan the design of a hybrid connectivity model, you might consider using third-party appliances for the on-premises side of the connectivity. Virtual WAN has a list of approved partners with how-to deployment guides as of this writing:

- Barracuda Networks
- Check Point
- Cisco Meraki
- Citrix
- Cloudgenix

- Fortinet
- HPE Aruba
- NetFoundry
- Nuage/Nokia
- Open Systems
- Palo Alto Networks
- Riverbed Technology
- Silver-Peak
- VMware SD-WAN
- Versa

> *NEED MORE REVIEW?* **PARTNER DEPLOYMENT GUIDES**
>
> For more information on the approved appliance partners and how-to guides, visit *https://docs.microsoft.com/en-us/azure/virtual-wan/virtual-wan-locations-partners*.

Create a hub in Virtual WAN

The first part of the Virtual WAN that is required is a hub. The hub is a virtual network that you create "within" the Virtual WAN. This hub network is the transitive network that will provide connectivity to the other services that you attach to your Virtual WAN.

When you create a hub, there are a couple of requirements that the hub must meet to be able to connect the various services. First, any on-premises or virtual network address spaces cannot overlap, including the private address space that you specify when creating the Virtual WAN. Second, any existing virtual networks cannot have a virtual network gateway associated with the virtual network. If the virtual network has a gateway, then it must be removed prior to connecting it to the hub.

To create a hub in an existing Virtual WAN, follow these steps:

1. Sign in to the Azure portal at *https://portal.azure.com*.
2. In the search bar, search for and select **Virtual WANs**.
3. On the Virtual WANs page, select the existing Virtual WAN resource.
4. On the Virtual WAN resource, click the **Hubs** blade.
5. On the Hubs blade, click **+ New Hub**.
6. In the Region dropdown menu, select the Azure region to deploy the hub to, such as **East US**.
7. In the Name field, provide a name for the hub, such as **vwan-eus-hub**.

8. In the Hub private address space field, provide an address space for the hub, such as **10.10.0.0/16**. Remember that this address space cannot overlap with any virtual network or on-premises environment that will connect to it. Figure 2-22 displays the Basics tab of the Create virtual hub page.

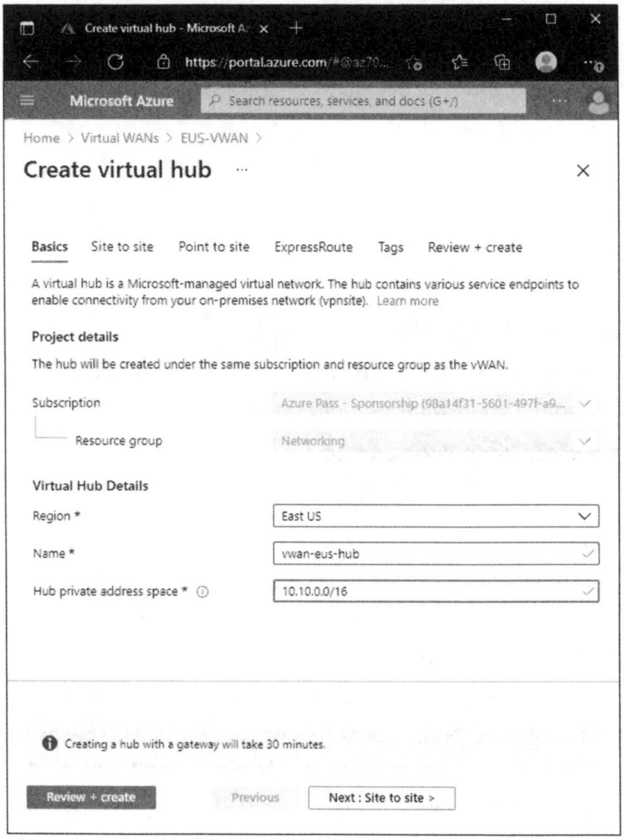

FIGURE 2-22 Virtual hub basics

9. The Site to site, Point to site, and ExpressRoute tabs allow you to create these connections at the same time as the hub, but they are not required at this time. Click **Review + Create**, and then click **Create**.

Connect a virtual network gateway to Azure Virtual WAN

As the title of this section suggests, the objective list for this exam references connecting a virtual network gateway to a Virtual WAN. However, the VPN sites that you define in a Virtual WAN are separate from virtual network gateways and the VPNs that you create there. You do not need to create a virtual network gateway and then associate the VPN to the Virtual WAN.

Instead, you create a VPN site within the virtual WAN. The VPN site can then have multiple links to the physical site you are connecting to. Additionally, you can configure scaling for the Virtual WAN solution as part of the site.

To create a VPN site in a Virtual WAN, follow these steps:

1. Sign in to the Azure portal at *https://portal.azure.com*.

2. In the search bar, search for and select **Virtual WANs**.

3. On the Virtual WANs page, select the existing Virtual WAN resource.

4. On the Virtual WAN resource, click the **VPN sites** blade.

5. On the VPN sites blade, click **Create site**.

6. In the Region dropdown menu, select a region for the VPN site, such as **East US**.

7. In the Name field, specify a name for the VPN site, such as **branch1-vpn**.

8. In the Device vendor field, specify the name of the vendor for the remote appliance, such as **Barracuda**.

9. In the Private address space field, specify the address space of the on-premises (or remote) location, such as **192.168.0.0/24**. Figure 2-23 shows the completed configuration.

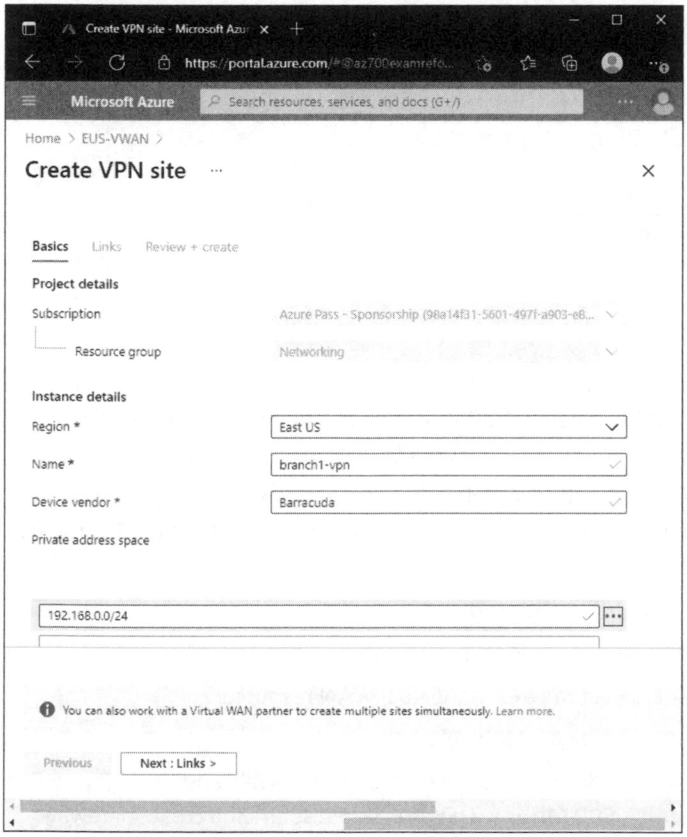

FIGURE 2-23 Create VPN site

10. Click **Next: Links**.

11. Complete the link fields using the following information, also shown in Figure 2-24:

- Link Name: Branch1-Link
- Link speed: 50
- Link provider name: Level 3
- Link IP address / FQDN: vpnlink.contoso.com
- Link BGP address: blank
- Link ASN: blank

12. Click **Next: Review + create**, and then click **Create**.

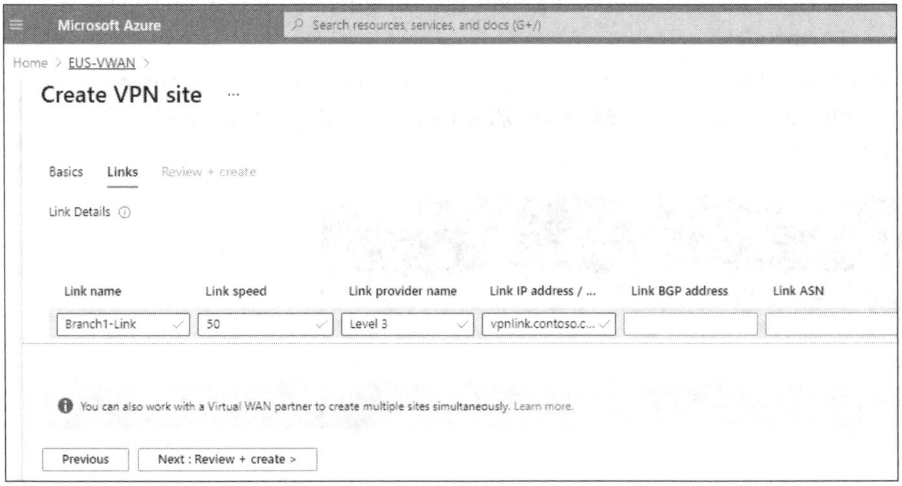

FIGURE 2-24 VPN site links

You can add up to four links per VPN site, allowing for a multi-homed connection over different providers. The link speed value is defined in Mbps and should represent the available speed at the branch office that is using the IP address or FQDN that you define.

After you create the VPN site, you need to associate the site with the hub that you previously created. But to do that, you first need a VPN gateway associated with the hub. To create a VPN gateway in Virtual WAN, follow these steps:

1. Sign in to the Azure portal at *https://portal.azure.com*.
2. In the search bar, search for and select **Virtual WANs**.
3. On the Virtual WANs page, select the existing Virtual WAN resource.
4. On the Virtual WAN resource, click the **Hubs** blade.
5. In the Gateway scale units dropdown menu, select the desired scale and throughput. For example, select **1 scale unit – 500 Mbps x 2**. Figure 2-25 displays the create gateway settings.
6. Click **Create**.

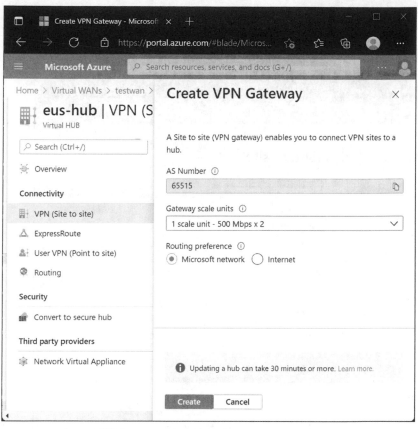

FIGURE 2-25 Create VPN Gateway

Note that the Create VPN Gateway interface does not let you edit the AS number for the device; it is set at 65515. It also takes around 30 minutes for the gateway to deploy and be associated with the hub. You cannot connect a VPN site until the gateway has been created.

After the gateway finishes deploying, you can connect the VPN site that was created earlier to the hub. This is also when you define the VPN settings, such as protocol, IPSec policy, and routing.

To connect the VPN site to the hub, follow these steps:

1. Sign in to the Azure portal at *https://portal.azure.com*.

2. In the search bar, search for and select **Virtual WANs**.

3. On the Virtual WANs page, select the existing Virtual WAN resource.

4. On the Virtual WAN resource, click the **Hubs** blade.

5. Select the name of the hub that you previously created, such as **vwan-eus-hub**.

6. On the hub page, click the **VPN (Site to site)** blade.

7. On the VPN blade, click **clear all filters** to display the hub.

8. Select the checkbox next to the hub that was previously created, and then click **Connect VPN sites**, as shown in Figure 2-26.

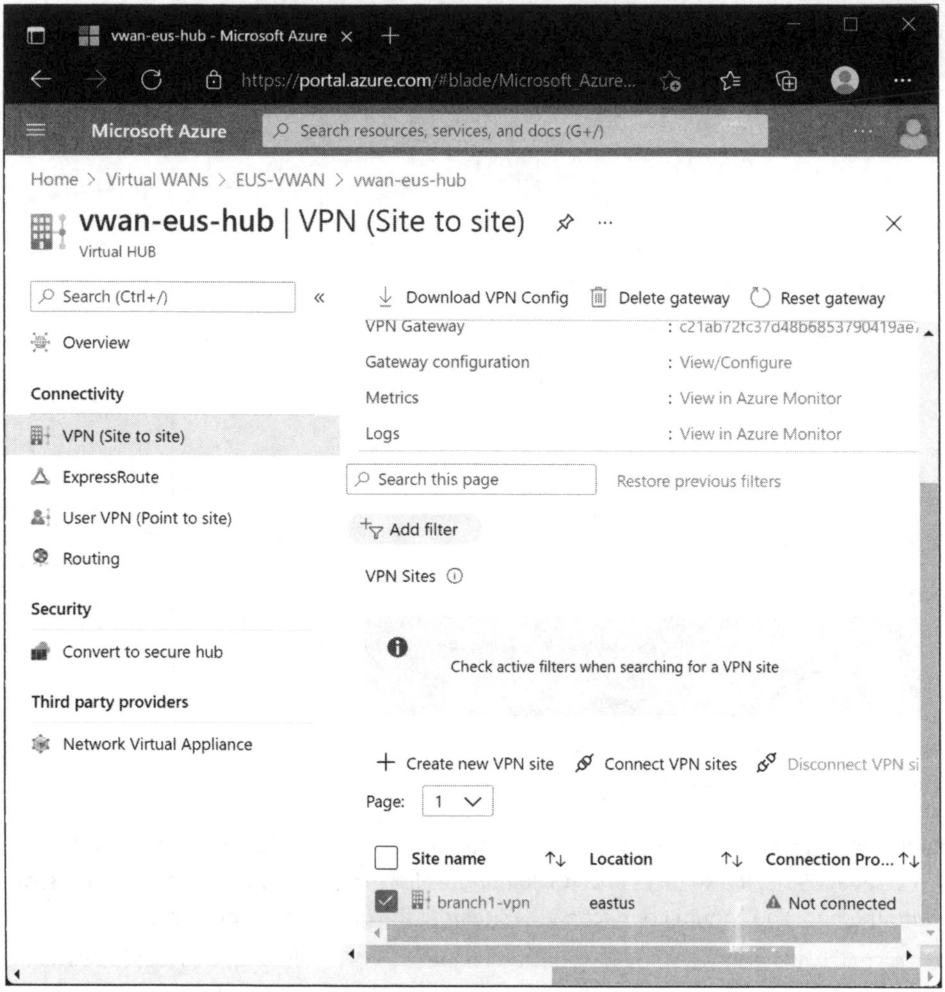

FIGURE 2-26 Connect VPN sites

9. In the Pre-shared key field, enter the secret that matches the remote configuration.

10. Leave the remaining fields set to their defaults and click **Connect**, as shown in Figure 2-27.

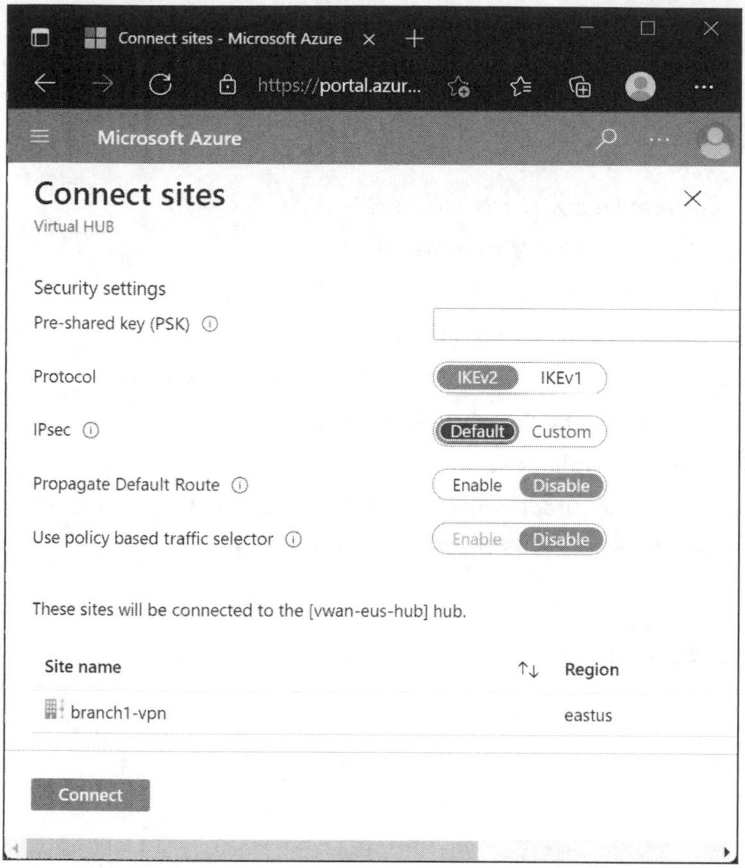

FIGURE 2-27 Connect sites

If you select Custom for the IPsec protocol, you can modify the SA lifetime, IKE phase 1, and IKE phase 2 settings for the VPN tunnel. When you click Connect, it will associate the branch office connection (VPN) to the virtual hub, creating the first spoke in the hub-and-spoke architecture.

Create a network virtual appliance in a virtual hub

As of this writing, there are three third-party providers for network virtual appliances (NVAs) in a Virtual WAN environment:

- Barracuda CloudGen WAN
- Cisco Cloud OnRamp for Multi-cloud
- VMware SD-WAN

These NVAs are intended to connect to the corresponding on-premises equipment to provide a holistic software-defined WAN (SD-WAN). When you deploy an NVA to a hub in Virtual WAN, it deploys the corresponding offer from the third-party vendor from the Azure marketplace.

To create an NVA in a hub, follow these steps:

1. Sign in to the Azure portal at *https://portal.azure.com*.

2. In the search bar, search for and select **Virtual WANs**.

3. On the Virtual WANs page, select the existing Virtual WAN resource.

4. On the Virtual WAN resource, click the **Hubs** blade.

5. Select the name of the hub that you previously created, such as **vwan-eus-hub**.

6. On the hub page, click the **Network virtual appliance** blade.

7. Click **Create network virtual appliance**.

8. In the Network Virtual Appliance dropdown menu, select the desired vendor's appliance. For example, select **baracudasdwanrelease**, as shown in Figure 2-28.

9. Click **Create**.

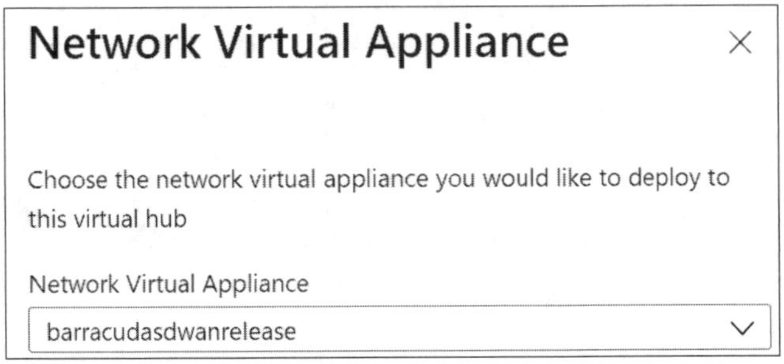

Network Virtual Appliance   ✕

Choose the network virtual appliance you would like to deploy to this virtual hub

Network Virtual Appliance

| barracudasdwanrelease | ∨ |

FIGURE 2-28 Network Virtual Appliance

10. You will be redirected to the Azure Marketplace, where you can deploy the vendor's appliance. Click **Get It Now**, as shown in Figure 2-29.

FIGURE 2-29 Azure Marketplace NVA

After you click Get It Now, you will be prompted to provide your contact details, which will be shared with the vendor before you can deploy the appliance.

Configure virtual hub routing

The virtual hub of the Virtual WAN is the central connection point for all site-to-site VPNs, point-to-site VPNs, ExpressRoute, and virtual networks. One of the benefits of the virtual hub is the transitive connectivity between these various connections, which can provide up to 50 Gbps of aggregate throughput.

When you create a virtual hub, two routing tables, named *None* and *Default,* are created within the hub. All connection types are initially associated with the Default routing table to allow the transitive connectivity across the various connections. Each connection that you add to the hub adds the routing prefix to the route table. The route table is propagated to the various connections using Border Gateway Protocol (BGP). If you need to prevent the routes from being propagated to the other connections, then you can associate the connection with the None route table.

You can control which connections receive route propagation by configuring additional route tables and customizing the associations between the connection and the various route tables. A way to make this easier is to create *labels* to identify the association between the connection and the route table.

To create a route table in a virtual hub, follow these steps:

1. Sign in to the Azure portal at *https://portal.azure.com*.

2. In the search bar, search for and select **Virtual WANs**.

3. On the Virtual WANs page, select the existing Virtual WAN resource.

4. On the Virtual WAN resource, click the **Hubs** blade.

5. Select the name of the hub that you previously created, such as **vwan-eus-hub**.

6. On the hub page, click the **Routing** blade.

7. Click **Create route table**.

8. Provide a name for the route table, such as **Branch2Branch**.

9. In the route table, specify a name for the route, such as **Branch1**.

10. In the Destination type dropdown menu, select **CIDR**.

11. In the Destination prefix field, provide the address range for the destination, such as **172.16.0.0/16**.

12. In the Next hop dropdown, select the hop that the traffic should be forwarded through. Figure 2-30 displays the Basics tab of the Create Route Table screen.

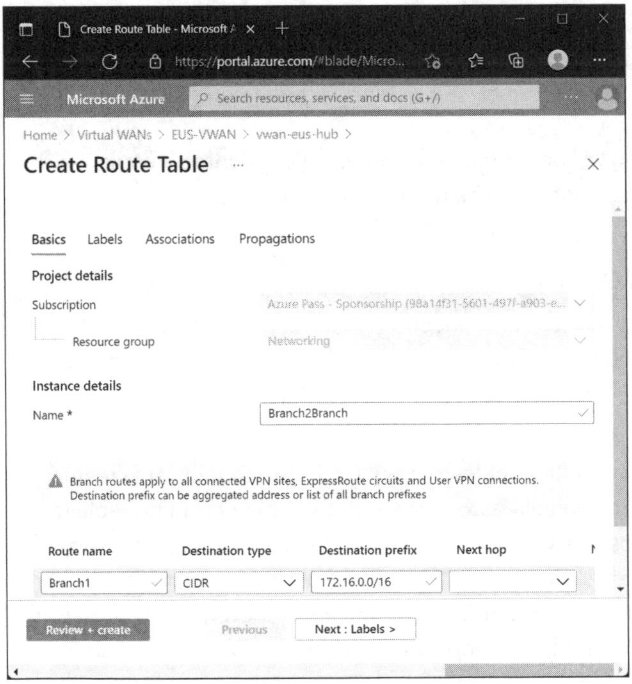

FIGURE 2-30 Create Route Table basics

13. Click **Next: Labels**.

14. In the Labels Name field, provide a label for the route table, such as **BranchOffices**. Figure 2-31 displays the Labels tab.

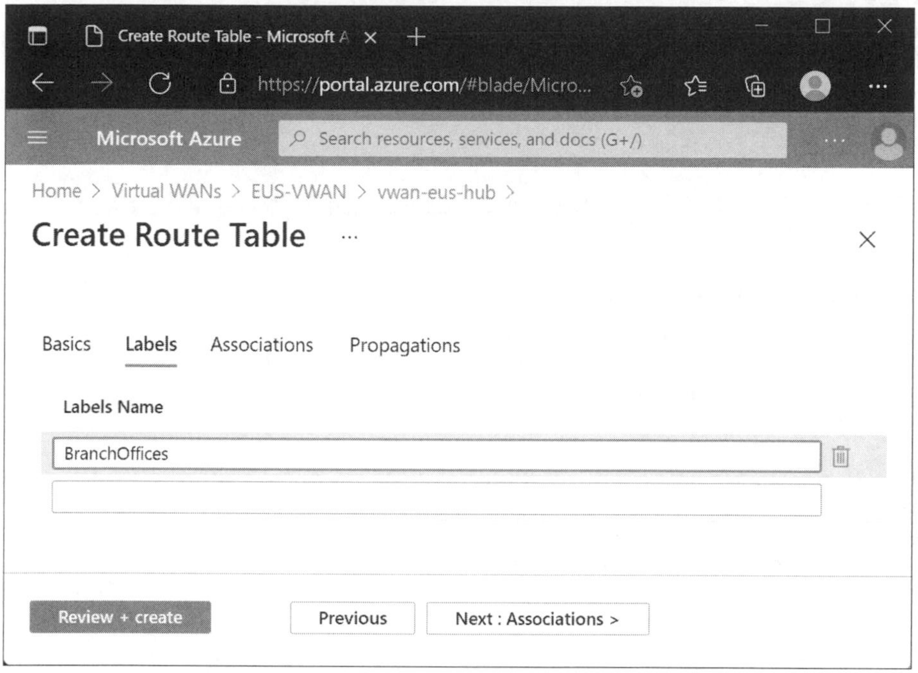

FIGURE 2-31 Create Route Table labels

15. Click **Next: Associations**. If you need to manage the association between the route table and various connections, you can configure them here.

16. Click **Next: Propagations**.

17. Set "Propagate routes from connections to this route table?" to **Yes**. You can also configure propagation from other route tables and virtual networks here. Figure 2-32 shows a portion of the configuration.

18. Click **Create**.

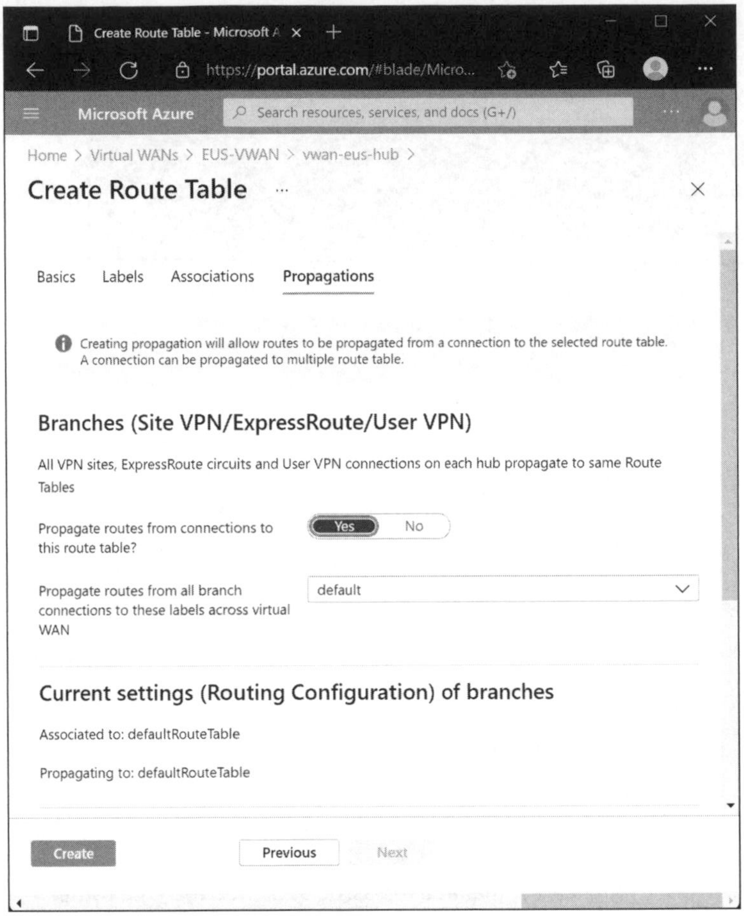

FIGURE 2-32 Create Route Table propagations

Chapter summary

- Virtual networks are the core communication infrastructure for an Azure subscription and resources.

- Virtual networks have an address space defined in CIDR notation, from which subnets are created.

- Multiple Azure services require dedicated subnets, sometimes with specific names, for each service, including virtual network gateways, firewalls, applications gateways, and Bastion.

- Subnet delegation enables other resources to manage networking automatically.

- Public DNS zones provide authoritative name resolution for custom domain names across the internet.

- Private DNS zones provide name resolution for internal resources within the Azure subscription.

- Virtual networks can be linked to private DNS zones to facilitate name resolution within the virtual network automatically.

- Virtual networks can be connected by using peering, but their address spaces cannot overlap.

- Address spaces in a virtual network are not advertised or propagated with peering and require additional route tables or virtual network gateways to create a service chain.

- Peering is not an encrypted tunnel; for scenarios that require IPsec connectivity, a VPN must be configured between virtual networks.

- In a larger-scale hybrid deployment, Virtual WAN provides a hub-and-spoke architecture across point-to-site, site-to-site, and ExpressRoute connections.

- A virtual hub in Virtual WAN facilitates the hub model to the various connections.

- A Virtual WAN can use third-party network virtual appliances to connect to on-premises solutions.

- Route propagation can be controlled with Virtual WAN by creating additional route tables.

Thought experiment

In this thought experiment, demonstrate your skills and knowledge of the topics covered in this chapter. You can find the answers in the section that follows.

An organization is migrating an application from an on-premises co-location to Azure. The current on-premises infrastructure supports multiple applications and will remain in place after the migration. The organization needs a hybrid network infrastructure configured between their main office, the co-location, and the selected Azure region.

The organization has an existing subscription with resources that run in the UK South Azure region. After the migration, the existing resources will need to communicate with the migrated application.

The application design includes using an application gateway for ingress traffic to the application and an Azure Firewall for egress traffic from the virtual network. The application also requires a dedicated custom domain for internal traffic. Most users will connect from Canada, and the organization has decided to deploy the application to the Canada East Azure region.

1. What resource should get created in Canada East?

2. What is the minimum number of subnets that will be required, and do any subnets require specific configuration?

3. What should be used to facilitate communication between the two Azure regions?

4. What should be deployed for the application's custom domain?

5. What should be deployed to facilitate the required hybrid connectivity?

With the above information, what should the organization deploy, and how should it be configured?

Thought experiment answers

This section contains the solution to the thought experiment. Each answer explains why the answer choice is correct.

1. The organization is using a different Azure region for the new migration, and therefore needs a new virtual network that is deployed in Canada East.

2. The virtual network would need at least three subnets defined: one for the application gateway, one for the Azure Firewall, and at least one for the application.

3. To facilitate communication between Canada East and UK South, the two virtual networks can be peered. However, the address spaces for the two virtual networks cannot overlap.

4. The Canada East region will need a private DNS zone to meet the requirement that the application must have a dedicated custom domain resolution for the internal traffic.

5. To address the hybrid connectivity requirements, we can consider using multiple virtual network gateways with custom routing tables; or the organization can deploy Virtual WAN and connect each site through a virtual hub. Without additional detail on future plans, Virtual WAN might be unnecessary for a two-site configuration. However, if the organization plans to scale to additional regions, this could better facilitate a hub-and-spoke architecture across VPNs.

CHAPTER 3

Design and implement routing

Routing traffic is a core component of any type of application deployment in your Azure environment. This can be an "east-west" type of traffic within the subscription, from one virtual network to another network or service. Or it can be a "north-south" type of traffic that flows in and out of the application.

The traffic flow in your virtual network can be manipulated by using user-defined routes (UDRs). Then, depending on the scenario, incoming traffic can be distributed across multiple backend resources using load balancers, application gateways, Azure Front Door, or Azure Traffic Manager. For outgoing traffic, you can represent multiple virtual machines with a single public IP using a NAT gateway. All of these services will be discussed in this chapter.

Skills in this chapter:

- Skill 3.1: Design, implement, and manage virtual network routing
- Skill 3.2: Design and implement an Azure load balancer
- Skill 3.3: Design and implement Azure Application Gateway
- Skill 3.4: Implement Azure Front Door
- Skill 3.5: Implement an Azure Traffic Manager profile
- Skill 3.6: Design and implement an Azure Virtual Network NAT

Skill 3.1: Design, implement, and manage virtual network routing

Routing is one of the core network infrastructure components that define how traffic leaves point A and arrives at point B. When you create a virtual machine in Azure, by default it can communicate outbound to the internet. In most organizations, there are security or compliance policies that require this traffic to be inspected or audited before going out to the internet. In these scenarios, it is required to create custom route tables to modify the traffic flow based on the destination. In this skill section, we discuss creating these UDRs and how to configure custom routing for a virtual network.

Design and implement user-defined routes

When you create a virtual network, there are default system routes that define how the resources attached to the virtual network can communicate with Azure services and the internet. Table 3-1 outlines the default system routes for a virtual network.

TABLE 3-1 Virtual network default routes

Destination address range	Next hop
Address space of the network	Virtual network
0.0.0.0/0	Internet
10.0.0.0/8	None
192.168.0.0/16	None
100.64.0.0/10	None

The first default route is determined by the address space that has been configured for the virtual network. Next, as long as the traffic is not destined to a reserved network from RFC 1918 or RFC 6598, then the traffic is sent to the internet. If you add any address ranges that are by default set to None to the virtual network, then it will change the next hop to *virtual network*.

If you add virtual network peering or a virtual network gateway or you configure service endpoints, the default routes are modified to include the service that you configure. When you configure virtual network peering, a default route is added for the address space of the peered virtual network, which is the underlying reason why peered virtual networks cannot have overlapping address spaces. Figure 3-1 outlines the bi-directional communication with virtual network peering.

Let's assume that in Figure 3-1, VM1 has an IP address of 10.0.0.4 and VM2 has an IP address of 10.1.0.4. The traffic flow would resemble this path:

1. Packets leave VM1 destined to VM2 through the default gateway of 10.0.0.1.
2. The gateway has a route to 10.1.0.0/16 through peering and forwards the packet to 10.1.0.1.

3. The virtual network at 10.1.0.0/16 recognizes that the packet is destined to VM2 and forwards accordingly.

4. VM2 receives the packet from VM1.

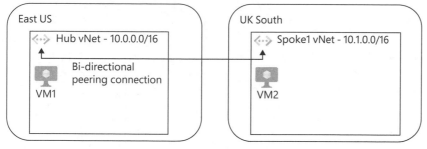

FIGURE 3-1 Bi-directional communication with virtual network peering

By default, when you deploy a virtual machine, it can and will communicate with the internet outbound through an Azure IP address, even if the virtual network does not have a firewall associated or if the VM does not have a public IP address assigned. The IP address that the VM would display to internet services would vary depending on the region.

There are several scenarios in which an organization will want to change this traffic flow and not allow VMs to communicate directly with the internet. Or, even if you decide to peer two virtual networks, instead of allowing all default communication, the traffic is first forwarded through a firewall or other type of network virtual appliance. The override mechanism for these scenarios is named a UDR, which you configure by using an Azure route table.

To create a route table, follow these steps:

1. Sign in to the Azure portal at *https://portal.azure.com*.

2. In the search bar, search for and select **Route tables**.

3. On the Route tables page, click **Create**.

4. In the Subscription dropdown, select the subscription to associate with the route table. This must be the same subscription as the virtual network.

5. In the Resource group dropdown, select a resource group to associate with the resource, such as **Networking**.

6. In the Region dropdown list, select the region to associate with the route table. This must also be the same location as the virtual network. In this example, select **East US**.

7. In the Name field, provide a name for the route table, such as **OutgoingProxy**.

8. Leave the default of **Yes** selected for Propagate gateway routes.

9. Click **Review + Create**, and then click **Create**. Figure 3-2 displays the completed configuration.

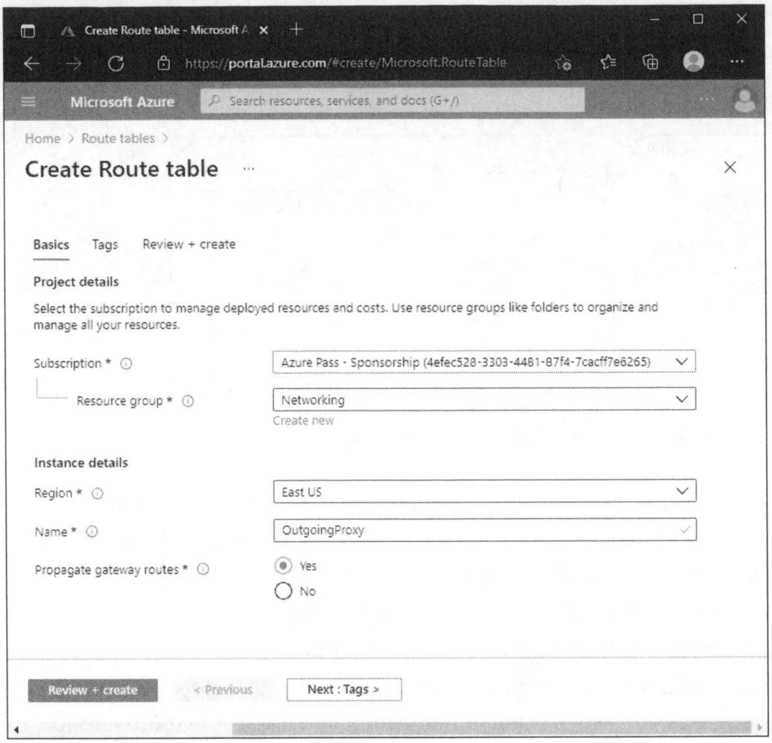

FIGURE 3-2 Create Route table

This creates a route table object in the specified subscription and region. Based on the name we provided for the route table, OutgoingProxy, we'll use the scenario of two VMs in different virtual networks and force outbound traffic through a network virtual appliance.

After creating the route table, there are two more steps to make the desired effect of changing the traffic flow: creating a route within the route table and associating the table with a subnet. To create a route within the table, follow these steps:

1. Sign in to the Azure portal at *https://portal.azure.com*.

2. In the search bar, search for and select **Route tables**.

3. Select the **OutgoingProxy** route table that was previously created.

4. From the table, click the **Routes** blade.

5. On the Routes blade, click **Add**.

6. In the Route name field, name the route **ToNVA**.

7. In the Address prefix field, enter the destination prefix that you want to modify traffic flow for. For example, to force all traffic through an NVA, specify **0.0.0.0/0**.

8. In the Next hop type dropdown, select **Virtual appliance**.

9. In the Next hop address field, specify the IP address of the NVA that will act as the proxy. For example, enter **10.0.0.250**.

10. Click **OK**. Figure 3-3 displays the completed route entry.

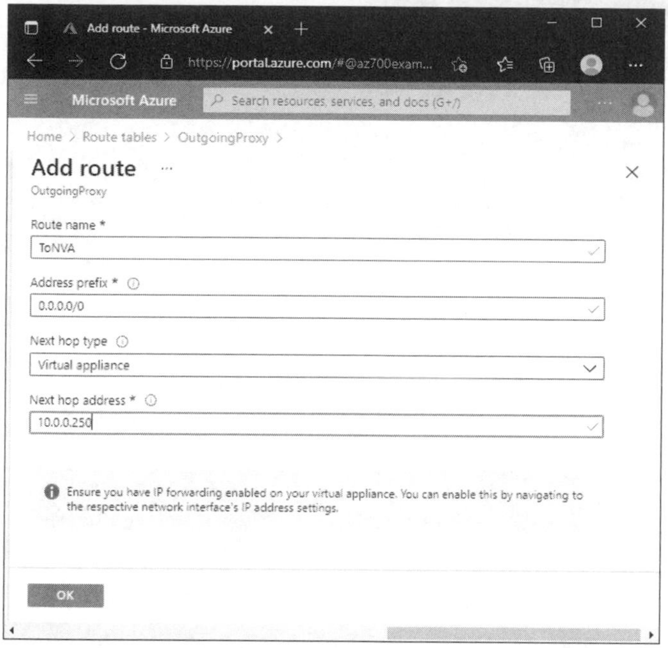

FIGURE 3-3 Add route entry

Associate a route table with a subnet

After you create the route table and add a route entry to the table, the final step to change the traffic flow is to associate the table with the subnets that you want to change the flow of traffic from.

To associate the table with a subnet, follow these steps:

1. Sign in to the Azure portal at *https://portal.azure.com*.
2. In the search bar, search for and select **Route tables**.
3. Select the **OutgoingProxy** route table that was previously created.
4. From the table, click the **Subnets** blade.
5. On the Subnets blade, click **Associate**.
6. In the Virtual network dropdown, select the network with the subnet to associate with the table; for example, select **hub-vnet-eus-01**.
7. In the Subnet dropdown, select the subnet to associate with the route table and modify the traffic flow for, such as **app1**.
8. Click **OK**. Figure 3-4 displays the completed configuration.

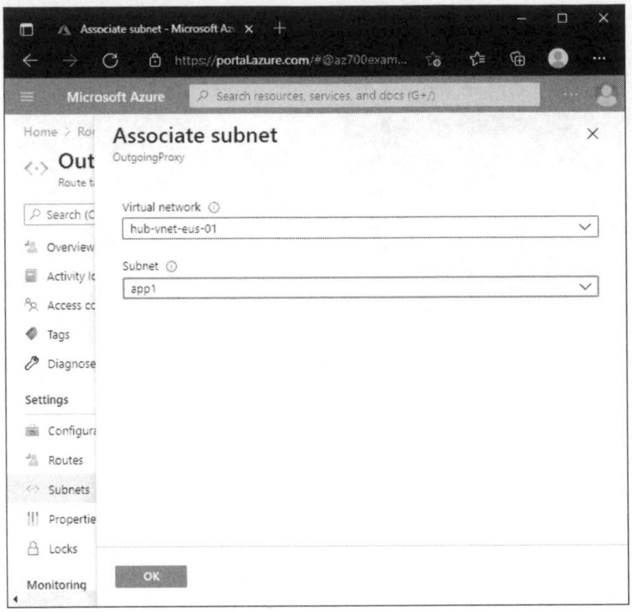

FIGURE 3-4 Associate subnet

In the scenario that the traffic from VM1 needs to flow through the NVA before communicating with VM2, we have made the route table entry and association if VM1 is in the app1 subnet. Table 3-2 outlines the IP address for the VMs in Figure 3-5.

TABLE 3-2 IP addresses

VM	IP address
VM1	10.0.0.4
NVA	10.0.0.250
VM2	10.1.0.4

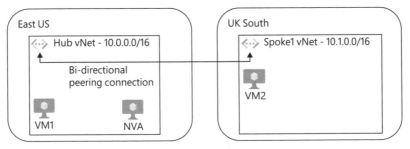

FIGURE 3-5 NVA proxy diagram

With the route table association to the app1 subnet, assuming VM1 is in the app1 subnet, then any traffic destined to VM2 will flow through the NVA. This NVA could be a proxy, a firewall, or any third-party appliance from Azure Marketplace.

Configure forced tunneling

Forced tunneling is a similar concept to using a network virtual appliance to route all traffic through as a proxy, but it incorporates either a site-to-site VPN or ExpressRoute to route any virtual network traffic back on-premises. This is typically designed in regulated or high-security environments where using the existing infrastructure is more convenient short-term than duplicating the requirements in the cloud.

For a forced tunneling design, the route table entry is similar to using an NVA. You change the next hop IP address to the on-premises address that is accessible through the VPN tunnel. Figure 3-6 represents the design of forced tunneling to on-premises.

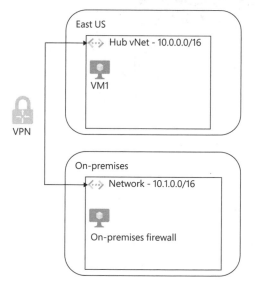

FIGURE 3-6 Forced tunneling diagram

If you are using ExpressRoute, either in addition to or instead of a VPN, the concept is the same except that the default route should be advertised as part of the BGP peering sessions. This does not require any additional route entry into a route table.

Diagnose and resolve routing issues

Routes in Azure are processed in the order of longest prefix match for any destination that has been defined. If a route has more than one match, then the processing priority is:

1. User-defined routes
2. BGP routes
3. System routes

If you need to troubleshoot the routing from a virtual machine perspective, there are two built-in tools in the Azure portal that can assist. From a VM, you can view the effective routes that apply to the VM based on the subnet that the NIC is associated with.

To view the effective routes, follow these steps:

1. Sign in to the Azure portal at *https://portal.azure.com*.

2. In the search bar, search for and select **Virtual machines**.

3. Select a virtual machine that you have deployed, for example **VM1**.

4. From the VM, click the **Networking** blade.

5. On the Networking blade, click the name of the network interface attached to the VM. Figure 3-7 shows an example of a NIC named **vm1623**.

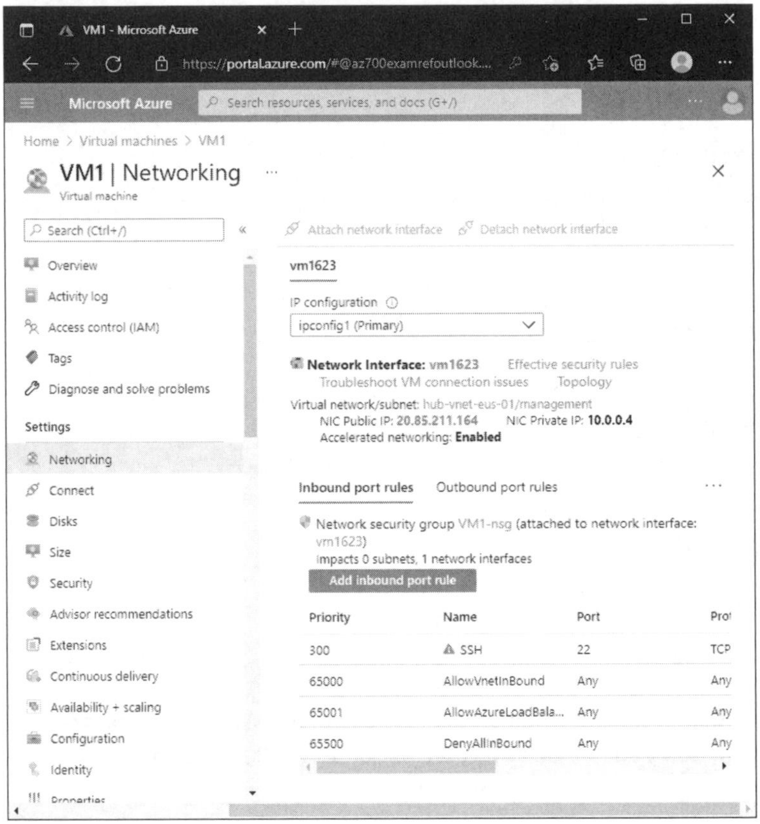

FIGURE 3-7 VM Networking

6. From the network interface, click the **Effective routes** blade. Figure 3-8 displays the effective routes for the network interface.

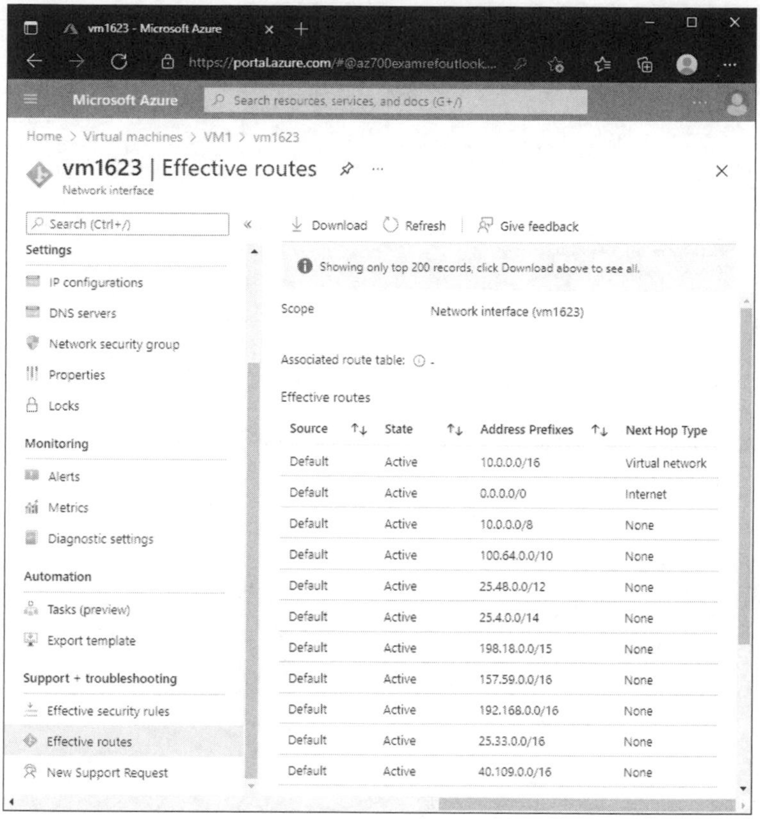

FIGURE 3-8 Effective routes

The Effective routes blade on the network interface card is a useful tool for an overview of the routes that are associated with the subnet that the NIC is associated with. Another method of troubleshooting the routing from a VM is to use Network Watcher.

Network Watcher is an Azure monitoring resource that is built into the Azure portal and is a collection of tools that can be used for troubleshooting. One of these tools, named Next hop, allows you to select a VM and identify the next hop for a specific address.

To use the Next hop tool, follow these steps:

1. Sign in to the Azure portal at *https://portal.azure.com*.

2. In the search bar, search for and select **Network Watcher**.

3. From Network Watcher, select the **Next hop** blade.

4. Complete the fields to select the desired virtual machine and network interface card.

5. In the Destination IP address field, specify the IP address that you want to test to identify what the configured next hop would be. For example, specify **8.8.8.8**.

6. Click **Next hop**. Figure 3-9 shows the completed form and that the next hop type is the internet based on the effective routes.

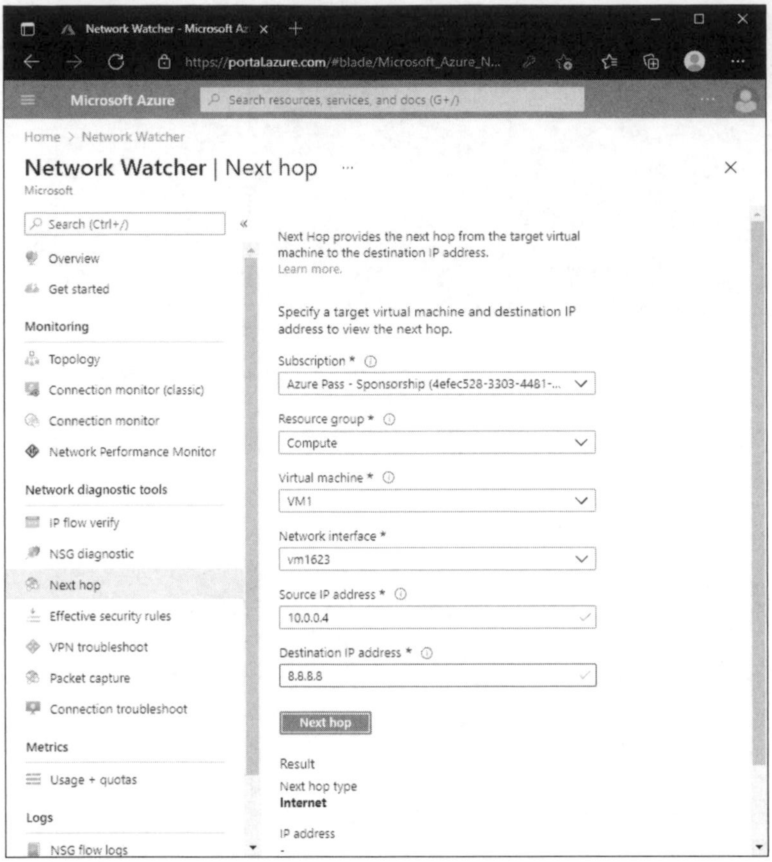

FIGURE 3-9 Next hop

Figure 3-9 shows that from the network interface card vm1623, which has a source IP address of 10.0.0.4 on the management subnet, if the VM were to communicate with the 8.8.8.8 destination IP address, the traffic would be forwarded to the internet.

Skill 3.2: Design and implement an Azure load balancer

There are a few options in Azure if you need to distribute incoming traffic to a pool of back-end resources. These options include Azure Load Balancer, Azure Application Gateway, and Azure Front Door. Each service has its own set of features and functionality that sets it apart. Azure Load Balancer is the simplest of the three options; it provides core layer 4 load balancing functionality for both public and internal scenarios.

This skill covers how to:

- Choose an Azure Load Balancer SKU
- Choose between public and internal
- Create and configure an Azure load balancer
- Implement a load balancing rule
- Create and configure inbound NAT rules
- Create explicit outbound rules for a load balancer

Choose an Azure Load Balancer SKU

As you are designing a solution that includes an Azure load balancer, there are two SKU options to select from: Basic and Standard. In general, the best practice is to use a Standard SKU load balancer for any production deployment. After you deploy a load balancer, you cannot change the SKU and must deploy a new resource. Table 3-3 outlines the feature differences between the SKUs.

TABLE 3-3 Load balancer SKUs

Feature	Standard load balancer	Basic load balancer
Backend pool size	Up to 1,000 instances	Up to 300 instances
Backend pool type	Virtual machines, VM scale sets	Availability sets or scale sets
Health probe protocols	TCP, HTTP, HTTPS	TCP, HTTP
Health probe failure behavior	Existing TCP connections stay alive	Single instance failures stay alive, all instance failures drop
Availability zones	Zone-redundant and zonal front-ends can be configured	Not available
Diagnostics	Azure Monitor	Not available
HA ports	With internal IP addresses	Not available
Security defaults	Closed by default	Open by default
Outbound rules	Outbound NAT	Not available
TCP Reset on Idle	Configured on rules	Not available
Multiple front-ends	Inbound and outbound	Inbound only
SLA	99.99%	None
Global virtual network peering	Supported with internal IP address	Not available

Of the feature differences outlined in Table 3-3, the standouts would be the number of instances, HTTPS as a health probe, and the SLA for the Standard SKU. For smaller development, test, quality assurance, or other non-production type environments, a Basic SKU might be acceptable.

Choose between public and internal

Determining whether a load balancer is public or internal is an architecture decision regarding where the load balancer is placed as part of the solution. Both Basic and Standard load balancers support internal and public IP addresses, so there is no placement restriction based on the SKU that you select. Both types of load balancer SKUs support both scenarios of internal or public. Whether you select internal or public determines which type of traffic the load balancer can accept traffic from. Internal load balancers can accept traffic only from private IP addresses, whereas public load balancers can accept traffic only from public IP addresses.

A likely scenario for public load balancers is to also perform outbound NAT for the backend pool virtual machines. However, only the Standard SKU load balancer supports configuring outbound NAT rules. Thus, most public load balancer scenarios would require a Standard SKU load balancer.

Other than the feature differences provided by the two types of SKUs, there is no performance benefit or restriction by choosing to configure a load balancer with a public or private IP address.

Create and configure an Azure load balancer

After you choose which SKU to use, and whether your load balancer will be internal or public-facing, you are ready to create the load balancer. To complete the configuration, you will also need virtual machines for the backend pool. There are a few configuration components that make up a complete load balancer configuration:

- Frontend IP address
- Backend pool
- Health probes
- Load balancer rules

In this section, we focus on configuring the frontend IP address and backend pools as we create the load balancer. We'll focus on load balancer health probes and rules in the next section. To create an Azure load balancer, follow these steps:

1. Sign in to the Azure portal at *https://portal.azure.com*.
2. In the search bar, search for and select **Load Balancers**.
3. On the Load Balancer page, click **Create**.
4. In the Resource group dropdown, select the desired resource group, such as **Networking**.
5. In the Name field, provide a name for the load balancer, such as **lb-eus-app1**.

6. In the Region dropdown menu, select the desired Azure region, such as **East US**.

7. For the SKU selection, select **Standard**.

8. For the Type selection, select **Public**.

9. For the Tier selection, select **Regional**.

10. Click **Next: Frontend IP Configuration**. Figure 3-10 shows the completed configuration on the Basics tab.

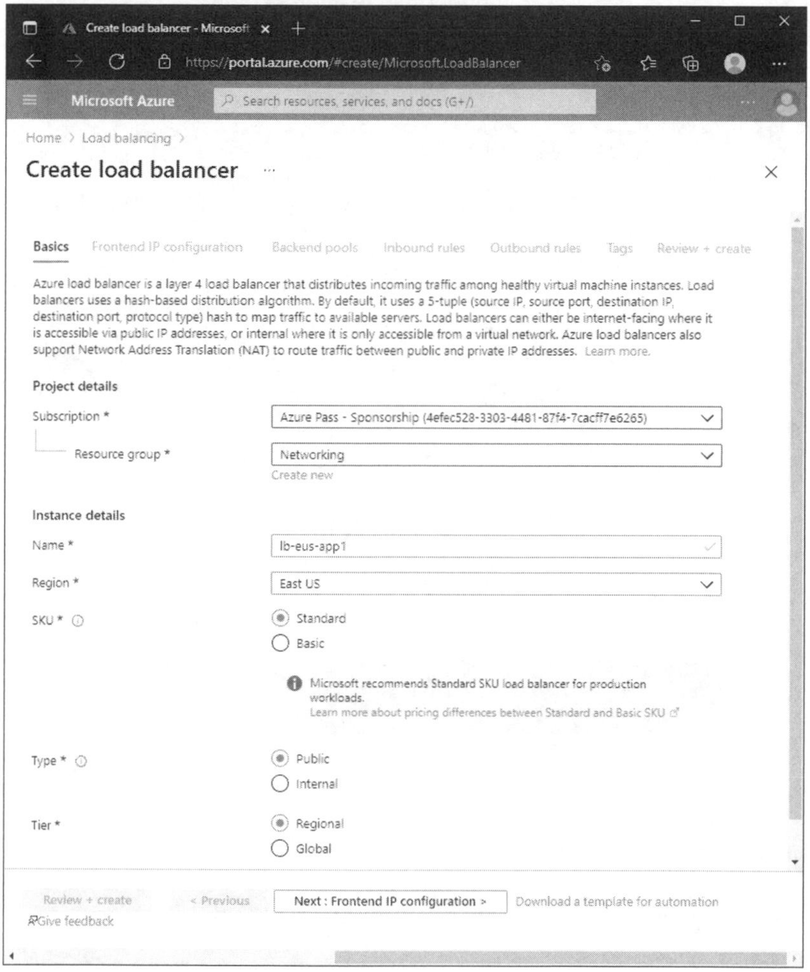

FIGURE 3-10 Load balancer basics

11. On the Frontend IP configuration tab, click **Add a frontend IP configuration**.

12. In the Name field, specify a name for the frontend IP address, such as **fe-app1**.

13. For the IP version, select **IPv4**.

14. For the IP type, select **IP address**.

15. For the Public IP address, click **Create new**.

16. In the Name field, provide a name for the IP address, such as **pip-fe-app1**.

17. Click **OK**, and then click **Add**. Figure 3-11 shows the example configuration.

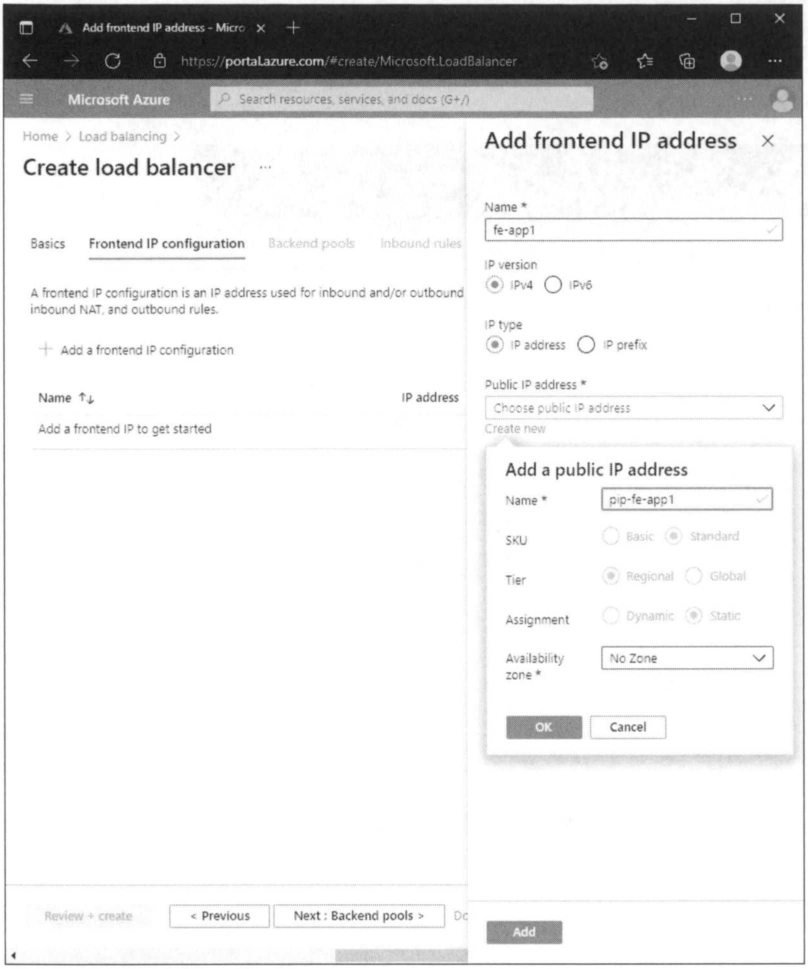

FIGURE 3-11 Load balancer frontend IP configuration

18. Click **Next: Backend pools**.

> **NOTE   COMPUTE DEPLOYMENT**
>
> These steps assume that you already have compute deployed, either individual virtual machines or a virtual machine scale set. Deploying compute options is not in the exam outline and is not covered in this book.

19. On the Backend pools tab, click **Add a backend pool**.

20. In the Name field, provide a name for the pool, such as **bep-vmss-app1**.

21. In the Virtual network dropdown menu, select the virtual network that the backend pool is connected to, such as **Compute-vnet**.

22. For the Backend Pool Configuration, select **NIC**.

23. For the IP Version, select **IPv4**.

24. Select the backend compute where the application is being run, whether individual virtual machines or a virtual machine scale set. In this example, select a virtual machine scale set named **vmss-app1**. Figure 3-12 displays the completed Add backend pool page.

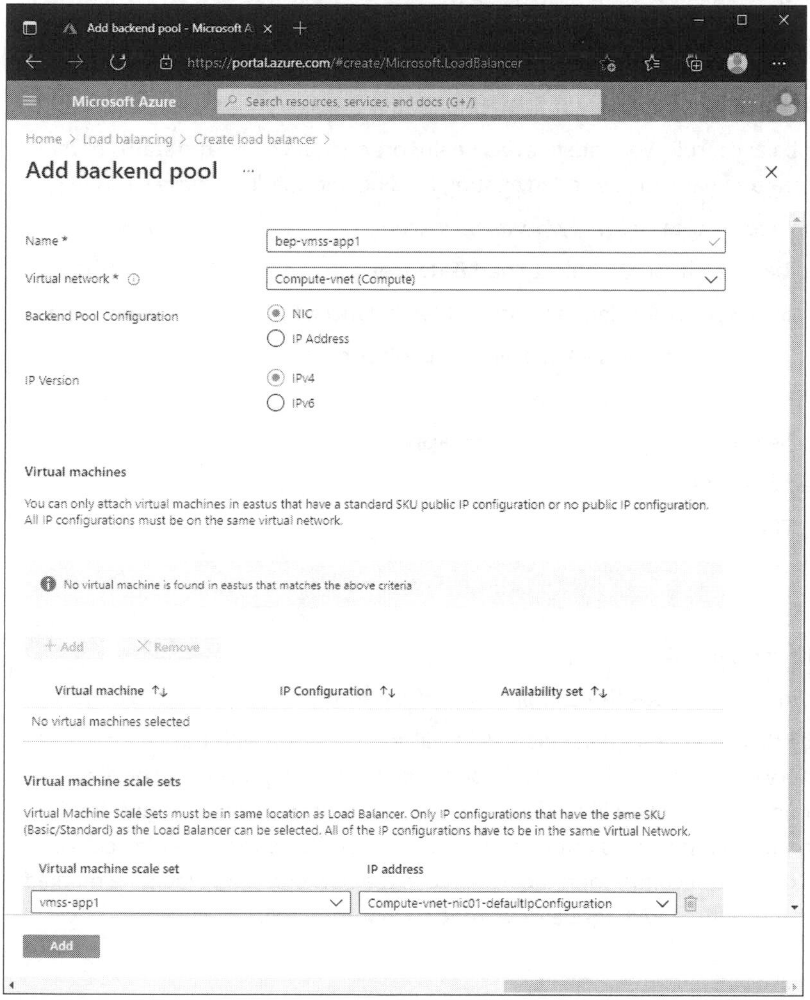

FIGURE 3-12 Load balancer backend pool

25. Click **Add**.

26. Click **Review + create**, and then click **Create**.

Adding at least one frontend IP address and one backend pool are the minimum requirements for creating a load balancer. For the load balancer to be functional, it will also need rules created.

Implement a load balancing rule

Load balancer rules are the configuration that ties together the frontend IP address, backend pool, health probe, protocol, and port number that you want to accept and distribute traffic on. Basic SKU load balancers can have up to 250 rules configured, and Standard SKU load balancers can have up to 1,500 rules.

Rules also allow you to configure port address translation. For example, if you need to allow port 443 (HTTPS) connections externally, but need to translate that to a custom port, 8443, internally, the load balancer rule can be configured to do this translation.

To create a load balancer rule, you must have a health probe that checks the status of the backend pool. To create a health probe for an existing load balancer, follow these steps:

1. Sign in to the Azure portal at *https://portal.azure.com*.

2. In the search bar, search for and select **Load Balancers**.

3. On the Load Balancer page, select an existing load balancer, for example **lb-eus-app1**.

4. On the selected load balancer, click the **Health probes** blade.

5. On the Health probes blade, click **Add**.

6. In the Name field, provide a name such as **hp-app1**.

7. Leave the remaining fields set to the defaults:

   - Protocol: **TCP**

   - Port: **80**

   - Interval: **5**

   - Unhealthy threshold: **2**

8. Click **Save**. Figure 3-13 shows the completed configuration.

The health probe that is configured in Figure 3-13 will communicate with the defined port number, TCP 80, every five seconds. The backend pool that the health probe is associated with through the load balancer rule will be deemed "Healthy" as long as the port number is accessible. If the communication times out or is otherwise unreachable for two consecutive attempts, or in this case ~10 seconds, then the resource in the backend pool would be marked "Unhealthy" and connections would not be forwarded to that resource.

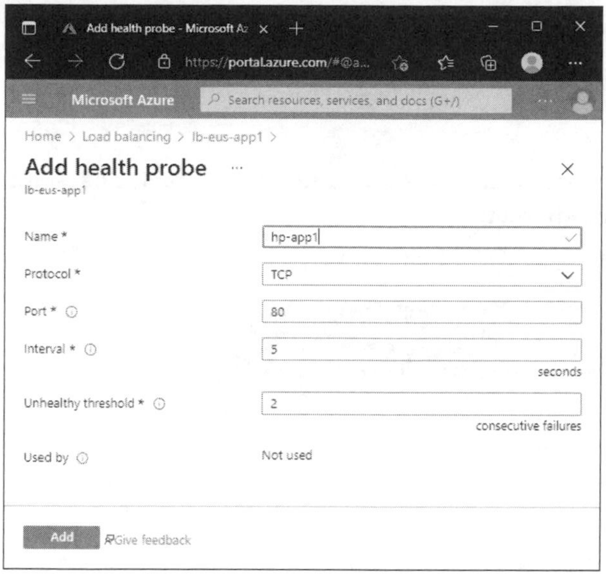

FIGURE 3-13 Add health probe

To create a rule that associates these components together for an existing load balancer, follow these steps:

1. Sign in to the Azure portal at *https://portal.azure.com*.
2. In the search bar, search for and select **Load Balancers**.
3. On the Load Balancer page, select an existing load balancer, for example **lb-eus-app1**.
4. On the selected load balancer, click the **Load balancing rules** blade.
5. On the Load balancing rules page, click **Add**.
6. In the Name field, provide a name for the rule, for example **app1-https**.
7. In the IP Version field, leave the default **IPv4** selected.
8. In the Frontend IP address dropdown, select the desired IP address to accept connections on. For example, select **fe-app1**.
9. In the Protocol field, leave the default of **TCP** selected.
10. In the Port field, specify the external port number to accept connections on. For example, specify **80**.
11. In the Backend port field, specify the internal or translated port number to forward the connection to on the backend pool. For example, specify **8080**.
12. In the Backend pool dropdown, select the desired backend pool. For example, select **bep-vmss-app1**.
13. In the Health probe dropdown, select the previously created health probe. For example, select **hp-app1**.

14. Leave the remaining fields set to their default values:

   ■ Idle timeout: **4 minutes**

   ■ TCP reset: **Disabled**

   ■ Floating IP: **Disabled**

   ■ Outbound source NAT: **(Recommended) Use outbound rules to provide backend pool members access to the internet.**

15. Click **Add**. Figure 3-14 displays the completed configuration.

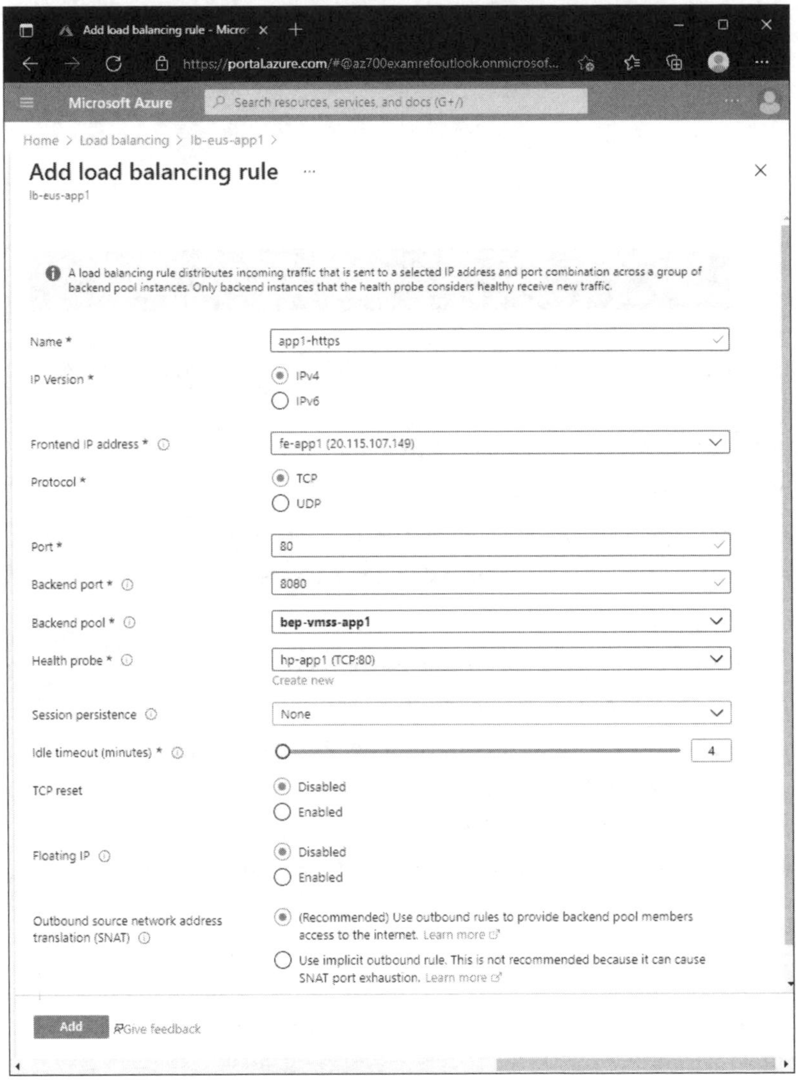

FIGURE 3-14 Add load balancing rule

The configuration displayed in Figure 3-14 creates a rule that brings together the individual components of the load balancer:

- Frontend IP address
- Backend pool
- Health probe

Along with these components, the protocol, external port number, and internal port number are defined. This will effectively distribute traffic incoming on public IP address 20.115.107.149 on TCP port 80 to the internal virtual machine scale set named bep-vmss-app1, internally on port 8080.

Azure load balancers also offer an option named *session persistence*, not to be confused with *session affinity*. Session persistence has three configuration options:

- None
- Client IP
- Client IP and protocol

The default option, None, uses a hash-based algorithm that allows successive requests from the same end user to be forwarded to any virtual machine in the backend pool. Client IP tracks the end user's IP address to ensure that successive requests from that IP address are forwarded to the same virtual machine in the backend pool, regardless of protocol. Client IP and protocol takes both the end user's IP address and the protocol that is being used, and if they are the same, then successive requests will be sent to the same virtual machine in the backend pool.

The idle timeout option defines the time period before a connection is considered dropped. The default timeout period is 4 minutes, but it can be configured up to 30 minutes for load balancer rules. By default, when a connection times out, there is no communication to the backend pool. If the application has its own timeout period, it may or may not release the connection. If you would prefer that the load balancer specifically sends a TCP reset packet when a timeout occurs, you can enable this setting.

Floating IP addresses allow you to reuse the same port number on the backend pool with multiple load balancer rules. Some applications or specific architectures might require this, including:

- High availability clustering
- Network virtual appliances
- Multiple TLS endpoints without re-encryption

For the outbound source network address translation (SNAT), the default option is the recommended setting of using outbound rules. This enables you to configure additional IP addresses to use as SNAT ports. This avoids exhausting the available number of ports, which can happen with the *Use implicit outbound rule* option. Outbound rules are further discussed later in this skill section.

Create and configure inbound NAT rules

An inbound NAT rule is similar to the load balancer rules, as it has a lot of the same configuration properties:

- Frontend IP address
- Protocol
- Port
- Idle timeout
- TCP reset

The difference is that instead of load balancing across multiple resources in a backend pool, an inbound NAT rule is to perform address translation for an individual virtual machine. This is useful if you have an administrative portal or custom port number for troubleshooting your application or service on a different port number. This gives you the ability to connect directly to a single VM in your backend pool through the load balancer.

To create an inbound NAT rule, follow these steps:

1. Sign in to the Azure portal at *https://portal.azure.com*.
2. In the search bar, search for and select **Load Balancers**.
3. On the Load Balancer page, select an existing load balancer, for example **lb-eus-app1**.
4. On the selected load balancer, click the **Inbound NAT rules** blade.
5. On the Inbound NAT rules blade, click **Add**.
6. In the Name field, specify a name such as **app1-vm1**.
7. In the Frontend IP address dropdown, select the desired IP address. For example, select **fe-app1**.
8. In the next four fields, leave the default settings:
   - Service: **Custom**
   - Protocol: **TCP**
   - Idle timeout: **4 minutes**
   - TCP Reset: **Enabled**
9. In the Port field, specify a port number to translate. For example, specify **8891**.
10. In the Target virtual machine dropdown menu, select a virtual machine that has been deployed. For example, select **VM1**. Note that the virtual machine cannot have a public IP address associated with it.
11. In the Network IP configuration dropdown menu, select the IP configuration of the NIC associated with the VM. For example, select **ipconfig1**.
12. In the Port mapping field, select **Custom**.

13. Leave the Floating IP option set to the default of **Disabled**.

14. In the Target port field, specify the internal port number on the virtual machine. For example, specify **8080**.

15. Click **Add**. Figure 3-15 displays the completed configuration.

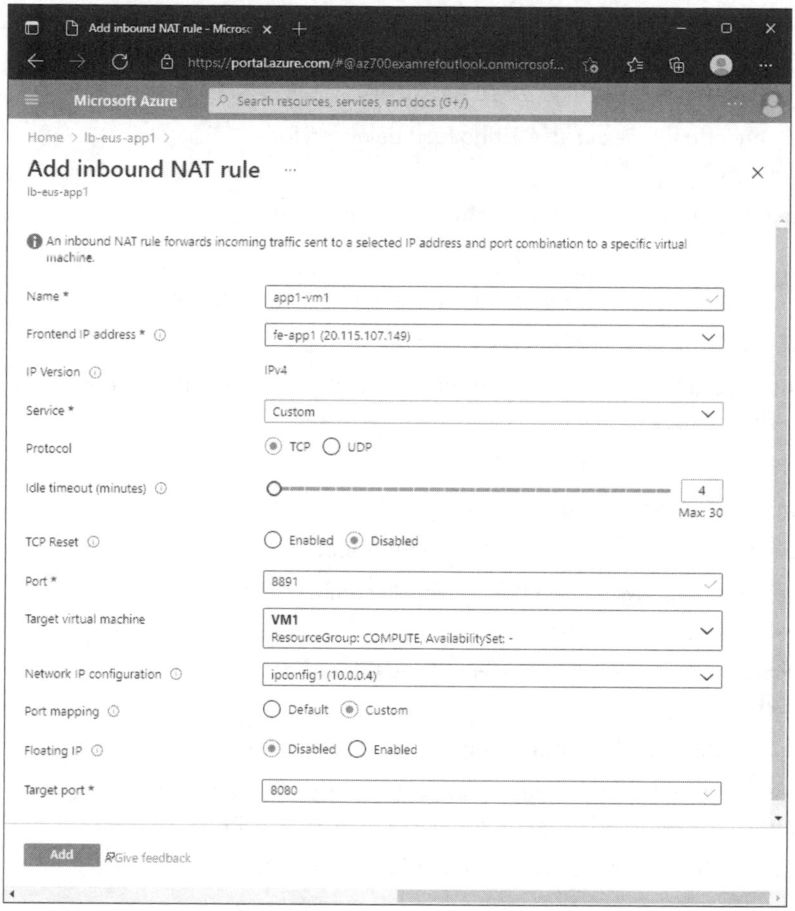

FIGURE 3-15 Add inbound NAT rule

As you can see in the configuration, instead of specifying a backend pool of multiple resources, you select a single target virtual machine. This is the primary difference between load balancing rules and inbound NAT rules. In the configuration displayed in Figure 3-15, any communication on port 8891 directed at the frontend IP address of 20.115.107.149 would be forwarded directly to VM1's private IP address of 10.0.0.4 but translated to port 8080.

Create explicit outbound rules for a load balancer

Outbound rules allow you to configure network address translation (NAT) for all of the virtual machines that are defined in the backend pools. Outbound rules are available only with Standard SKU load balancers that have a public frontend IP address.

To configure an outbound rule, follow these steps:

1. Sign in to the Azure portal at *https://portal.azure.com*.

2. In the search bar, search for and select **Load Balancers**.

3. On the Load Balancer page, select an existing load balancer, for example **lb-eus-app1**.

4. On the selected load balancer, click the **Outbound rules** blade.

5. On the Outbound rules blade, click **Add**.

6. In the Name field, provide a name for the rule. For example, enter **ob-rule1**.

7. In the IP Version field, leave the default **IPv4** selected.

8. In the Frontend IP address dropdown, select the previously configured IP address. For example, select **fe-app1**.

9. In the Protocol field, leave the default of **All** selected.

10. In the Idle timeout field, leave the default setting of **4**.

11. In the TCP Reset field, leave the default setting of **Enabled**.

12. In the Backend pool dropdown, select the previously configured backend pool. For example, select **bep-vmss-app1**.

13. In the Port allocation dropdown menu, select **Manually choose number of outbound ports**.

14. In the Choose by field, select **Maximum number of backend instances**.

15. In the Maximum number of backend instances field, specify the maximum number of instances the VM scale set could increase to. For example, specify **20**.

16. Click **Add**. Figure 3-16 displays the completed configuration.

An outbound rule configures the source network address translation for the resources defined in the backend pool to communicate outbound through the load balancer. The available frontend ports are determined by the number of frontend IP addresses that you select. These available frontend ports are then distributed across the virtual machines in the backend pool. In the above configuration, the 63,984 possible frontend ports across a maximum of 20 virtual machines would result in approximately 3,192 ports per instance.

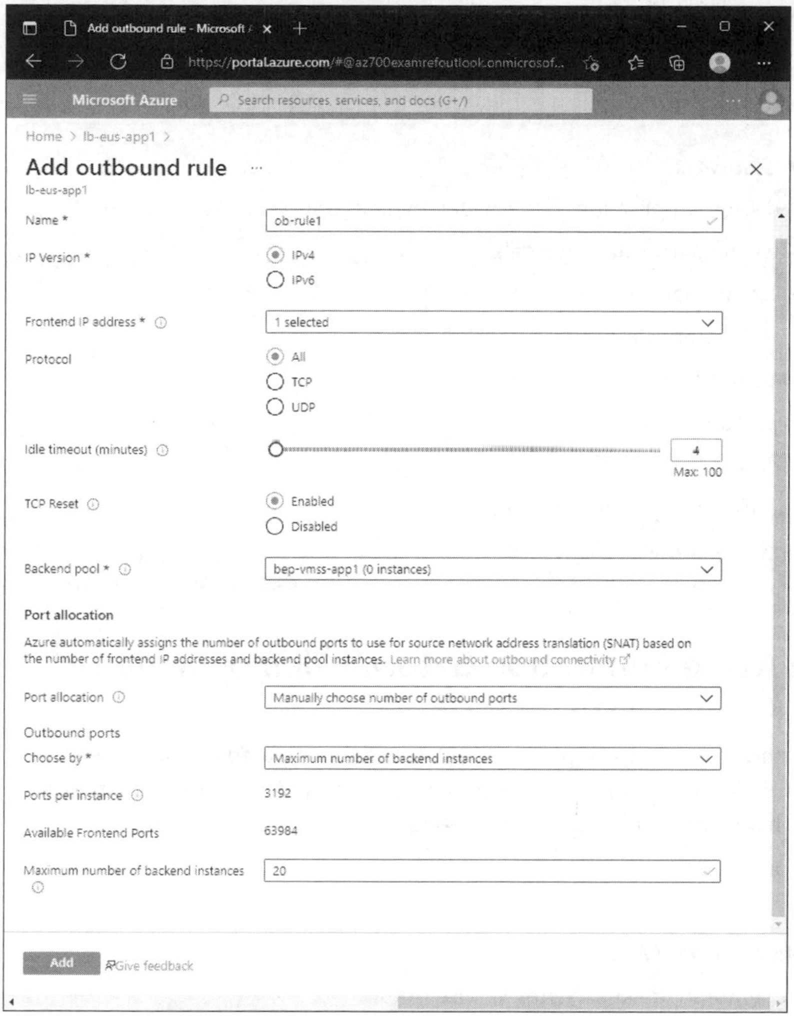

FIGURE 3-16 Add outbound rule

Skill 3.3: Design and implement Azure Application Gateway

Application gateways are the region-based load balancing option that focuses on layer 7 of the OSI model. By operating at layer 7, an application gateway provides many more features than a traditional load balancer. It can perform the basic functionality of distributing traffic across a backend pool of resources, but it also has the ability to redirect to certain backend pools based on the URL or headers of an incoming request. You can optionally enable a Web Application

Firewall (WAF), perform TLS termination, and enable end-to-end TLS encryption. This skill section introduces the application gateway and how to configure the various components.

> **This skill covers how to:**
> - Recommend Azure Application Gateway deployment options
> - Choose between manual and autoscale
> - Create a backend pool
> - Configure HTTP settings
> - Configure health probes
> - Configure listeners
> - Configure routing rules
> - Configure Transport Layer Security (TLS)
> - Configure rewrite policies

Recommend Azure Application Gateway deployment options

Azure application gateways operate at layer 7 of the OSI model, compared to layer 4 for traditional and Azure load balancers. By operating at layer 7, there are additional features that an application gateway has compared to a traditional load balancer:

- SSL termination
- Autoscaling
- Web Application Firewall (WAF)
- Ingress Controller for Azure Kubernetes Service (AKS)
- URL-based routing
- Multiple-site hosting
- Session affinity
- Connection draining
- Custom error pages
- HTTP header and URL rewrites

Application gateways are deployed into an Azure region and can be deployed to be zone-redundant. This is important when considering the deployment options that are available with Azure Front Door, which is discussed more in the next skill section. For applications that will be deployed into one or two regions and require SSL termination or any of the other features listed above, an application gateway is a good choice to recommend. If the application will reside in more than two regions or require some of the other features outlined with Azure Front Door, such as a content delivery network (CDN), then Azure Front Door might be a better option.

After you decide that an application gateway is the recommended ingress point for an application, there are a few SKUs to decide between. First, you can decide whether you want a v1 or a v2 SKU. The v1 SKUs have three preset configuration sizes:

- Small
- Medium
- Large

The v1 SKUs do not provide autoscaling and must be manually configured to one of the predefined sizes. The v2 SKUs include these features that v1 gateways do not:

- Autoscaling
- Zone redundancy
- Static virtual IPs
- AKS Ingress controller
- Azure Key Vault integration
- HTTPS header rewrites
- WAF custom rules

After you decide whether to deploy a v1 or a v2 SKU, both options have a separate SKU for enabling a WAF. For example, there is WAF v1, Medium size; or WAF v2 with autoscaling available.

Choose between manual and autoscale

The first factor in choosing between manual and autoscale is the SKU that you decide to deploy. If you choose to deploy a v1 SKU, then autoscaling is not available and you must choose from one of the predetermined sizes and set the instance count manually, up to 32 instances.

If you choose to deploy a v2 SKU, then you also have the choice of using manual instance counts or autoscaling. In either scale, you can scale up to 125 instances with a v2 SKU. When you choose to use autoscaling, you also set minimum and maximum guardrails. If you know for your application that you need at least two instances at any given time, you can set the minimum to two. If for budget and cost management, you don't expect the peak traffic to go beyond the need for 10 instances, you can set the maximum to 10.

Whether you decide to use manual or autoscale, each scale instance represents approximately 10 *compute units*. Compute units define the amount of compute behind the application gateway when you decide to use a v2 SKU type instead of the Small, Medium, or Large preset sizes. Each compute unit can accept approximately 50 concurrent connections per second without the WAF enabled, or 10 concurrent connections per second when using the WAF.

Compute units are also a component of the overall *capacity unit*. A capacity unit defines the compute, throughput, and consistent connections that an instance supports. A v2 SKU can process approximately 2.2 Mbps of throughput with each capacity unit, and a total of 2,500 persistent connections. For additional compute, throughput, or connections, additional instances are required.

To create an application gateway, follow these steps:

1. Sign in to the Azure portal at *https://portal.azure.com.*

2. In the search bar, search for and select **Application Gateways**.

3. On the Application Gateway page, click **Create**.

4. In the Subscription dropdown menu, select the subscription that has the resources you would like to put the application gateway in front of.

5. In the Resource group dropdown, select a resource group to put the application gateway in. For example, select **Networking**.

6. In the Application gateway name field, provide a name for the gateway. For example, enter **appgw-eus-01**.

7. In the Region dropdown menu, select the Azure region to deploy the gateway to. This must be the same as the resources you will add to the backend pool. For example, select **East US**.

8. In the Tier dropdown menu, select **WAF V2**.

9. In the Enable autoscaling field, set the value to **Yes**.

10. In the Minimum instance count field, set the value to **2**.

11. In the Maximum instance count field, set the value to **5**.

12. Leave the next fields at their default values:

    Firewall status: **Enabled**

    Firewall mode: **Detection**

    Availability zone: **None**

    HTTP2: **Disabled**

13. In the Virtual network dropdown menu, select the virtual network to associate the application gateway with. For example, select **hub-vnet-eus-01**.

14. In the Subnet field, select an available subnet that does not have resources connected. For example, select a dedicated subnet named **AppGW**. Figure 3-17 displays the completed configuration on the Basics tab.

15. Click **Next: Frontends**.

16. Leave the Frontend IP address type at the default, **Public**.

17. In the Public IP address field, click **Add new**.

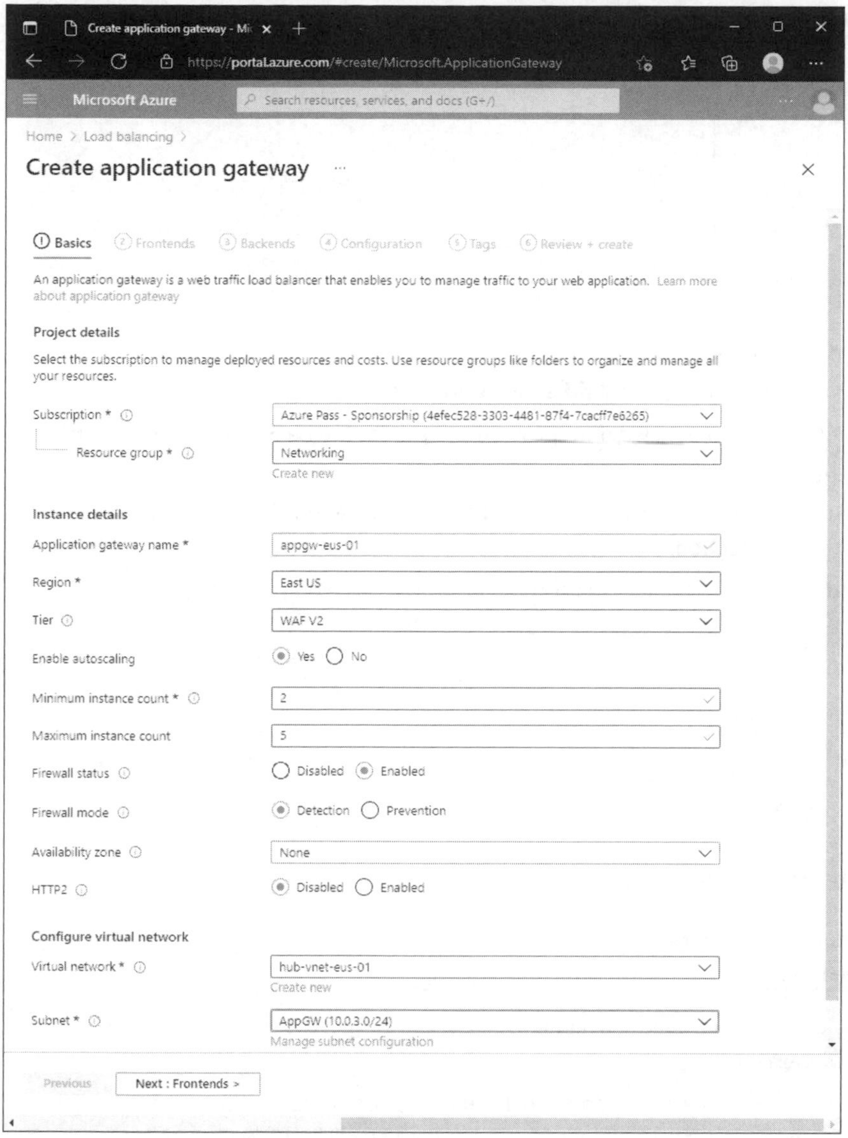

FIGURE 3-17 Create application gateway basics

18. The Add a public IP window will pop up. In the Name field, name the public IP address object. For example, enter **appgw-pip1**. Because the IP address is being associated with an application gateway, the IP SKU must be Standard with a Static assignment. These values are not available to configure.

19. Click **OK**. Figure 3-18 displays the Add a public IP popup.

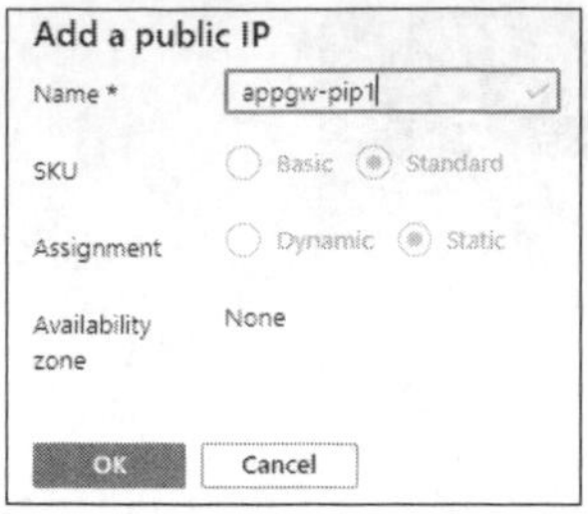

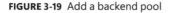

Add a public IP

Name *	appgw-pip1
SKU	○ Basic ● Standard
Assignment	○ Dynamic ● Static
Availability zone	None

OK   Cancel

FIGURE 3-18 Add a public IP

20. Click **Next: Backends**.

21. On the Backend pool tab, click **Add a backend pool**.

22. In the Add a backend pool window, provide a name for the backend pool. For example, enter **appgw-bep1**.

23. Set the Add backend pool without targets field to **Yes**. Backend pools are discussed more in the next section.

24. Click **Add**. Figure 3-19 displays the completed Add a backend pool page.

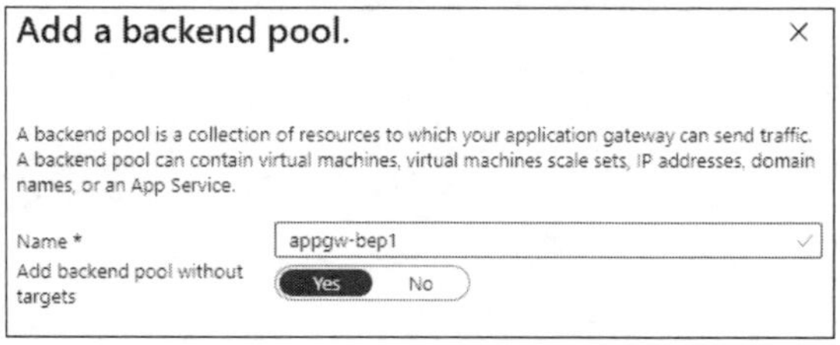

Add a backend pool.   ✕

A backend pool is a collection of resources to which your application gateway can send traffic.
A backend pool can contain virtual machines, virtual machines scale sets, IP addresses, domain
names, or an App Service.

Name *	appgw-bep1
Add backend pool without targets	Yes No

FIGURE 3-19 Add a backend pool

25. Click **Next: Configuration**.

26. On the Configuration tab, click **Add a routing rule**.

27. In the Rule name field, specify a name for the routing rule. For example, specify **public-to-bep1**.

28. In the Listener name field, enter a name for the listener. For example, enter **listener-app1**. Listeners are discussed in more detail later in this skill section.

29. In the Frontend IP dropdown, select **Public**.

30. Leave the remaining values set to their defaults:

    Protocol: **HTTP**

    Port: **80**

    Listener type: **Basic**

    Error page url: **No**

31. Figure 3-20 displays the completed Listener tab. Click the **Backend targets** tab.

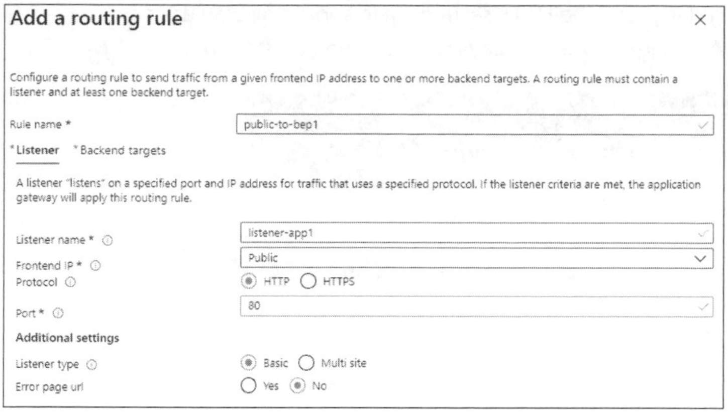

FIGURE 3-20 Add a routing rule – Listener tab

32. On the Backend targets tab, leave the default target type as **Backend pool**.

33. In the Backend target dropdown menu, select the previously configured backend pool. For example, select **appgw-bep1**.

34. In the HTTP settings field, click **Add new**.

35. In the Add a HTTP setting page, provide a name for the settings. For example, enter **app1-settings**. HTTP settings are discussed in more detail later in this skill section.

36. Leave all other fields set to default values and click **Add**. Figure 3-21 displays the configured HTTP settings.

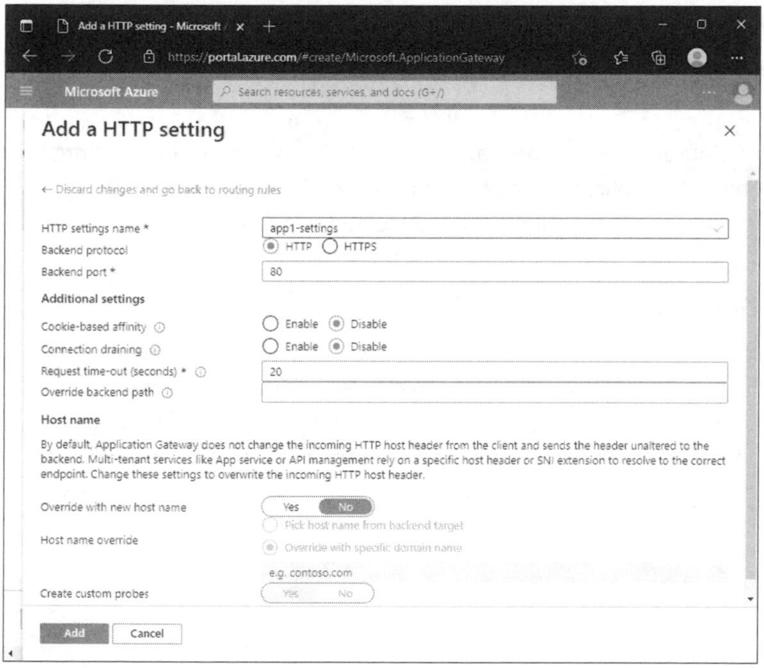

FIGURE 3-21 Add a HTTP setting

37. On the Add a routing rule page, the HTTP settings field should display the new app1-settings. Click **Add**. Figure 3-22 displays the Backend targets tab.

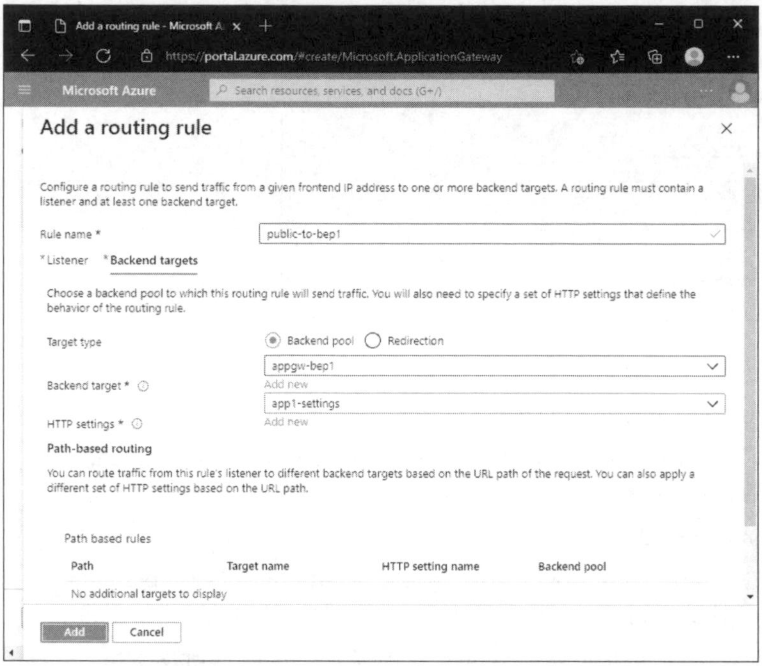

FIGURE 3-22 Add a routing rule – Backend targets tab

38. Click **Next: Tags**.
39. Click **Next: Review + Create**.
40. Click **Create**.

These steps deploy a simple application gateway with the minimum requirements to get the first instance up and running. An application gateway supports multiple backend pools, health probes, listeners, routing rules, and more. All these are discussed in the next sections.

Create a backend pool

When you deploy an application gateway, there are a number of required components during deployment and more that you can configure after it is deployed, including backend pools. Backend pools are the resources "behind" the application gateway in a network topology or architecture design. Supported services for a backend pool in an application gateway include:

- IP addresses or fully qualified domain names
- Virtual machines
- Virtual machine scale sets
- App services

Essentially, as long as the application gateway can communicate with the resource, it can be added as a backend pool. This is true even if the resource is in another Azure region, on-premises, or in another cloud. After you have created a backend pool object that identifies these resources, you associate the pool with a listener by using a routing rule. Listeners and routing rules are discussed in a later section.

To create a new backend pool for an existing application gateway, follow these steps:

1. Sign in to the Azure portal at *https://portal.azure.com*.

2. In the search bar, search for and select **Application Gateways**.

3. On the Application Gateway page, select the application gateway that was previously created, for example **appgw-eus-01**.

4. On the Application Gateway page, click the **Backend pools** blade.

5. On the Backend pools blade, click **Add**. Note that one backend pool already exists from when you created the application gateway, but additional backend pools can be created.

6. On the Add backend pool screen, provide a name for the backend pool. For example, enter **bep-as-app1**.

7. In the Target type dropdown menu, select **App Services**.

8. In the Target dropdown menu, select an app service that you have deployed. For example, select **az700demoapp1**. Note that this requires an app service to be created in advance. App services are not covered on the AZ-700, and the steps to create one are not outlined here. If you would like to use a different target type, select and configure it here.

9. Click **Add**. Figure 3-23 shows the completed backend pool page.

FIGURE 3-23 Add backend pool

A backend pool is really just an object definition of the resource that the application gateway needs to direct traffic to. However, the backend pool is only the object definition. To be able to forward requests that the application gateway receives, then health probes, listeners, and routing rules must also be configured.

Configure HTTP settings

An application gateway relies on the HTTP settings that you configure to understand the specifics of forwarding traffic to the backend pool. HTTP settings are required to configure both health probes and routing rules.

HTTP settings are essentially a definition of the protocol and port number that should be used to communicate with a backend pool. The HTTP settings are also where you can configure cookie-based session affinity, as well as connection draining if you are taking a resource offline.

To add an HTTP setting to an application gateway, follow these steps:

1. Sign in to the Azure portal at *https://portal.azure.com*.

2. In the search bar, search for and select **Application Gateways**.

3. On the Application Gateway page, select the application gateway that was previously created, for example **appgw-eus-01**.

4. On the Application Gateway page, click the **HTTP settings** blade.

5. On the HTTP settings blade, click **Add**.

6. On the Add HTTP setting page, in the Name field provide a name for the collection of settings. For example, enter **settings-as-app1**.

7. In the Backend protocol and Port fields, leave the defaults of **HTTP** and **80**.

8. In the Cookie-based affinity field, select **Enable**, and then leave the cookie name the default value.

9. Leave the remaining settings at their default values and click **Save**. Figure 3-24 displays the completed configuration.

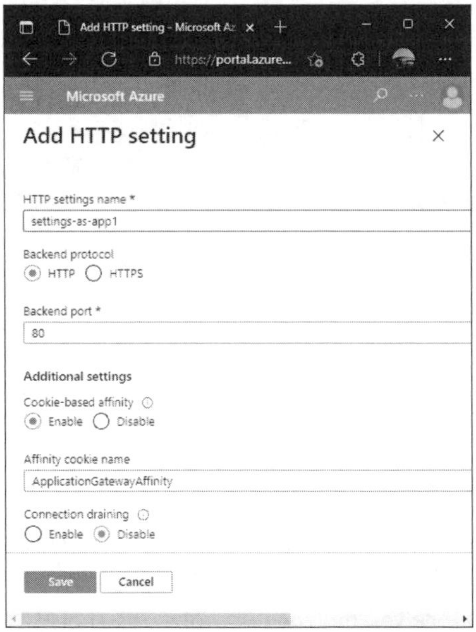

FIGURE 3-24 Add HTTP setting

Configure health probes

Application gateways automatically monitor the resources defined in the backend pool to ensure that they are healthy before sending connection requests and traffic to that resource. In the event that a resource becomes unavailable, the health probes are configured with a failure threshold to indicate to the application gateway that the resource is unavailable. If all resources become unavailable, then the application gateway will present HTTP 502 (Bad Gateway) errors to the client connections.

For example, if the resource does not respond to three consecutive requests at 30-second intervals, it would be deemed unhealthy. The default values of a health probe are to test the connection every 30 seconds, with a 30 second timeout, and to mark the resource as unhealthy at three consecutive requests.

You can also configure custom health probes to be used with HTTP settings and rules so that you can customize the hostname, port number, interval, timeout period, or unhealthy threshold. Health probes require the following information to be configured:

- Name
- Backend host
- Virtual directory path
- Interval
- Timeout
- Unhealthy threshold

To configure a health probe on an existing application gateway, follow these steps:

1. Sign in to the Azure portal at *https://portal.azure.com*.
2. In the search bar, search for and select **Application Gateways**.
3. On the Application Gateway page, select the application gateway that was previously created, for example **appgw-eus-01**.
4. On the Application Gateway page, click the **Health probes** blade.
5. On the Health probes blade, click **Add**.
6. On the Add health probe page, in the Name field provide a name for the health probe. For example, enter **hp-as-app1**.
7. In the Protocol field, leave the default of **HTTP** selected.
8. In the Host field, enter the IP address or fully qualified domain name of the host to monitor. For example, enter **az700demoapp1.azurewebsites.net**.
9. Leave the Pick host name and Pick port from settings at their default values.
10. In the Path field, specify the path of the host to monitor. For example, to monitor the root of the path, enter **/**. You can specify the full path if there are certain virtual directories of your app to monitor.

11. In the Interval (seconds) field, set the desired interval to check with the resource. For example, set it to **15**.

12. In the Timeout (seconds) field, set the desired timeout value. For example, set it to **10**.

13. In the Unhealthy threshold field, set the desired consecutive failed attempts before marking the resource unhealthy. For example, set it to **2**. Overall, these settings would mark a resource unhealthy faster than would the default settings.

14. In the HTTP settings dropdown menu, select the settings that you previously created. For example, select **settings-as-app1**.

15. Click **Test**. Figure 3-25 shows the completed configuration. At this point, if you have followed the steps in the book, you will receive a message that the HTTP setting that has been selected is not associated with a backend pool. This is because the HTTP setting must also be configured with the routing rule, which then creates the backend pool association.

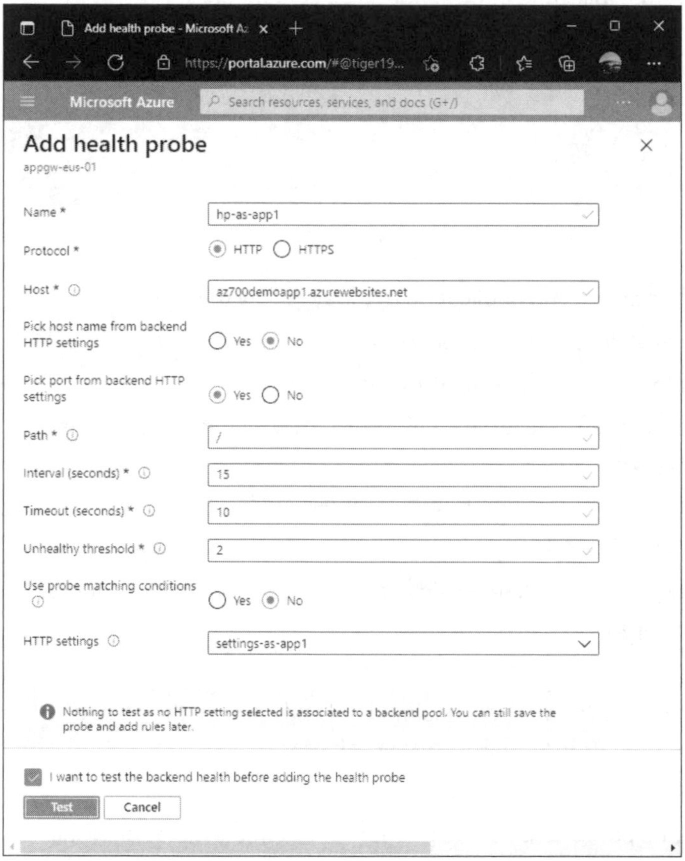

FIGURE 3-25 Add health probe

16. Clear the checkbox next to I want to test the backend health before adding the health probe, and then click **Add**.

Configure listeners

A listener is the component that "listens" to the frontend IP address of the application gateway for incoming connections. The listener defines the protocol, port number, hostname, and IP address that an incoming request is attempting to connect to and matches it with the configuration that you have defined. An application gateway can have multiple listeners for different hostnames, virtual directory paths, different backend pools, and many other scenarios.

As listeners identify the incoming traffic and connection requests, listeners support four protocols:

- HTTP
- HTTPS
- HTTP/2
- WebSocket

When you configure the listener, you can select either HTTP or HTTPS. WebSocket support is enabled by default and does not have a configurable setting. To create a listener on an existing application gateway, follow these steps:

1. Sign in to the Azure portal at *https://portal.azure.com*.
2. In the search bar, search for and select **Application Gateways**.
3. On the Application Gateway page, select the application gateway that was previously created, for example **appgw-eus-01**.
4. On the Application Gateway page, click the **Listeners** blade.
5. On the Health probes blade, click **Add listener**.
6. On the Add listener screen, provide a name for the listener. For example, enter **listener-as-app1**.
7. In the Frontend IP dropdown menu, select the frontend IP address that you configured when you deployed the application gateway. For example, select **Public**.
8. In the Port field, enter a port number that the listener should expect incoming traffic on. For example, enter **8080**.
9. In the remaining fields, leave the default values:
   - Protocol: **HTTP**
   - Listener type: **Basic**
   - Error page url: **No**
10. Click **Add**. Figure 3-26 displays the completed configuration.

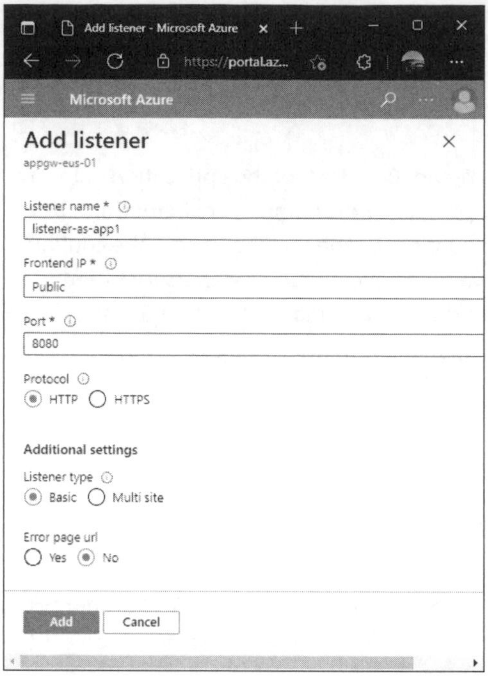

FIGURE 3-26 Add listener

Configure routing rules

Routing rules are the glue that holds together the listener, backend pool, and HTTP settings that you have created. There are two types of routing rules:

- Basic
- Multi-site

Basic routing rules map a single fully qualified domain name (FQDN) to one backend pool that has been configured. A multi-site listener allows you to define multiple FQDNs to a back-end pool. As of this writing, there is a preview feature to also allow wildcards to be used as part of domain names or as portions of sub-domain names.

To create a new routing rule, follow these steps:

1. Sign in to the Azure portal at *https://portal.azure.com*.
2. In the search bar, search for and select **Application Gateways**.
3. On the Application Gateway page, select the application gateway that was previously created, for example **appgw-eus-01**.
4. On the Application Gateway page, click the **Rules** blade.
5. On the Rules blade, click **Request routing rule**.
6. On the Add a routing rule page, in the Rule name field, provide a name for the rule. For example, enter **public-to-as-app1**.

7. In the Listener dropdown menu, select the listener that you previously created. For example, select **listener-as-app1**. Figure 3-27 shows the completed Listener tab.

FIGURE 3-27 Add a routing rule – listener

8. Click the **Backend targets** tab.

9. In the Target type, leave the default value, **Backend pool**.

10. In the Backend target dropdown menu, select the desired backend target. For example, select **bep-as-app1**.

11. In the HTTP settings dropdown menu, select the HTTP settings that you previously created. For example, select **settings-as-app1**.

12. Click **Add**. Figure 3-28 shows the completed Backend targets tab.

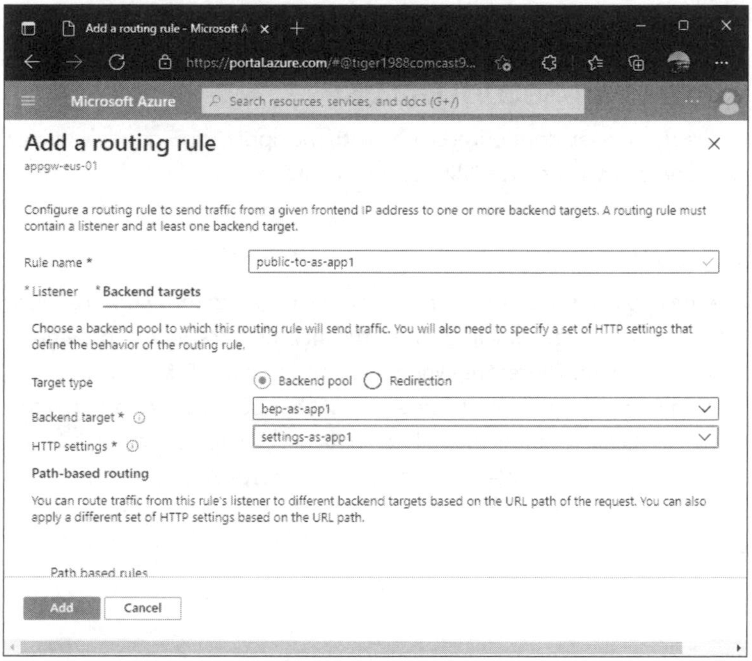

FIGURE 3-28 Add a routing rule – Backend targets

The above steps will create the rule that associates the frontend IP address of the application gateway, through the listener, with the backend pool and HTTP settings. Figure 3-29 outlines the various components of the application gateway that have been configured and how they are associated.

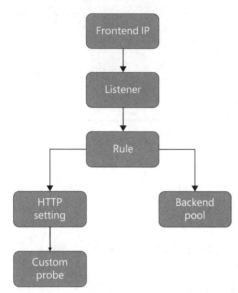

FIGURE 3-29 Application gateway diagram

Configure Transport Layer Security (TLS)

All the examples and steps that have been configured so far with the application gateway have used HTTP. Application gateways can also use TLS/SSL in two scenarios:

- TLS termination
- End-to-end TLS encryption

TLS termination is where the application gateway presents a certificate to the client through the listener. This enables the application gateway to decrypt the incoming traffic and provide an encrypted response back to the client. Therefore, when you configure the TLS certificate it must be a Personal Information Exchange (PFX) certificate file that has both public and private keys. For TLS termination, the certificate requires the full trust chain to be uploaded, including the root certificate from the CA, any intermediates, and the leaf certificate. Application gateway can use the following certificate types:

- Certificate Authority
- Extended Validation
- Wildcard
- Self-signed

Allowing the application gateway to terminate the TLS connection typically provides better performance by the backend resources. This is especially true using larger key sizes for the certificates. By decrypting the traffic at the application gateway, it can view the request content and perform the URL or path-based routing to the various backend pools that you might define.

If you have a PFX certificate file to upload to an application gateway, follow these steps to add a new listener that uses HTTPS:

1. Sign in to the Azure portal at *https://portal.azure.com*.

2. In the search bar, search for and select **Application Gateways**.

3. On the Application Gateway page, select the application gateway that was previously created, for example **appgw-eus-01**.

4. On the Application Gateway page, click the **Listeners** blade.

5. On the Listeners blade, click **Add listener**.

6. On the Add listener screen, provide a name for the listener. For example, enter **listener-as-app2**.

7. In the Frontend IP dropdown menu, select the frontend IP address that you configured when you deployed the application gateway. For example, select **Public**.

8. In the Protocol field, select **HTTPS**. This will automatically set the port number to **443**.

9. Additional fields will appear for HTTPS settings. In the Choose a certificate field, leave the default value of **Upload a certificate**.

10. In the Cert name field, provide a name for the certificate. For example, enter **HugeLab**.

11. In the PFX certificate file field, browse and select your PFX certificate file.

12. In the Password field, provide the password to the PFX certificate file.

13. In the remaining fields, leave the default values:

    - Listener type: **Basic**
    - Error page url: **No**

14. Click **Add**. Figure 3-30 displays the completed configuration.

Some security requirements or compliance policies might require that all communication in the end-to-end process be encrypted. The process for this works similarly to TLS termination, except that the application gateway will perform an encrypted connection to the backend pool. The application gateway still decrypts the session when it arrives to identify the path and any other features that might be enabled, such as cookie-based session affinity, header rewrites, and more.

For an application gateway to be able to establish a new TLS session with a backend pool, the host settings must match the common name in the certificate that is being used. If the backend pool is using a self-signed certificate, then the certificate must be provided to the application gateway. The certificate must be defined in the HTTP settings that the routing rule is configured to use.

FIGURE 3-30 Add listener

To configure settings that use HTTPS, follow these steps.

1. Sign in to the Azure portal at *https://portal.azure.com*.

2. In the search bar, search for and select **Application Gateways**.

3. On the Application Gateway page, select the application gateway that was previously created, for example **appgw-eus-01**.

4. On the Application Gateway page, click the **HTTP settings** blade.

5. On the HTTP settings blade, click **Add**.

6. On the Add HTTP setting page, in the Name field provide a name for the collection of settings. For example, enter **settings-as-app2**.

7. In the Backend protocol and Port fields, select **HTTPS**. The backend port will automatically adjust to **443**.

8. In the CER certificate field, browse to and select your certificate file to communicate with the backend pool.

9. In the Cert Name field, provide a name for the certificate. For example, enter **HugeLab**.

10. In the Cookie-based affinity field, select **Enable**, and then leave the cookie name the default value.

11. Click **+Add certificate**.

12. Leave the remaining settings at their default values and click **Save**. Figure 3-31 displays the completed configuration.

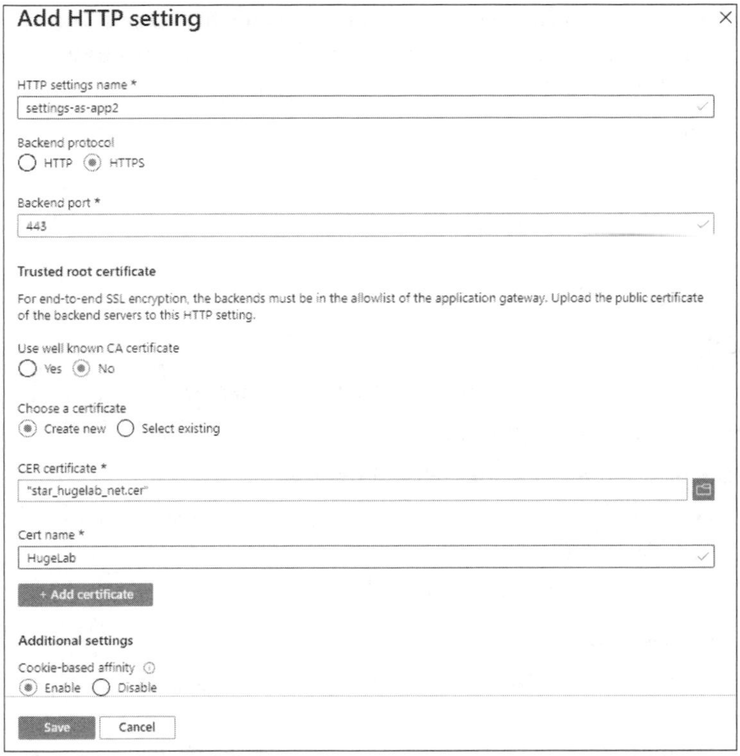

Add HTTP setting   ×

HTTP settings name *
settings-as-app2

Backend protocol
○ HTTP   ◉ HTTPS

Backend port *
443

Trusted root certificate

For end-to-end SSL encryption, the backends must be in the allowlist of the application gateway. Upload the public certificate of the backend servers to this HTTP setting.

Use well known CA certificate
○ Yes   ◉ No

Choose a certificate
◉ Create new   ○ Select existing

CER certificate *
"star_hugelab_net.cer"

Cert name *
HugeLab

[+ Add certificate]

Additional settings

Cookie-based affinity ⓘ
◉ Enable   ○ Disable

[Save]   [Cancel]

FIGURE 3-31 Add HTTP setting

Configure rewrite policies

With an application gateway V2 SKU, you can create header rewrite sets to add, update, or remove various HTTP headers and server variables. When you create a rewrite set, you base the rewrites on rules, conditions, and actions based on actions, conditions, or variables. All headers in connection requests and responses can be modified, except for the *Connection* and *Upgrade* headers.

Each rule that you create has a rule sequence number that determines the order in which the rules are processed. Rules with the lower sequence number are processed first. If you configure two rules with the same sequence number, there is no predefined method of guaranteeing which rule is processed first.

Conditions in a rewrite set are simply if–then statements that identify the type of variable to check—either HTTP header or server variable—and then the value within that might need to be added or modified. Conditions can optionally be configured to be case-sensitive and to be looking for specific patterns to match in the header. Conditions are not required to be configured as part of a rewrite set if you want all traffic to be inspected or modified by the rule.

After identifying the component that needs to change, whether it is all packets or only the packets that meet the condition, the action defines what to change within the headers. The rewrite set can then set or delete a request header or response header, or modify the URL. These rewrite sets are associated with a routing rule when they are created.

Common scenarios for using header rewrites include:

- Removing port information from the X-Forwarded-For header
- Modifying a redirection URL
- Implementing security HTTP headers
- Deleting unwanted headers
- Parameter-based path selection

To create a rewrite set that sets a security HTTP header, follow these steps:

1. Sign in to the Azure portal at *https://portal.azure.com*.
2. In the search bar, search for and select **Application Gateways**.
3. On the Application Gateway page, select the application gateway that was previously created, for example **appgw-eus-01**.
4. On the Application Gateway page, click the **Rewrites** blade.
5. On the Rewrites blade, click **+ Rewrite set**.
6. On the Create rewrite set page, in the Name field provide a name for the set. For example, enter **rewrite-app1**.
7. In the Routing Rules | Paths section, select a previously created routing rule to associate the rewrite set with. For example, select **public-to-as-app1**.
8. Click **Next**. Figure 3-32 shows the completed Name and Association tab.
9. On the Rewrite rule configuration tab, click **Add rewrite rule**.
10. In the rewrite rule name field, provide a name for the new rule. For example, enter **SetTransportSecurity**. Leave the Rule sequence value at the default, **100**. Figure 3-33 displays the relevant portion of the Create rewrite set page.
11. In the Do section, select **Click to fix configuration this action**.
12. The Do section will expand. In the Rewrite type dropdown field, select **Response Header**.
13. In the Action type dropdown field, leave the default value of **Set**.

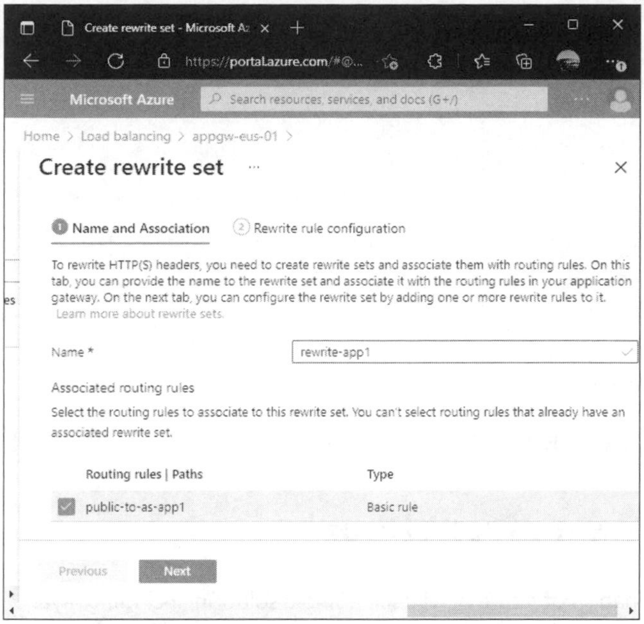

FIGURE 3-32 Create rewrite set

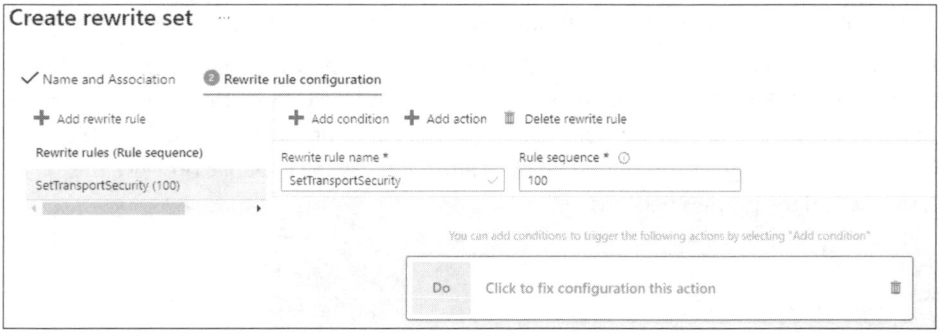

FIGURE 3-33 Rewrite rule configuration

14. In the Header name field, leave the default value of **Common header** selected.

15. In the Common header dropdown field, select **Strict-Transport-Security**.

16. In the Header value field, provide a value for the header. For example, enter **max-age=31536000**.

17. Click **OK**. Figure 3-34 displays the completed Do section.

18. Click **Create**.

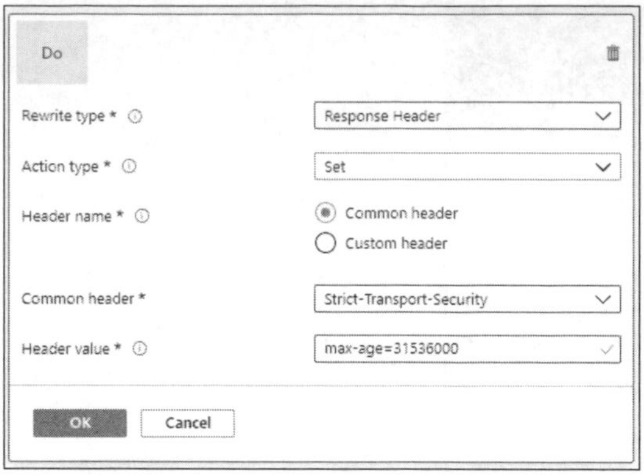

FIGURE 3-34 Rewrite rule action

Skill 3.4: Implement Azure Front Door

Azure Front Door provides a combination of Azure services in a single solution, including layer 7 load balancing, web app firewall, security reporting, and content delivery and optimization. Unlike most other Azure services, Front Door is considered a global service that you do not deploy into a specific Azure region. Instead, when you create a Front Door endpoint, it is accessible from all of Azure's regions, edge locations, and points of presence (POPs) across the world.

As of this writing, *Azure Front Door* is the generally available product. A new deployment option named *Azure Front Door Standard/Premium* is currently in public preview and separates some of the features and functionality of the core product into the two versions. The Objectives list includes choosing an appropriate SKU, so although it is still in public preview, this skill section focuses on the preview versions.

> **This skill covers how to:**
> - Choose an Azure Front Door SKU
> - Configure health probes
> - Configure SSL termination and end-to-end SSL encryption
> - Configure multisite listeners and configure back-end targets
> - Configure routing rules

Choose an Azure Front Door SKU

There are two SKUs of Azure Front Door: Standard and Premium. The Standard SKU offers optimized content delivery across the world, not only in a single Azure region. Both SKUs of Azure Front Door are considered a global load balancer, which uses anycast IP addresses to locate the nearest Microsoft point of presence (POP) to access the Azure network backbone. Table 3-4 outlines the feature difference between the two SKU options.

TABLE 3-4 Azure Front Door SKU comparison

Feature	Standard	Premium
Custom domain	Yes	Yes
SSL Offloading	Yes	Yes
Caching	Yes	Yes
Compression	Yes	Yes
Global load balancing	Yes	Yes
Layer 7 routing	Yes	Yes
URL rewrites	Yes	Yes
Rules engine	Yes	Yes
Private Link	No	Yes
WAF	Custom rules only	Yes
Bot protection	No	Yes
Enhanced metrics and monitoring	Yes	Yes
Traffic report	Yes	Yes
Security report	No	Yes

As Table 3-4 outlines, the Premium SKU has all of the features of the Standard SKU, plus adds more rule options for the WAF, bot protection, integration with Microsoft Threat Intelligence and security analytics with reporting, and integration with Azure Private Link. To deploy an Azure front door with your choice of SKU, follow these steps:

1. Sign in to the Azure portal at *https://portal.azure.com*.
2. In the search bar, search for and select **Front Doors Standard/Premium**.
3. On the Front Doors Standard/Premium page, click **Create**.
4. In the Compare offerings screen, accept the default to deploy a Quick create Azure front door Standard/Premium, and click **Continue to create a front door**.
5. In the Subscription dropdown menu, select the desired subscription to deploy the front door in.

6. In the Resource Group dropdown, select the resource group. For example, select **Networking**.

7. In the Name field, provide a name for the front door. For example, enter **fd-app1**.

8. In the Tier field, select the desired SKU. For example, select **Standard**.

9. In the Endpoint name field, provide a globally unique name for the front door URL. For example, enter **az700fdapp**.

10. In the Origin type dropdown menu, select the origin component. For example, select **App Services**.

11. In the Origin host name dropdown menu, select the app service that you previously created. For example, select **az700demoapp1.azurewebsites.net**.

12. Leave the remaining fields at their default blank values, and click **Review + create**. Figure 3-35 displays the completed configuration.

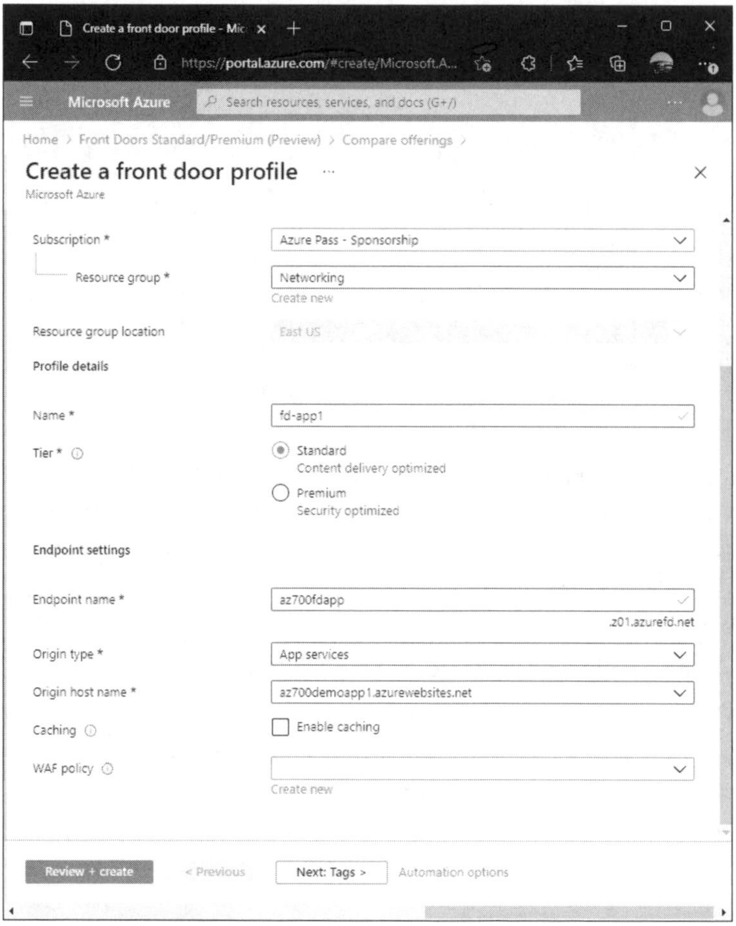

FIGURE 3-35 Create a front door profile

13. Click **Create**.

Configure health probes

Health probes are associated with the origin group that contains the resources (origins) that Front Door will send the client connections to. When you create the front door profile, it will automatically enable the health probe for the selected origin.

With Front Door, health probes perform two primary functions. First is to verify that the backend resource is online and healthy. Second, the health probe assists Front Door in determining the best backend resource to send the client requests to. Front Door also relies on POPs, and there can be many health probes that cause additional network traffic. The default health probe frequency is 30 seconds, which can result in approximately 200 health probe requests per minute, per backend source.

> **NEED MORE REVIEW?** **AZURE POINTS OF PRESENCE**
>
> For more information on Azure regions, edge locations, and points of presence, visit *https://infrastructuremap.microsoft.com/*.

Health probes in Front Door have two possible probe methods: GET and HEAD. Using a GET probe retrieves information from the backend resource, including a message body. This can incur more costs and throughput with each health check. A HEAD request is the default value, and requires that the backend resource not include a message body in the response.

When a backend resource responds to a probe, both GET and HEAD requests should result in an HTTP 200 (OK) status code. Any other response type will count as a failed attempt. The response time in latency is also measured to assist the Front Door service in choosing the most responsive backend resource.

To modify the settings of a health probe associated with an origin group, follow these steps:

1. Sign in to the Azure portal at *https://portal.azure.com*.
2. In the search bar, search for and select **Front Doors Standard/Premium**.
3. On the Front Doors Standard/Premium page, select the Front Door instance that you previously created. For example, select **fd-app1**.
4. Click the **Origin groups** blade.
5. On the Origin groups blade, click the **default-origin-group**.
6. In the Update origin group screen, scroll down to the **Health probes** section.
7. Verify that the **Enable health probes** checkbox is already selected and that the path is set to **/**.
8. In the Protocol field, select **HTTPS**.
9. In the Interval field, set the time to **30** seconds.
10. Click **Update**. Figure 3-36 displays the updated Health probes section.

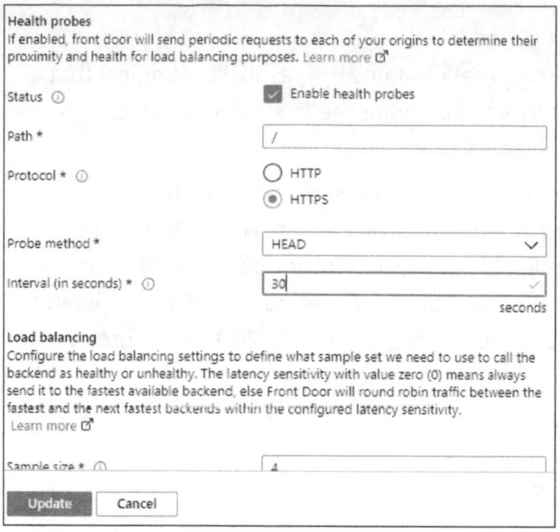

FIGURE 3-36 Origin group health probes

Configure SSL termination and end-to-end SSL encryption

By default and without any additional configuration, Azure Front Door supports using HTTPS on the default hostname that you configure when you first deploy the service. This is the *azurefd.net* domain that you customize when you create the service. There is no additional configuration required if you are using this domain to access the service.

If you plan on using a custom domain with your own certificate, then there is additional configuration required. As of this writing, Front Door only supports using a certificate that is in an Azure Key Vault in the same subscription. Azure Key Vault is a requirement, and it is not currently supported to be in a different subscription than the Front Door service. Additionally, the certificate must have a complete certificate chain, and the root CA listed must be on the Microsoft Trusted CA list. Finally, the certificate that you use cannot use an elliptic-curve (EC) cryptography algorithm.

The overall steps for allowing the Front Door service to access a Key Vault certificate are:

1. Register a service principal in Azure Active Directory associated with Azure Front Door.

2. Grant the Get permission to the service principal for Secrets and Certificates in Azure Key Vault.

3. Select the certificate from Front Door and associate it with a custom domain.

Register a service principal

The application ID for Azure Front Door is *ad0e1c7e-6d38-4ba4-9efd-0bc77ba9f037*. You can run this PowerShell command from Azure Cloud Shell to create a service principal that is associated with the Front Door application ID. The user identity that runs this command must be a Global Administrator in the Azure Active Directory environment.

```
New-AzADServicePrincipal -ApplicationId "205478c0-bd83-4e1b-a9d6-db63a3e1e1c8"
```

If you run the command from Azure Cloud Shell, you should receive information back about the newly created service principal. Note that the DisplayName is *Microsoft.Azure.FrontDoor-Cdn*.

```
ServicePrincipalNames : {205478c0-bd83-4e1b-a9d6-db63a3e1e1c8,
    https://microsoft.onmicrosoft.com/033ce1c9-f832-4658-b024-ef1cbea108b8}
ApplicationId         : 205478c0-bd83-4e1b-a9d6-db63a3e1e1c8
ObjectType            : ServicePrincipal
DisplayName           : Microsoft.AzureFrontDoor-Cdn
Id                    : a1d4a221-de6f-4b32-aa0d-d9873deeebd4
Type                  : ServicePrincipal
```

Azure Key Vault permissions

After you create the service principal, the object needs permission in Azure Key Vault to access the certificate that you upload. To use a Key Vault access policy to assign the permissions, follow these steps:

1. Sign in to the Azure portal at *https://portal.azure.com*.

2. In the search bar, search for and select **Key Vault**.

3. Select an existing key vault that you have deployed.

4. On the Key vault page, click the **Access policies** blade.

5. On the Access policies page, click **Add Access Policy**.

6. In the Key permissions dropdown menu, select **Get**.

7. In the Secret permission dropdown menu, select **Get**.

8. In the Select principal field, click **None selected**.

9. The Principal screen will appear. Search for the application ID, *205478c0-bd83-4e1b-a9d6-db63a3e1e1c8*, and select **Microsoft.Azure.FrontDoor-Cdn**.

10. Click **Select**. Figure 3-37 displays the search portion of the Principal screen.

FIGURE 3-37 Select a principal

11. On the Add access policy screen, click **Add**. Figure 3-38 displays the completed configuration.

12. On the Access policies page, click **Save**.

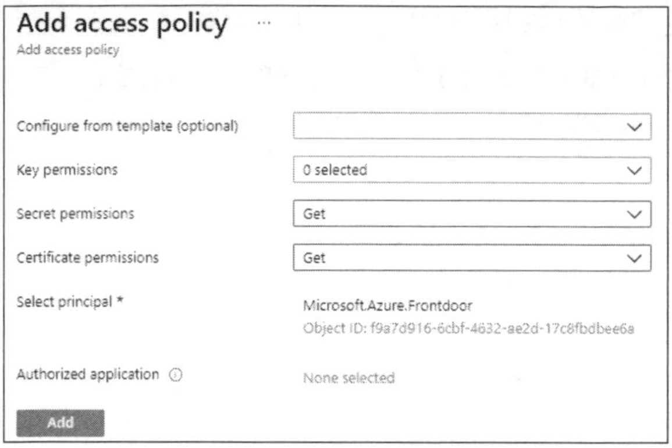

FIGURE 3-38 Add access policy

Add custom domain to endpoint

After you have the certificate uploaded to Azure Key Vault and you have the Front Door service principal with the appropriate access policy, you can configure the custom domain on your Front Door endpoint. To add the custom domain to the endpoint with your own certificate, follow these steps:

1. Sign in to the Azure portal at *https://portal.azure.com*.

2. In the search bar, search for and select **Front Doors Standard/Premium**.

3. On the Front Doors Standard/Premium page, select the front door instance that you previously created. For example, select **fd-app1**.

4. Click the **Secrets** blade.

5. On the Secrets blade, click **Add certificate**.

6. On the Add certificate screen, expand the key vault with your certificate, then select the checkbox next to the certificate name.

7. Click **Add**. Figure 3-39 displays the selected certificate.

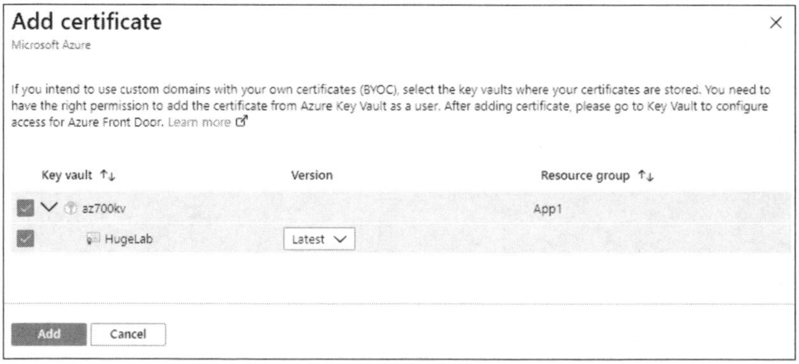

FIGURE 3-39 Add certificate

8. Click the **Endpoint manager** blade.

9. On the Endpoint manager screen, click **Edit endpoint** for the endpoint you want to configure the custom domain on.

10. In the Domains section, click **Add**.

11. In the Add a domain field, select **Add a new domain**.

12. In the DNS management field, select the appropriate DNS option for your domain. For example, select **All other DNS services**.

13. In the Custom domain field, enter the FQDN of your domain. For example, enter **fd.hugelab.net**.

14. In the HTTPS field, select **Bring Your Own Certificate (BYOC)**.

15. In the Secret dropdown menu, select the certificate that you added to Front Door from Key Vault. Figure 3-40 displays the completed Add a domain screen.

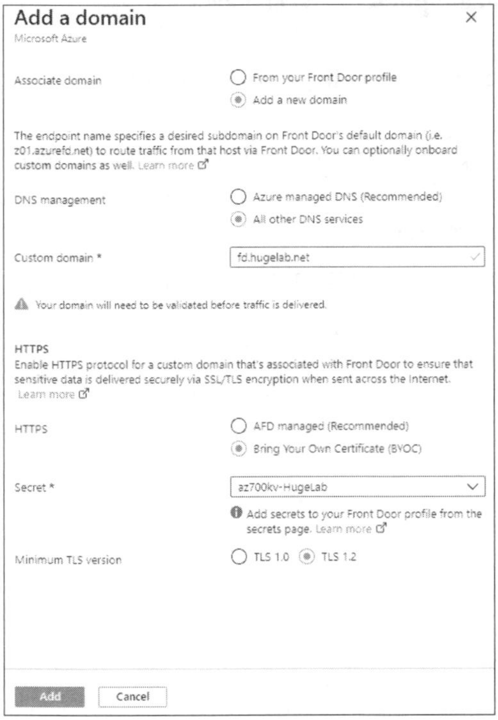

FIGURE 3-40 Add a domain with a certificate

16. Click **Add**.

Completing these steps will add the certificate for the domain that you specified to the Front Door configuration. A CNAME record is also required at the DNS provider to forward requests for the custom domain that you added—for example, **fd.hugelab.net**. This would need to be redirected to the **azurefd.net** endpoint. This provides TLS termination at the Front Door endpoint.

End-to-end encryption

After configuring the HTTPS termination at the endpoint, the next step for your deployment might be to ensure end-to-end encryption. In an Azure Front Door Standard or Premium deployment, the forwarding protocol is configured in the routing rule. By default, the endpoint will accept both HTTP and HTTPS requests and then forward the request using the same incoming protocol.

To force end-to-end encryption and use only HTTPS, you must modify the routing rule. To modify the routing rule, follow these steps:

1. Sign in to the Azure portal at *https://portal.azure.com*.

2. In the search bar, search for and select **Front Doors Standard/Premium**.

3. On the Front Doors Standard/Premium page, select the front door instance that you previously created. For example, select **fd-app1**.

4. Click the **Endpoint manager** blade.

5. On the Endpoint manager screen, click **Edit endpoint** for the endpoint you want to configure the custom domain on.

6. In the Routes section, click the name of the route to modify. For example, click **default-route.**

7. On the Update route screen, locate the Accepted protocols dropdown menu and select **HTTPS only**.

8. In the Forwarding protocol field, select **HTTPS only**.

9. Click **Update**. Figure 3-41 displays the updated configuration.

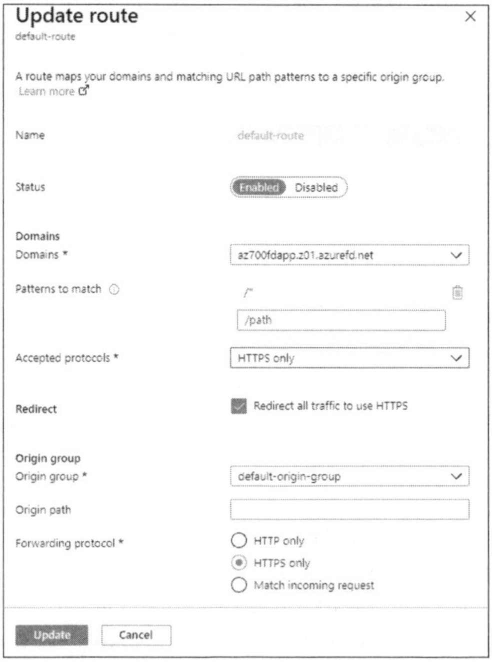

FIGURE 3-41 Update route

Configure multisite listeners and configure backend targets

With Azure Front Door Standard and Premium, the names of the components that are configured are different from application gateways and the original Front Door service. Figure 3-42 outlines how the named components connect.

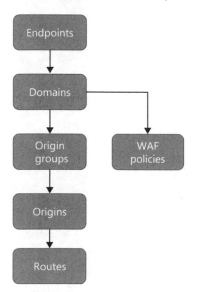

FIGURE 3-42 Azure Front Door Standard/Premium components

You can configure multiple endpoints per Azure Front Door instance. Each endpoint would have its own azurefd.net FQDN. Each endpoint can then have one or more domains associated with it. This would be the equivalent of a multi-site listener on an application gateway.

Each domain that you add must be verified if the DNS zone is not managed in your Azure subscription. The verification process is to add a TXT record with the confirmation string. Domains are then associated with origin groups, as well as WAF policies.

Origin groups are the equivalent of backend pool for application gateways. In an origin group, you create individual origins, which are the resources that you want to be able to communicate with through Front Door. These could be Azure resources such as App Services or Traffic Manager, or public IP addresses for on-premises or other applications hosted in other cloud providers.

Configure routing rules

Routes specify how the domains are associated with the origin groups. You can specify specific patterns to match in the incoming request URL to restrict which URLs Front Door responds to. By default, the first route will accept requests on **/***, which would be any directory on the endpoint. Routes are also where you can set whether to use HTTP, HTTPS, or both protocols on the incoming connection and the forward to the origin.

To configure the routing rules for an existing front door instance, follow these steps:

1. Sign in to the Azure portal at *https://portal.azure.com*.

2. In the search bar, search for and select **Front Doors Standard/Premium**.

3. On the Front Doors Standard/Premium page, select the front door instance that you previously created. For example, select **fd-app1**.

4. Click the **Endpoint manager** blade.

5. On the Endpoint manager screen, click **Edit endpoint** for the endpoint you want to configure the custom domain on.

6. In the Routes section, click the name of the route to modify. For example, click **default-route**.

7. In the Update route screen, locate the "Patterns to match" field and click the trashcan icon to delete the entry for **/***.

8. In the Patterns to match field, enter **/app1**.

9. Click **Update**. Figure 3-43 displays the updated configuration.

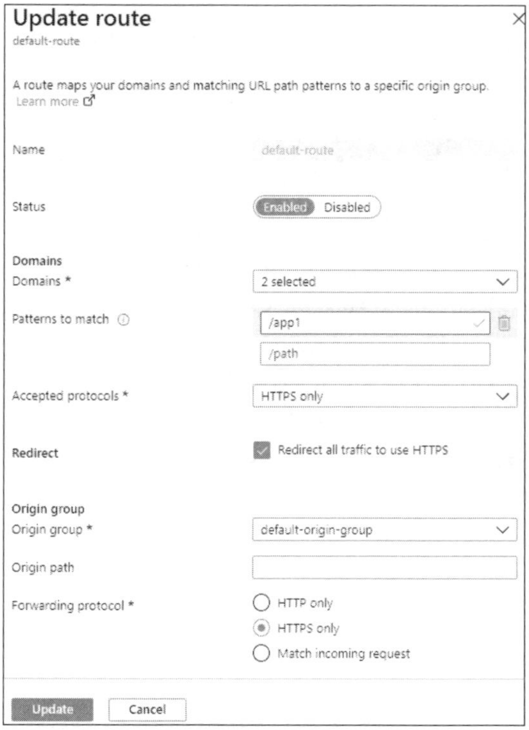

FIGURE 3-43 Update route

Making the change to the Patterns to match field will require that incoming traffic include /app1 on the incoming request to the endpoint. If the pattern matches, then the traffic will be forwarded to the origin group using HTTPS.

Skill 3.5: Implement an Azure Traffic Manager profile

Traffic Manager falls into the load balancer discussion because it provides a way to distribute traffic across multiple backend resources, whether they are Azure resources in a single region, in multiple regions, or even hosted outside of Azure. However, instead of load balancing at either layer 4 or layer 7, Traffic Manager load balances by using DNS.

When a client initiates a connection that uses Traffic Manager, the routing method that you configure determines which backend resource the client should connect to. But instead of facilitating the connection as an application gateway or Front Door does, Traffic Manager provides the client with the DNS name of the resource to connect to, and the client connects directly to the resource. Therefore, Traffic Manager is simply a DNS-based load balancer.

This skill covers how to:

- Configure a routing method
- Configure endpoints
- Create HTTP settings

Configure a routing method

A routing method is required when you configure a Traffic Manager profile and determines how a backend resource, called an endpoint in Traffic Manager, is selected for the client connection. There are six routing methods that are available, and you must select one for the Traffic Manager profile. The routing methods are:

- **Performance.** Performance relies on the latency to the endpoint to provide the client connection with the lowest latency connection possible at that time. Traffic Manager tracks the latency for each endpoint by using an internal Internet Latency Table to track round-trip time.

- **Weighted.** Weighted enables you to distribute traffic across multiple endpoints at the ratio that you specify. If you provide the same weight to all endpoints, then the traffic would be distributed evenly.

- **Priority.** Priority enables you to set a priority for each endpoint to allow for active/passive types of configurations. The endpoint that has the lowest integer is considered to be the highest priority.

- **Geographic.** Geographic relies on the client connection's geography to direct users to specific endpoints. This is useful in compliance or data sovereignty scenarios where the end-user location can determine which endpoint to connect to.

- **MultiValue.** MultiValue enables the service to respond with multiple endpoints with one DNS query. MultiValue can be used only with External endpoints that are IPv4 or IPv6 addresses, not FQDNs.

- **Subnet.** Subnet routing allows you to map IP ranges to certain endpoints. Then, if a connection request is received from an IP in that range, Traffic Manager responds with the endpoint that you have configured. If you need one endpoint for certain IP ranges and a different endpoint for other ranges, this routing method is useful.

To configure a Traffic Manager profile in an active/passive configuration, follow these steps:

1. Sign in to the Azure portal at *https://portal.azure.com*.
2. In the search bar, search for and select **Traffic Manager profiles**.
3. On the Traffic Manager page, click **Create**.
4. In the Name field, provide a name for the Traffic Manager profile. The name must be globally unique, as it creates a **.trafficmanager.net** domain name. For example, name the profile **az700tm**.
5. In the Routing method dropdown menu, select **Priority**.
6. In the Subscription dropdown menu, select the desired subscription for the Traffic Manager resource. This does not have to be in the same subscription as the endpoints.
7. In the Resource group field, select an appropriate resource group. For example, select **Networking**.
8. Click **Create**. Figure 3-44 displays the completed configuration.

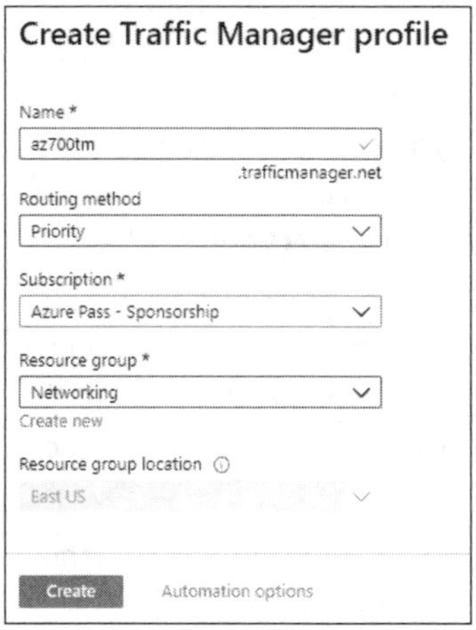

FIGURE 3-44 Create Traffic Manager profile

These steps create the Traffic Manager profile with the Priority routing method. This would then require at least two endpoints to be defined in the profile with priority values added for each endpoint. The endpoint with the lowest integer value would receive all of the traffic, as long as the health probe shows the endpoint as healthy.

To change the routing method of an existing Traffic Manager profile, follow these steps.

1. Sign in to the Azure portal at *https://portal.azure.com*.
2. In the search bar, search for and select **Traffic Manager profiles**.

3. On the Traffic Manager page, select the previously created profile, **az700tm**.

4. On the Traffic Manager profile page, click the **Configuration** blade.

5. In the Routing method dropdown menu, select the desired routing method. For example, select **Performance**.

6. Click **Save**. Figure 3-45 displays a portion of the Configuration blade.

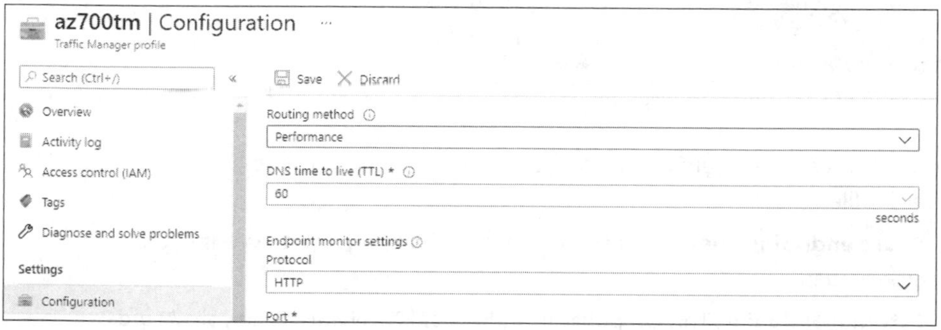

FIGURE 3-45 Traffic Manager configuration

Configure endpoints

Traffic Manager profiles require endpoints as the backend resources that clients connect directly to. Traffic Manager acts as a recursive DNS service that responds with an endpoint based on the routing method. The overall steps for this process are:

1. A client sends a request to connect to an app, such as a website at *app1.contoso.com*.

2. The client's IP configuration asks the configured DNS server the IP address of app1.contoso.com.

3. This FQDN is a CNAME that points to a Traffic Manager profile. The profile handles the DNS request and responds to the DNS server with an endpoint, based on the routing method.

4. The DNS server provides the endpoint information to the client as the DNS response.

5. The client connects directly to the endpoint and caches the DNS query for the TTL configured in Traffic Manager.

Figure 3-46 diagrams the process for each of these steps.

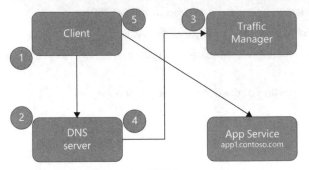

FIGURE 3-46 Traffic Manager DNS diagram

There are three types of endpoints that you can configure in a Traffic Manager profile:

- **Azure endpoint.** These are resources that you have deployed in your Azure environment.
- **External endpoint.** This is a public IP address or FQDN outside of your Azure environment.
- **Nested endpoint.** This is for high-availability deployments where one endpoint is another Traffic Manager profile in a different region for failover.

To create an app service as an Azure endpoint, follow these steps:

1. Sign in to the Azure portal at *https://portal.azure.com*.
2. In the search bar, search for and select **Traffic Manager profiles**.
3. On the Traffic Manager page, select the previously created profile, **az700tm**.
4. On the Traffic Manager profile page, click the **Endpoints** blade.
5. On the Endpoints blade, click **Add**.
6. Ensure that the Type dropdown menu is set to **Azure endpoint**.
7. In the Name field, provide a name for the endpoint. For example, enter **as-eus-app1**.
8. In the Target resource type dropdown field, select **App Service**.
9. In the Target resource dropdown field, select an app service that you previously deployed. For example, select **az700demoapp1**.
10. In the Priority field, set a priority for the target resource. The lower the integer, the higher in priority the resource will be. For example, set this to **50**.
11. Leave the remaining fields set to default and click **Add**. Figure 3-47 displays the completed configuration.

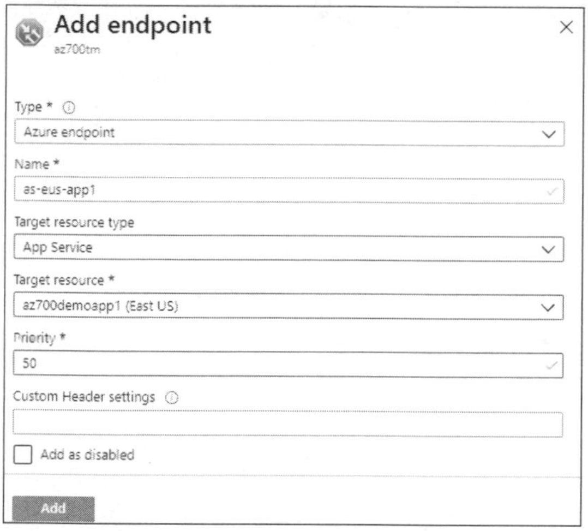

Add endpoint
az700tm

Type * ⓘ

Azure endpoint

Name *

as-eus-app1

Target resource type

App Service

Target resource *

az700demoapp1 (East US)

Priority *

50

Custom Header settings ⓘ

☐ Add as disabled

Add

FIGURE 3-47 Add endpoint

If you navigate to the Traffic Manager profile URL, you will now be redirected to the app service because it is the only endpoint that has been added. Repeat these steps as many times as necessary to add the backend resources to the Traffic Manager profile. Note that you cannot mix Azure endpoints and External endpoints in the same profile configuration.

Create HTTP settings

The objective "Create HTTP settings" is interesting because as we discussed in this skill section, Traffic Manager is a recursive DNS service that does not handle application (HTTP/HTTPS) traffic. The only settings that you can configure in a Traffic Manager profile that contain HTTP are the health probe and custom headers that can be added. You can add up to eight pairs of custom headers and values to the Custom Header settings field.

To customize the health probe settings, follow these steps:

1. Sign in to the Azure portal at *https://portal.azure.com*.
2. In the search bar, search for and select **Traffic Manager profiles**.
3. On the Traffic Manager page, select the previously created profile, **az700tm**.
4. On the Traffic Manager profile page, click the **Configuration** blade.
5. In the Custom Header settings field, enter any headers to add to the health probe in the **header:value** format.
6. In the Expected Status Code Ranges field, specify additional HTTP status codes for the health probe to accept. For example, enter **200-202**.
7. Click **Save**. Figure 3-48 displays the updated configuration.

FIGURE 3-48 Traffic Manager configuration

Skill 3.6: Design and implement an Azure Virtual Network NAT

When you deploy virtual machines, you associate the network interface card of that VM to a subnet. The subnet is then part of a broader virtual network. If you've read the chapter that includes Network Security Groups, then you might remember that all outbound traffic is allowed by default from a virtual machine. By default, if the virtual machine does not have a public IP address assigned to the NIC, it connects to the internet using a random IP address that is allocated to that Azure region.

> **This skill covers how to:**
> - Choose when to use a Virtual Network NAT
> - Allocate public IP or public IP prefixes for a NAT gateway
> - Associate a Virtual Network NAT with a subnet

Choose when to use a Virtual Network NAT

Having a random outgoing IP address could be problematic if the VM needs to connect to specific external services that require a firewall rule or to know the source IP of your VM. You can achieve this by using a NAT gateway. A NAT gateway is a resource that you configure with a public IPv4 address, or range of public IPv4 addresses, and associate with a virtual network. Then any VM within the virtual network will use an IP address that you configure when communicating with the internet. Figure 3-49 displays the basic design of using a NAT gateway.

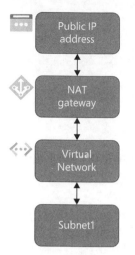

FIGURE 3-49 NAT gateway design

Allocate public IP addresses for a NAT gateway

When you create a NAT gateway, you need at least one public IP address to the gateway. This is the IP address that will be put in the header of the outbound packet from any VMs in the virtual network.

To create a NAT gateway, follow these steps:

1. Sign in to the Azure portal at *https://portal.azure.com*.

2. In the search bar, search for and select **NAT gateways**.

3. On the NAT gateways page, click **Create**.

4. In the Subscription dropdown, select the desired subscription for the NAT gateway. This must be the same as the virtual network that you plan to associate the NAT gateway with.

5. In the Resource group dropdown, select the desired resource group. For example, select **Networking**.

6. In the NAT gateway name field, provide a name for the gateway. For example, enter **nat-vnet1**.

7. In the Region dropdown, select the desired Azure region. This must be the same region as your virtual network. For example, select **East US**.

8. Leave the remaining fields set to their default values, and click **Next: Outbound IP**. Figure 3-50 displays the completed Basics tab.

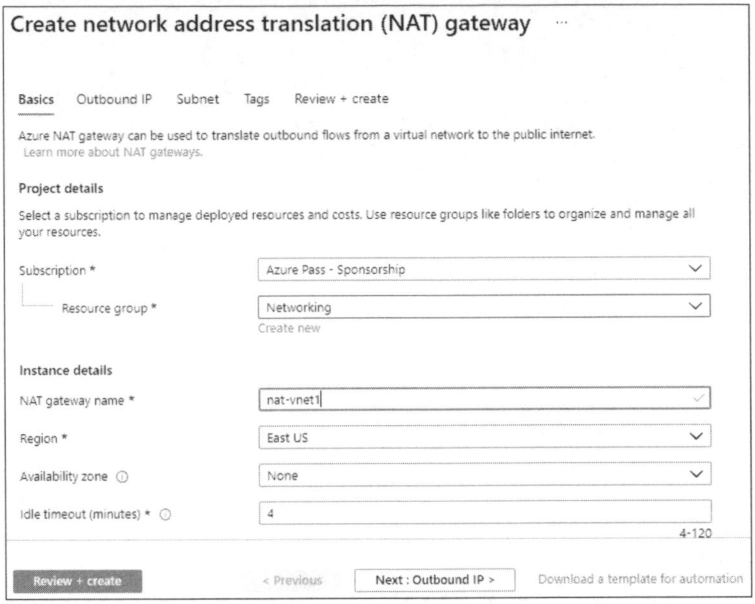

FIGURE 3-50 Create NAT gateway basics

9. On the Outbound IP tab, click **Create a new public IP address**.

10. In the Add a public IP address field, name the new public IP address **nat-pip1**.

11. Click **OK**. Figure 3-51 displays the Add a public IP address screen.

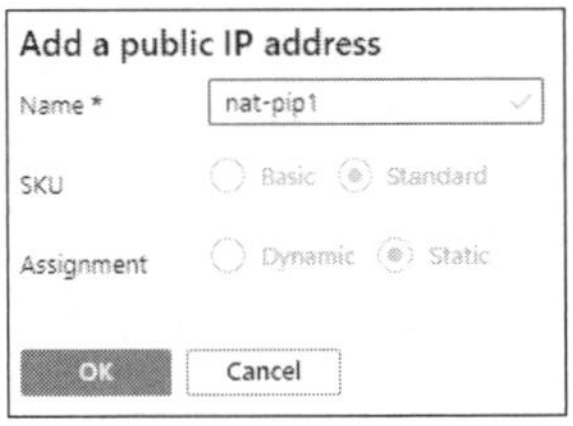

FIGURE 3-51 Add a public IP address

12. Click **Next: Subnet**.

13. In the Virtual network dropdown menu, select the desired virtual network to associate the NAT gateway with. For example, select **hub-vnet-eus-01**.

14. The available subnets will display below the selection. Select the checkboxes next to the desired subnets to include with the NAT gateway.

15. Click **Review + create**. Figure 3-52 displays the completed Subnet tab.

16. Click **Create**.

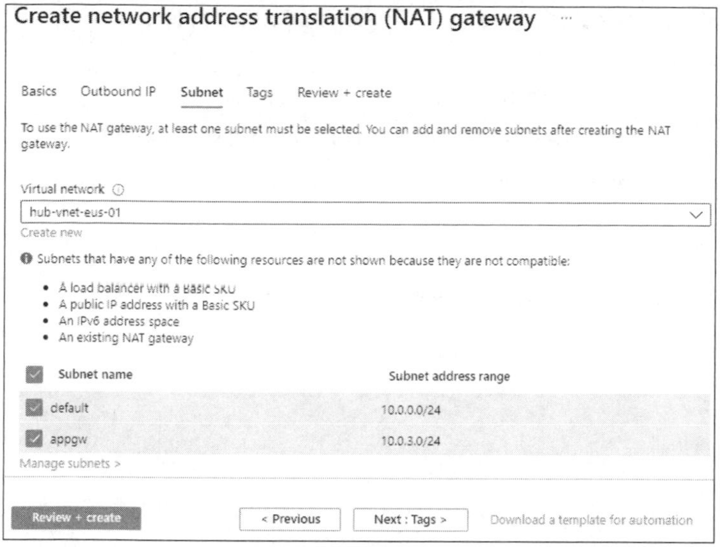

FIGURE 3-52 Create NAT gateway - Subnets

Associate a virtual network NAT with a subnet

When you create the NAT gateway, you can select the subnets that exist at that time to associate the NAT gateway with. However, if you add subnets to the same virtual network, they are *not* associated with the NAT gateway by default.

You can make the association either from the subnets page within the virtual network or from the NAT gateway. To associate the subnet with the NAT gateway from the subnet page, follow these steps:

1. Sign in to the Azure portal at *https://portal.azure.com*.
2. In the search bar, search for and select **Virtual networks**.
3. On the virtual network page, select the previously associated virtual network. For example, select **hub-vnet-eus-01**.
4. On the selected virtual network blade, select the **Subnets** blade.
5. On the Subnets page, click the newly created subnet. For example, click **app2**.
6. In the NAT gateway dropdown menu, select the NAT gateway. For example, select **nat-vnet1**.
7. Click **Save**. **Note:** As of this writing, there is a UI bug that prevents you from saving the configuration using this method.

If you want to make the association from the NAT gateway, follow these steps:

1. Sign in to the Azure portal at *https://portal.azure.com*.
2. In the search bar, search for and select **NAT gateways**.

3. On the NAT gateways page, select the existing NAT gateway. For example, select **nat-vnet1**.

4. On the NAT gateway, click the **Subnets** blade.

5. Select the checkbox next to the newly created subnet. For example, select **app2**.

6. Click **Save**. Figure 3-53 displays the updated subnet association.

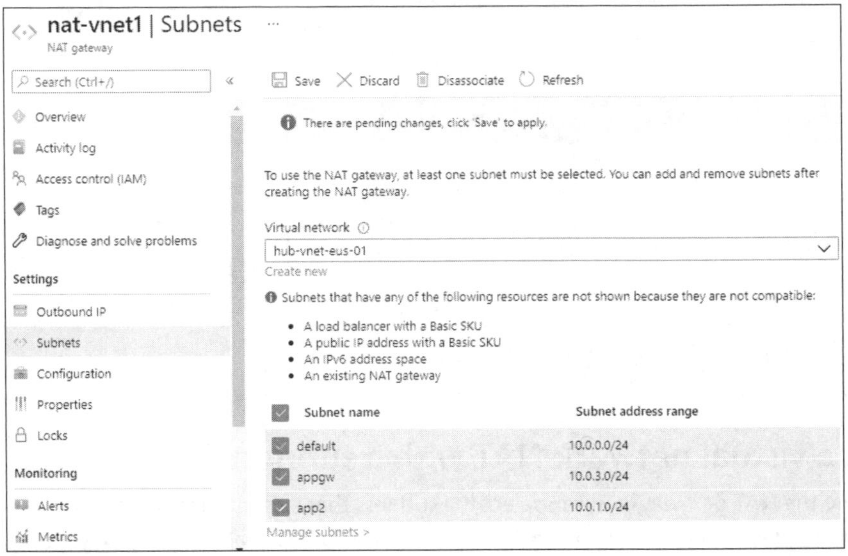

FIGURE 3-53 NAT gateway subnets

Chapter summary

- The built-in system routes allow outbound traffic from VMs in a virtual network to the internet.

- Subnets within a virtual network can communicate with each other without any additional routing requirements.

- User-defined routes can manipulate the traffic flow to deviate from the default routing.

- When you create user-defined routes to forward traffic through an on-premises firewall, the concept is named forced tunneling.

- Azure load balancers are available in Basic and Standard SKUs.

- Load balancers provide layer 4 load balancing across the backend pool that you specify.

- Load balancers can be either internal, with a private IP address, or external, with a public IP address.

- Load Balancer Basic SKU is a free load balancer service but has limited backend pool options and is not highly available.

- Load balancers have a frontend IP address, backend pool, health probes, and rules that define how traffic is forwarded.

- Load balancers can include NAT rules to translate incoming addresses and port numbers.

- Azure application gateways provide layer 7 load balancing across the backend pool that you specify.

- Application gateways can be scaled to multiple instances either manually or with auto-scaling rules.

- Application gateways provide domain-based and path-based routing to specific back-end resources.

- Application gateways include frontend IP addresses, backend pools, listeners, health probes, and rules that define how traffic is forwarded.

- Application gateways can rewrite headers before forwarding to a backend pool.

- Application gateways can perform both TLS termination and end-to-end TLS encryption.

- Azure Front Door combines layer 7 load balancing, security, content delivery and content optimization into one service.

- Front Door is a global service that is not deployed into a single region.

- Front Door is deployed as an endpoint that can have custom domains associated with it.

- Front Door has origin groups that contain origins, or backend resources, that clients connect to.

- Azure Traffic Manager is a DNS-based routing service that uses recursive DNS to point client connections to a backend resource.

- Traffic Manager uses routing methods to determine how to select an endpoint, or back-end resource, to the client.

- When using Traffic Manager, clients connect directly to the endpoint and only use Traffic Manager for DNS.

- NAT gateways provide a way for VMs to share an outbound IP address.

- NAT gateways are associated with one virtual network and selectable subnets within that virtual network.

- NAT gateways only support IPv4 public IP addresses.

Thought experiment

In this thought experiment, demonstrate your skills and knowledge of the topics covered in this chapter. You can find the answers in the section that follows.

An organization is planning to deploy a new Azure subscription for a three-tier application. The first tier, the web tier, will be the frontend of a web app that is hosted in Azure App Services. The app service communicates with a custom API in a logic tier that will be hosted on a virtual machine scale set (VMSS). The third tier is the data tier, which will be hosted on Azure SQL Managed Instances.

The VMSS will communicate with a third-party reporting software. The third-party vendor has a requirement that all incoming traffic must be from the same IP address. All outgoing traffic from the VMs must use the same public IP address

The organization plans to deploy this application into four Azure regions across North America and Europe. As users connect to the web app, they should be directed to the nearest instance of the application based on their geographic location. The ingress solution must provide the ability to do end-to-end TLS encryption and provide security reporting.

1. What should the organization use as an ingress solution?

2. What should the organization deploy for the app services to communicate with the VMSS?

3. What should the organization deploy for the VMSS to communicate with the third-party vendor?

Thought experiment answers

This section contains the solution to the thought experiment. Each answer explains why the answer choice is correct.

1. What should the organization use as an ingress solution?

   Based on the overall scenario, it might seem that either an application gateway or Azure Front Door would work as an ingress solution. However, the requirement for security reporting points the solution toward Azure Front Door. Additionally, because the organization is using at least four Azure regions, Front Door would most likely be a better cost option than deploying application gateways in every region, which would most likely cost more.

2. What should the organization deploy for the app services to communicate with the VMSS?

   As an inbound solution to the VMSS, an Azure load balancer would be sufficient to distribute traffic from the app services to the VMSS.

3. What should the organization deploy for the VMSS to communicate with the third-party vendor?

The virtual network that the VMSS is associated with should be configured with a NAT gateway. The NAT gateway can have a single public IP address associated with it, which will represent the VMSS as it communicates outbound. This IP address can be given to the third-party vendor to be allow-listed in their firewall.

NEED MORE REVIEW? **SCALABLE WEB APP**

For more information on a reference architecture for a scalable web app, visit *https:// docs.microsoft.com/en-us/azure/architecture/reference-architectures/app-service-web-app/scalable-web-app*.

CHAPTER 4

Secure and monitor networks

This chapter introduces additional security and monitoring solutions for virtual networks and the resources that will be connected. This starts with the Azure Firewall service, which gets associated with a virtual network. All inbound and outbound traffic can then traverse the firewall. Then within the virtual network, you can configure network security groups to filter traffic from subnet to subnet. Additionally, Web Application Firewall policies can be used with either Azure Front Door or Azure Application Gateway to manage rule sets. Finally, there are several tools in Network Watcher to assist with monitoring the virtual network and resources.

Skills in this chapter:

- Skill 4.1: Design, implement, and manage an Azure Firewall deployment
- Skill 4.2: Implement and manage network security groups (NSGs)
- Skill 4.3: Implement a Web Application Firewall (WAF) deployment
- Skill 4.4: Monitor networks

Skill 4.1: Design, implement, and manage an Azure Firewall deployment

Azure Firewalls provide both packet filtering and stateful packet inspection. That means that you can filter at the layer 3 level based on source or destination IP address, port, and protocol. You can also protect resources at the layer 7 level by having the firewall inspect the headers for the fully qualified domain name (FQDN) or the Azure service tag that the packet might be trying to communicate with. In this skill section, we discuss where an Azure Firewall is included in a design and how to deploy and configure the firewall.

> **This skill covers how to:**
> - Design an Azure Firewall deployment
> - Create and implement an Azure Firewall deployment
> - Configure Azure Firewall rules
> - Create and implement Azure Firewall Manager policies
> - Create a secure hub by deploying Azure Firewall inside an Azure Virtual WAN hub

Design an Azure Firewall deployment

An Azure Firewall is a managed stateful firewall that you can deploy to inspect traffic in both east–west and north–south deployment models. Azure Firewalls can perform filtering and packet inspection from OSI model layers 3 through 7. There are two SKUs of an Azure Firewall: *Standard* and *Premium*. The Standard SKU includes the following features:

- High availability, including availability zones
- Unrestricted scalability
- Application FQDN filtering rules
- Network traffic filtering rules
- FQDN tags
- Service tags
- Threat intelligence with packet inspection
- DNS proxy
- Custom DNS
- Forced Tunnel Mode
- Outbound SNAT support
- Inbound DNAT support
- Multiple public IP addresses
- Azure Monitor logging
- Web category filtering
- Industry certifications

If you choose to deploy the Premium SKU, you receive all of the Standard features plus gain these additional features:

- TLS inspection
- Intrusion detection and prevention
- URL filtering
- Advanced web category filtering

The Premium SKU requires that you use Firewall Manager policies to configure the features of the firewall. The Standard SKU has the ability to use Firewall Manager or to configure individual rules on a single firewall.

The SLA that your design can support is determined by how you decide to deploy the Azure Firewall. If you deploy one firewall in a region that does not support zones, or you deploy to only one zone, then the SLA of the firewall is 99.95%. If you deploy a firewall to at least two zones, then the SLA is increased to 99.99%.

When you deploy a firewall, it must be associated with a single virtual network. The firewall will act as a gate for any traffic that is entering or leaving the virtual network. You can combine this with peering connections to other virtual networks and user-defined routes to force east–west traffic through the firewall before leaving the region. Figure 4-1 displays a sample architecture with an on-premises VPN connection and two spoke networks that are peered with a hub network.

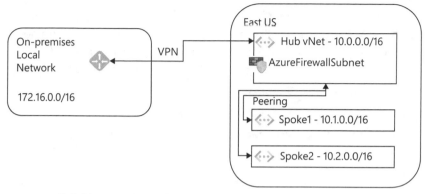

FIGURE 4-1 Hybrid connection with Azure Firewall

The filtering rules that you configure enable you to specifically allow or deny network traffic based on source and destination IP address, port number, protocol, or FQDN. FQDN filter is considered application filtering, and the remaining options are considered network filtering.

Create and implement an Azure Firewall deployment

When you create an Azure Firewall, the basic resource requirements exist: a subscription, resource group, and region. The Azure Firewall must be deployed in the same region as the virtual network. The virtual network cannot have another firewall already deployed or associated with the virtual network.

To deploy an Azure Firewall, follow these steps:

1. Sign in to the Azure portal at *https://portal.azure.com*.
2. In the search bar, search for and select **Firewalls**.
3. On the Firewalls page, click **Create**.
4. In the Subscription dropdown menu, select the subscription that contains the virtual network you want to associate the firewall with.
5. In the Resource group field, select or create a resource group to group the firewall in. For example, select **Networking**.
6. In the Name field, provide a name for the firewall. For example, enter **fw-eus-vnet1**.
7. In the Region dropdown menu, select an Azure region to deploy the firewall in. This must be the same as the virtual network. For example, select **East US**.

8. In the Availability zone field, leave the default of **None**.

9. For the Firewall tier option, leave the default of **Standard**.

10. In the Firewall management field, select **Use Firewall rules (classic) to manage this firewall**. We will start with this setting and take a look at Firewall Manager policies later in this skill section.

11. In the Choose a virtual network field, select **Use existing**. You also have the ability to create a new virtual network if you have not already created one.

12. In the Virtual network dropdown menu, select the desired virtual network. For example, select **hub-vnet-eus-01**. The virtual network must already have a subnet named *AzureFirewallSubnet*; you cannot create the subnet from the Create a firewall page.

13. In the Public IP address field, click **Add new**.

14. Name the public IP address **pip-fw01**, and then click **OK**.

15. Click **Review + create**, and then click **Create**. Figure 4-2 displays the completed Create a firewall screen.

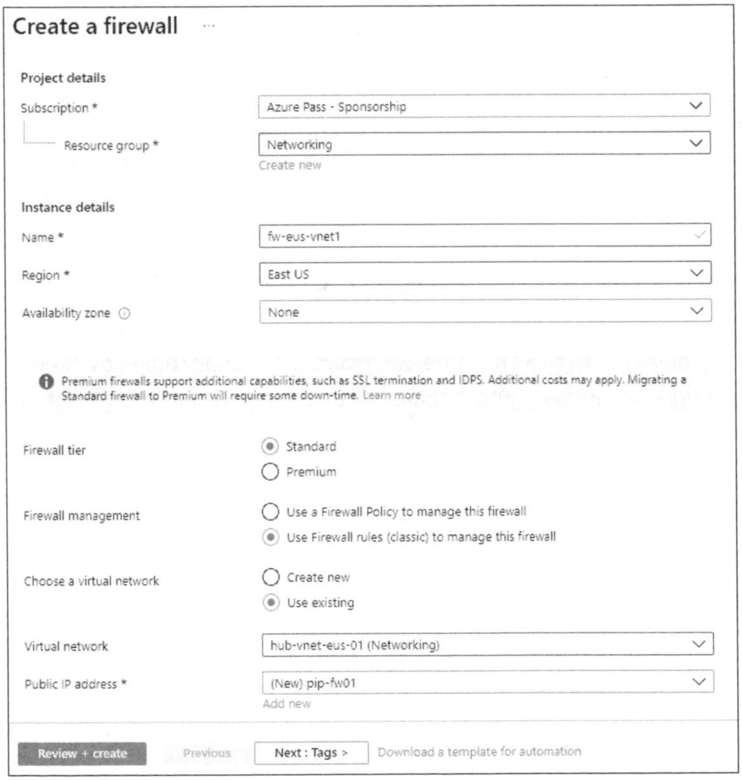

Create a firewall ...

Project details

Subscription *
Azure Pass - Sponsorship

Resource group *
Networking
Create new

Instance details

Name *
fw-eus-vnet1

Region *
East US

Availability zone ⓘ
None

ⓘ Premium firewalls support additional capabilities, such as SSL termination and IDPS. Additional costs may apply. Migrating a Standard firewall to Premium will require some down-time. Learn more

Firewall tier
◉ Standard
○ Premium

Firewall management
○ Use a Firewall Policy to manage this firewall
◉ Use Firewall rules (classic) to manage this firewall

Choose a virtual network
○ Create new
◉ Use existing

Virtual network
hub-vnet-eus-01 (Networking)

Public IP address *
(New) pip-fw01
Add new

[Review + create]   Previous   [Next : Tags >]   Download a template for automation

FIGURE 4-2 Hybrid connection with Azure Firewall

Configure Azure Firewall rules

Azure Firewall rules can be managed from two places, depending on how you deployed the firewall. By using the "Firewall Rules (classic)" setting during deployment, you can create and configure rules directly on the firewall. If you choose to use Firewall Manager, you can create policies, which can then contain rules (and other settings) that can be applied to multiple firewalls. Policies will be discussed more in the next section.

Classic firewall rules can be created in three categories:

- NAT rule collections
- Network rule collections
- Application rule collections

The network and application rules can be set to either allow or deny as the action to take on the packets. The NAT rule collection is simply a translation of address and port numbers from the public IP address to an internal address. Each collection also has a priority value that you configure, which is an integer between 100 and 65,000. As with other priority lists in Azure, the lower the integer, the higher the precedence of the rule.

To create a NAT rule collection, follow these steps:

1. Sign in to the Azure portal at *https://portal.azure.com*.

2. In the search bar, search for and select **Firewalls**.

3. On the Firewalls page, select the firewall that you previously created. For example, select **fw-eus-vnet1**.

4. On the firewall page, click the **Rules (classic)** blade.

5. On the Rules (classic) page, ensure that you are on the NAT rule collection tab. Click **Add NAT rule collection**.

6. In the Name field, provide a name for the first rule collection. For example, enter **NAT-External-HTTPS**.

7. In the Priority field, provide a priority for the rule. For example, enter **500**.

8. In the Rules field, use the following information to create the rule:

   - Name: **8443HTTPS**
   - Protocol: **TCP**
   - Source type: **IP address**
   - Source: *****
   - Destination Address: **<Your Public IP address>**
   - Destination Ports: **8443**
   - Translated address: **10.0.1.4**
   - Translated Port: **443**
   - Click **Add**. Figure 4-3 displays the completed NAT rule collection.

Add NAT rule collection ✕

Name *	NAT-External-HTTPS	✓
Priority *	500	✓
Action	Destination Network Address Translation (DNAT)	⌄

Rules

name	Protocol	Source type	Source	Destination Addr...	Destination Ports	Translated address	Transl
8443HTTPS ✓	TCP ⌄	IP address ⌄	* ✓	23.96.113.155 ✓	8443 ⌄	10.0.1.4 ⌄	443
	0 selected ⌄	IP address ⌄	*, 192.168.10.1, 192...	192.168.10.0	8080	192.168.10.0	8080

Add

FIGURE 4-3 Add NAT rule collection

The completed rule collection will look for TCP traffic destined for the public IP address of the firewall and translate that to an internal address with a destination port of 8443. The firewall will modify the packet and translate the destination port to 443. This would allow you to use a custom port number for an application and obscure the actual port that is being used internally.

Adding network and application rule collections are similar, but they enable you to select whether the network traffic is allowed or denied. Network rule collections can be based on IP addresses, service tags, or FQDNs. Service tags are predefined categories of Azure services that you can choose from as a global service or for each specific region. For example, if you want an IP range to be able to communicate with Azure Storage in East US but not West US, you could allow the storage service tag for East US and then deny the storage service tag for West US.

To create a network rule collection using this example, follow these steps:

1. Sign in to the Azure portal at *https://portal.azure.com*.
2. In the search bar, search for and select **Firewalls**.
3. On the Firewalls page, select the firewall that you previously created. For example, select **fw-eus-vnet1**.
4. On the firewall page, click the **Rules (classic)** blade.
5. On the Rules (classic) page, click the **Network rule collection** tab.
6. On the Network rule collection page, click **Add network rule collection**.
7. In the Name field, provide a name for the rule collection. For example, enter **Allow-Azure-Storage-Subnet1**.
8. In the Priority field, enter a priority for the rule. For example, enter **500**.
9. In the Action dropdown menu, leave the default setting of **Allow**.
10. In the Service Tags section, use the following information to complete the configuration:
    - Name: **AllowStorage**
    - Protocol: **Any**
    - Source type: **IP address**

- Source: **10.0.1.0/24**
- Service Tags: **Storage.EastUS**
- Destination Ports: *

11. Click **Add**. Figure 4-4 displays the completed configuration.

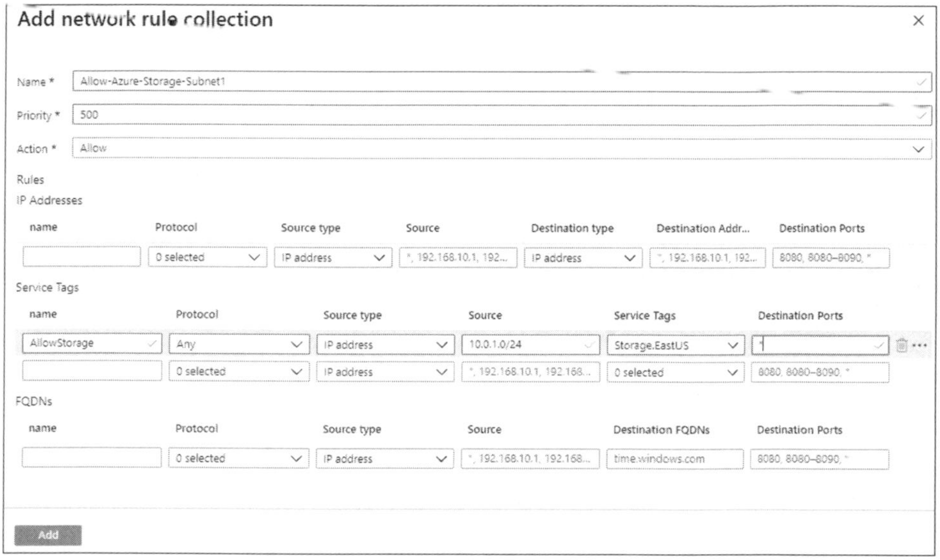

FIGURE 4-4 Add network rule collection

The preceding example assumes that subnet1 has an address range of 10.0.1.0/24, as identified in the Source field. In this scenario, if the traffic is destined for Azure Storage in the East US region, it will be allowed, assuming that there is not another rule with a higher-precedence priority that might deny it.

Application rule collections are similar, but instead they are configured based on FQDN tags or target FQDNs. For example, if you need to block access to contoso.com, you can block the domain based on protocol or port numbers.

To create an application rule collection using this example, follow these steps:

1. Sign in to the Azure portal at *https://portal.azure.com*.
2. In the search bar, search for and select **Firewalls**.
3. On the Firewalls page, select the firewall that you previously created. For example, select **fw-eus-vnet1**.
4. On the firewall page, click the **Rules (classic)** blade.
5. On the Rules (classic) page, click the **Application rule collection** tab.
6. On the **Application** rule collection tab, click **Add application rule collection**.
7. In the Name field, provide a name for the rule collection. For example, enter **Deny-Contoso**.
8. In the Priority field, enter a value for the priority. For example, enter **500**.

9. In the Action dropdown menu, select **Deny**.

10. In the Target FQDN section, use the following information to configure the rule:

   - Name: **Contoso**
   - Source type: **IP address**
   - Source: **10.0.1.0/24**
   - Protocol:Port: **HTTP, HTTPS**
   - Target FQDNs: **www.contoso.com**

11. Click **Add**. Figure 4-5 displays the completed configuration.

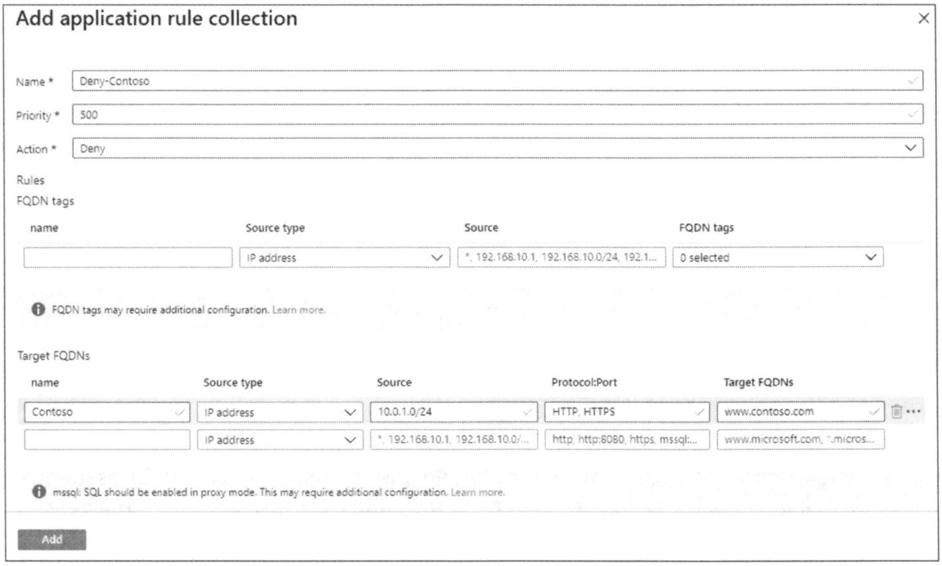

FIGURE 4-5 Add application rule collection

Create and implement Azure Firewall Manager policies

In an enterprise where you might deploy to several Azure regions and need multiple firewalls, managing rules at each firewall can become an administrative nightmare. Therefore, it's recommended to use policies with Firewall Manager and then associate the policies with the firewalls. This gives you an easy way to manage the rules for all firewalls in a single location.

To create a policy using Firewall Manager, follow these steps:

1. Sign in to the Azure portal at *https://portal.azure.com*.

2. In the search bar, search for and select **Firewall Manager**.

3. On the Firewalls page, select the **Azure Firewall Policies** blade.

4. On the Azure Firewall Policies page, click **Create Azure Firewall Policy**.

5. In the Subscription dropdown menu, select the subscription that contains the Azure Firewall.

6. In the Resource group field, select or create a resource group to group the policy in. For example, select **Networking**.

7. In the Name field, provide a name for the firewall. For example, enter **fwpolicy-eus-01**.

8. In the Region dropdown menu, select the region for the policy. For example, enter **East US**. Unlike other resources, the policy can be in any region and be applied to firewalls that are in different regions.

9. In the Policy tier field, select **Standard**. This matches the SKU of the firewall that was deployed earlier in this skill section.

10. Click **Next: DNS Settings**. Figure 4-6 displays the completed Basics tab.

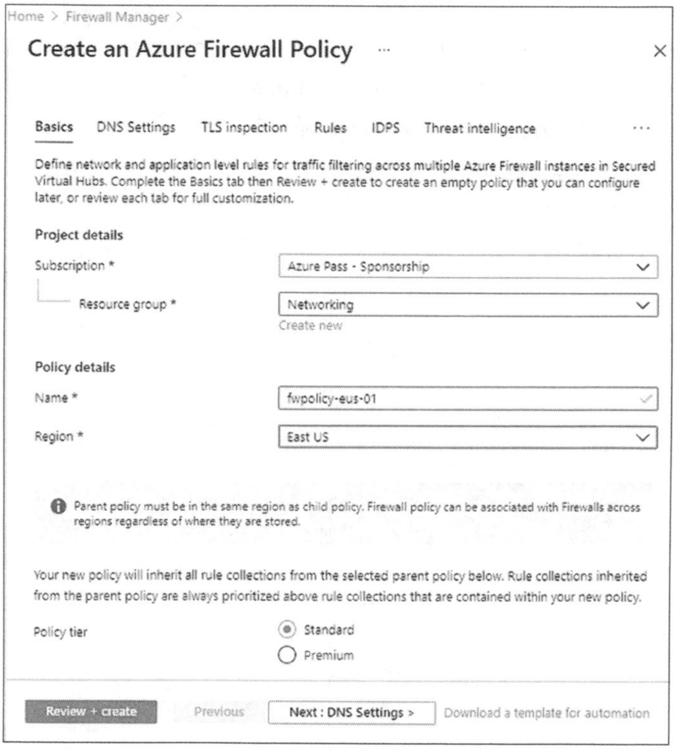

FIGURE 4-6 Firewall policy basics

11. On the DNS Settings tab, set the policy to **Enabled** and leave the default settings.

12. Click **Next: TLS inspection**. Figure 4-7 displays the configured DNS Settings tab.

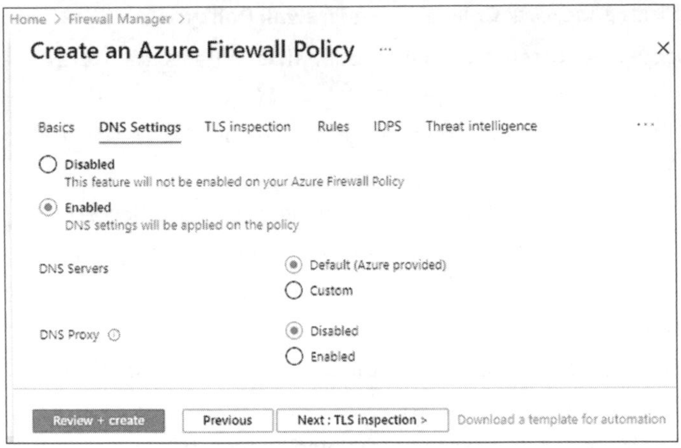

FIGURE 4-7 Firewall policy DNS settings

13. On the TLS inspection page, notice that the options are not available. This is because Standard policy was selected on the Basics tab. Click **Next: Rules**.

14. On the Rules tab, click **Import rules from an Azure Firewall**.

15. Select the firewall that was previously deployed and configured with rules in the previous section, and then click **Import**.

16. Click **Next: IDPS**. Figure 4-8 displays the imported rules.

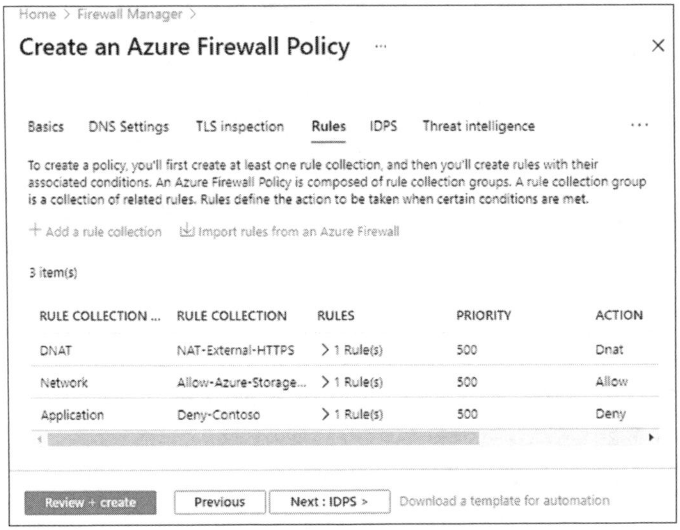

FIGURE 4-8 Firewall policy rules

17. On the IDPS page, notice that the options are not available. This is because Standard policy was selected on the Basics tab. Click **Next: Threat intelligence**.

18. On the Threat intelligence tab, leave the default mode set to **Alert only**.

19. Click **Review + create**, and then click **Create**.

Create a secure hub by deploying Azure Firewall inside an Azure Virtual WAN hub

You can also use an Azure Firewall to filter and protect traffic in an Azure Virtual WAN. Virtual WANs were discussed in Chapter 2 but provide hybrid connectivity across various connection types: virtual networks, VPNs, and ExpressRoute. If you already have an Azure Virtual WAN hub, you can associate a firewall and firewall policy to the existing hub, or you can create a new virtual hub.

To create a secured hub, follow these steps:

1. Sign in to the Azure portal at *https://portal.azure.com*.

2. In the search bar, search for and select **Firewall Manager**.

3. On the Firewalls page, select the **Virtual Hubs** blade.

4. On the Virtual Hubs blade, click **Create new secured virtual hub**.

5. In the Subscription dropdown menu, select the subscription that contains the Azure Firewall.

6. In the Resource group field, select or create a resource group to group the policy in. For example, select **Networking**.

7. In the Name field, provide a name for the firewall. For example, enter **shub-eus-01**.

8. In the Region dropdown menu, select the region for the policy. For example, select **East US**.

9. In the Hub address space field, provide an address range for the hub. This range cannot overlap with other ranges in the Virtual WAN. For example, enter **172.16.0.0/16**.

10. In the Choose an existing vWAN or create a new one field, select the desired setting if you have an existing virtual WAN. For this example, select **New vWAN**.

11. In the Virtual WAN Name field, provide a name for the virtual WAN. For example, enter **vwan-eus-01**.

12. Leave the remaining fields at default values and click **Next: Azure Firewall**. Figure 4-9 displays the completed Basics tab.

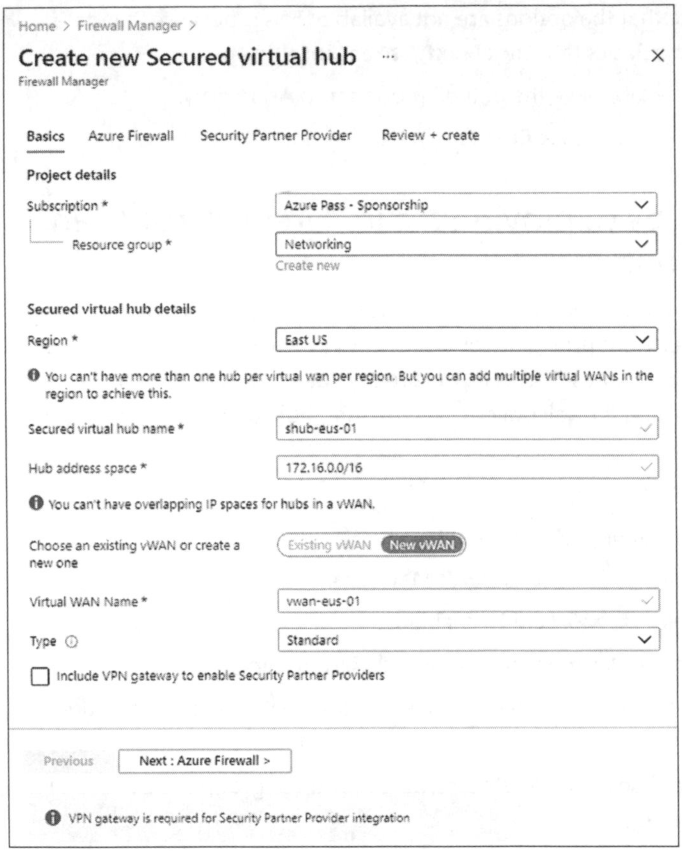

FIGURE 4-9 New secured virtual hub basics

13. On the Azure Firewall tab, review the default values as shown in Figure 4-10. These values are appropriate for this example; click **Next: Security Partner Provider**.

14. On the Security Partner Provider tab, review the available third-party security providers. If you decide that you want to use one of these providers, then you must also deploy a virtual network gateway to connect to the third-party appliance. Leave the Security Partner Provider field set at **Disabled**, and then click **Next: Review + Create**.

15. Click **Create**.

When you create a secured hub with Virtual WAN, you are presented with the option of integrating with a third-party provider. As of this writing, there are three third-party providers that are supported with secure virtual hubs:

- Check Point
- iboss
- Zscaler

If you choose to integrate with one of these providers, you must also deploy a virtual network gateway to establish a secure connection (VPN) with the appliance.

Create new Secured virtual hub ···   ×

Firewall Manager

Basics   **Azure Firewall**   Security Partner Provider   Review + create

Secured virtual hubs must have at least one, and can have at most two security providers. You may use two
security providers to secure different types of connections. You can choose to enable Azure Firewall for this
virtual hub and associate a policy. You can also select "None" and associate a policy later.

Azure Firewall   (Enabled) Disabled

Azure Firewall tier   ⦿ Standard
                                    ○ Premium

Availability zone | None   ∨ |

Enabling Azure Firewall will create an Azure Firewall resource as part of this hub creation process. This action
will have an immediate billing impact. Learn more

Specify number of Public IP addresses ⓘ   ○──────────────────────── | 1 |
                                    1   30   60   90   120   150   180   210   340

Subscription(s) | Azure Pass - Sponsorship   ∨ |

| Firewall Policy ↑↓ | Inherits From ↑↓ | Firewall Policy Ti..↑↓ | Subscription ↑↓ | Resour |
| ☑ Default Deny Policy | | | | |

‹   ›

| Previous | | Next : Security Partner Provider > |

FIGURE 4-10 New secured virtual hub Azure Firewall

Skill 4.2: Implement and manage network security groups (NSGs)

Network security groups (NSGs) provide packet filtering at the subnet or network interface
card layer. Compared to on-premises hardware, you might be familiar with these types of rules
by another name: *access control lists (ACLs)*. If you have configured ACLs before, NSGs operate
in a very similar way. NSGs look at the header of a packet and validate the packet against the
configured rules to determine if the packet should be allowed or denied. NSGs are a funda-
mental security concept within a virtual network, as by default, subnet-to-subnet communication is allowed on all ports and protocols.

> **This skill covers how to:**
> - Create a network security group
> - Associate an NSG to a resource
> - Create an application security group (ASG)
> - Associate an ASG to a NIC
> - Create and configure NSG rules
> - Interpret and validate NSG flow logs
> - Verify IP flow

Create a network security group

An NSG provides packet filtering at the subnet or virtual machine network interface level. Note the distinction between *packet filtering* and *packet inspection*. An NSG does not look at the payload of the packet to identify a fully qualified domain name. The NSG only looks at the header of the packet and provides filtering based on the headers: source and destination IP address, port, and protocol. This means that you can allow or deny traffic that is both entering (inbound) or leaving (outbound) the resource that you associate the NSG with. NSGs can be associated with both subnets and network interface cards (NICs).

When you create a virtual network or a NIC, there is not by default an NSG associated with the resources. From a NIC perspective, this means that any traffic would be allowed inbound and outbound from the VM it is attached to. This is also true at the subnet level, which is why subnet-to-subnet communication is open by default in a virtual network.

An NSG on its own is a separate resource from NICs, virtual networks, and subnets. One NSG can be associated with multiple NICs or subnets. However, each NIC or subnet can be associated with only one NSG. You can also create an NSG that is not associated with either resource for later use.

To create an NSG, follow these steps:

1. Sign in to the Azure portal at *https://portal.azure.com*.

2. In the search bar, search for and select **Network security groups**.

3. On the Network security groups page, click **Create**.

4. In the Subscription dropdown menu, select the subscription to place the NSG in.

5. In the Resource group field, select or create a resource group to group the NSG in. For example, select **Networking**.

6. In the Name field, provide a name for the NSG. For example, enter **nsg-eus-app1**.

7. In the Region dropdown menu, select an Azure region to deploy the firewall in. This must be the same as the virtual network. For example, select **East US**.

8. Click **Review + create**. Figure 4-11 displays the completed configuration.

9. Click **Create**.

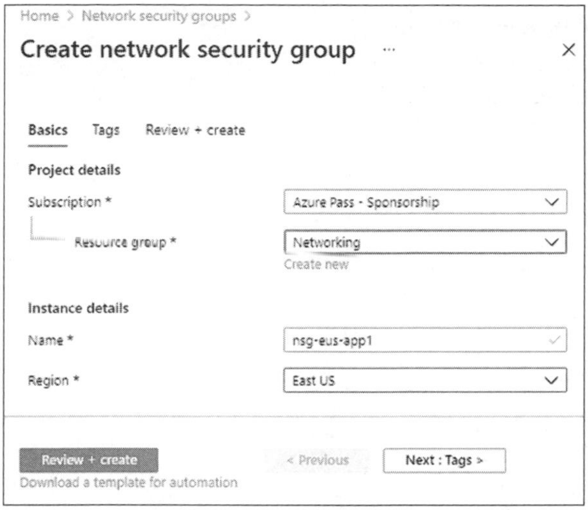

FIGURE 4-11 Create network security group

Associate an NSG to a resource

NSGs can be associated with either network interface cards or subnets in a virtual network. You can configure this association either from the NSG or from the resource that you are linking it to.

To link an NSG to a resource from the NSG, follow these steps:

1. Sign in to the Azure portal at *https://portal.azure.com*.

2. In the search bar, search for and select **Network security groups**.

3. On the Network security groups page, select the NSG that you previously created, **nsg-eus-app1**.

4. On the NSG page, select the desired blade for the resource type you plan to associate with, either Network interfaces or Subnets. For this example, select the **Network interfaces** blade.

5. On the Network interfaces page, click **Associate**.

6. In the Network interface associations field, select the desired NIC. For example, select **nic-eus-vm1**.

7. Click **OK**. Figure 4-12 displays the completed configuration.

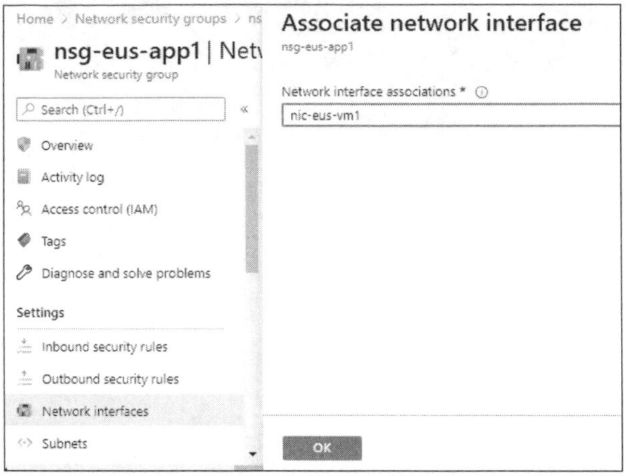

FIGURE 4-12 Associate network interface

You can also configure the association from the resource. To associate the NSG with a subnet from the virtual network, follow these steps:

1. Sign in to the Azure portal at *https://portal.azure.com*.

2. In the search bar, search for and select **Virtual networks**.

3. In the list of networks, select an existing virtual network. For example, select **hub-vnet-eus-01**.

4. From the virtual network, select the **Subnets** blade.

5. In the list of subnets, select a subnet that was previously created. For example, select **app1**.

6. On the app1 subnet page, in the Network security group dropdown menu, select the desired NSG. For example, select **nsg-eus-app1**.

7. Click **Save**. Figure 4-13 displays the completed configuration.

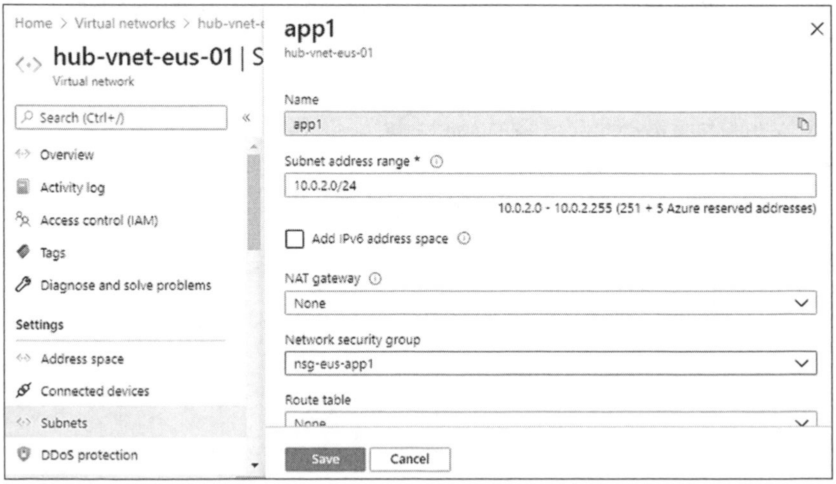

FIGURE 4-13 Subnet NSG association

Create an application security group (ASG)

Application security groups (ASGs) allow you to group NICs for use with NSG rules. For example, you might have 20 web servers for which you need to allow port 443, but then deny any other traffic on other port numbers. You have a few options with varying amounts of administrative overhead:

- **Create a rule for the entire subnet.** This might be the easiest from an administrative perspective, but it would require that the subnet only ever be used for the web servers. Otherwise, port 443 would be open for any other VMs that you place in the same subnet.

- **Create rules for each VM.** This would be the biggest headache from an administrative perspective. Not only would you have to create 20 rules, but any IP address changes or the addition of VMs would require rule changes. It would work, but it is not recommended.

- **Create one ASG for the VM NICs.** Similarly to using groups to manage user permissions, you can create one ASG that represents the individual NICs of the web VMs as a group. Then you create one rule that references the ASG. Regardless of the IP addresses that get assigned to the NICs, the traffic would be allowed. Any new VMs only need to be added to the ASG.

ASGs are similar to the other resources that have been discussed. You create the ASG as a shell of an object and then associate it with another resource—in this case NICs.

To create an application security group, follow these steps:

1. Sign in to the Azure portal at *https://portal.azure.com*.
2. In the search bar, search for and select **Application security groups**.
3. On the Application security groups page, click **Create**.
4. In the Subscription dropdown menu, select the subscription to place the NSG in.
5. In the Resource group field, select or create a resource group to group the NSG in. For example, select **Networking**.
6. In the Name field, provide a name for the NSG. For example, enter **asg-eus-web1**.
7. Click **Review + create**. Figure 4-14 displays the completed configuration.
8. Click **Create**.

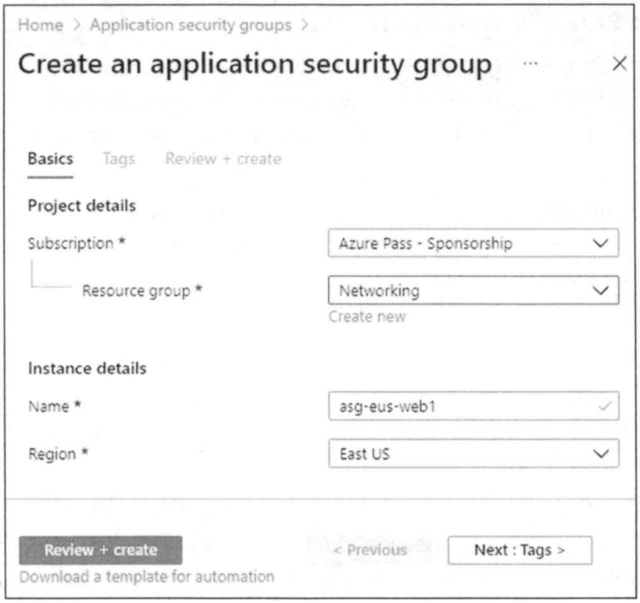
Home > Application security groups >
Create an application security group
Basics
Tags
Review + create
Project details
Subscription *
Azure Pass - Sponsorship
Resource group *
Networking
Create new
Instance details
Name *
asg-eus-web1
Region *
East US
Review + create
< Previous
Next : Tags >
Download a template for automation

FIGURE 4-14 Create an application security group

Associate an ASG to a NIC

After you create the ASG you must associate the NICs that you want to group. ASGs are highly scalable and allow up to 4,000 IP configurations per ASG. You can then have up to 3,000 ASGs in a subscription. To associate a NIC with an ASG, the NIC must already be associated with a virtual machine (VM). All resources (VM, NIC, and ASG) must be in the same Azure region.

To associate a NIC with an existing ASG, follow these steps:

1. Sign in to the Azure portal at *https://portal.azure.com*.
2. In the search bar, search for and select **Virtual machines**.
3. From the list of VMs, select the VM that has the NIC configured that you want to associate with an ASG.
4. On the VM page, select the **Networking** blade.
5. On the Networking blade, select the **Application security groups** tab.
6. On the Application security groups tab, click **Configure the application security groups**. Figure 4-15 displays the location of this tab and button.

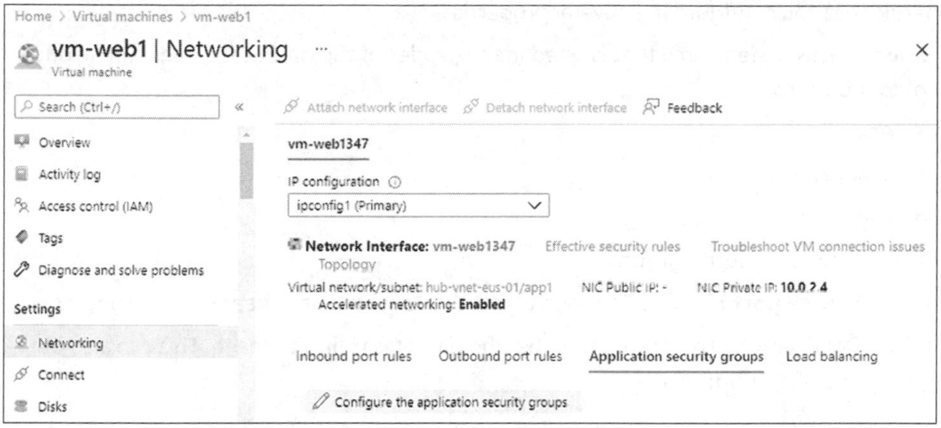

FIGURE 4-15 VM Networking blade

7. On the Configure the application security groups page, in the Application security groups dropdown menu, select the ASG that you previously created. For example, select **asg-eus-web1**.

8. Click **Save**. Figure 4-16 displays the completed configuration.

FIGURE 4-16 Configure the ASG

Create and configure NSG rules

The NSG rules are what you would like to filter the inbound or outbound packets on. Both inbound and outbound rules are processed the same way, just depending on whether that specific packet is entering or leaving the subnet or NIC.

Each rule that you configure has several properties:

- **Source.** This is the source that is listed in the header of the packet. Sources can be one of four options:
  - Any
  - IP addresses
  - Service tag
  - Application security group
    - **Source port ranges.** The source port that is listed in the header of the packet.
    - **Destination.** The destination that the packet is trying to reach. This can also be one of four options:
      - Any
      - IP addresses
      - Service tag
      - Application security group
    - **Service.** Allows you to specify a destination port number by selecting the service name instead of memorizing the port number. For example, selecting RDP automatically fills and locks the destination port range field with 3389. The default option is **Custom**.
    - **Destination port ranges.** The target port(s) that the packet is trying to reach.
    - **Protocol.** The protocol that the packet is using to communicate, which has four available options:
      - Any
      - TCP
      - UDP
      - ICMP
    - **Action.** The action to take if a packet matches the configuration, either *Allow* or *Deny*.
    - **Priority.** An integer between 100 and 4,096 that specifies the order in which the rule should be processed. Rules with a lower integer, *100* for example, are processed first.
    - **Name.** The display name of the rule in the NSG.
    - **Description.** The description is the only optional field in the configuration and can be used for administrative notes.

As a virtual network grows, so can the number of rules in an NSG. The design of the rules, in particular the *Priority* that is assigned to each rule, becomes critical. An NSG processes the rules from the lowest integer (100) to the highest integer (4096). As soon as a packet matches a rule, that rule is processed regardless of whether it is an *Allow* or a *Deny* rule. Table 4-1 displays a simple set of rules for an NSG.

TABLE 4-1 Network security group rules

Source IP	Source Port	Destination IP	Destination Port	Priority	Action
Any	Any	192.168.0.0/24	443	500	Deny
Any	Any	192.168.0.4/32	443	600	Allow

In Table 4-1, there are two rules that are configured with similar properties. Regardless of the source, both rules are configured for destination port 443, signaling a web server. However, the first rule, which references the entire subnet, *192.168.0.0/24*, is a *Deny* rule with a priority of *500*. This means that any traffic destined to this subnet on port 443 will be denied, and any future rules with a lower priority (higher integer) will not be reviewed or processed. This effectively makes the second rule in the table useless because it has the lower priority (*600*). If you need to allow 443 to 192.168.0.4 specifically, and deny access to all other resources on the subnet, then the rule priorities would need to swap.

To create an NSG rule that allows HTTPS traffic to an ASG that contains the web VMs, follow these steps:

1. Sign in to the Azure portal at *https://portal.azure.com*.
2. In the search bar, search for and select **Network security groups**.
3. On the Network security groups page, select the previously created NSG.
4. On the NSG, click the **Inbound security rules** blade.
5. On the Inbound security rules blade, click **Add**.
6. Use the following information to complete the NSG rule:
   - Source: **Any**
   - Source port ranges: *****
   - Destination: Application security group
   - Destination ASG: **asg-eus-web1**
   - Service: **HTTPS**
   - Action: **Allow**
   - Priority: **300**
   - Name: **web1-HTTPS**
7. Click **Add**. Figure 4-17 displays the completed configuration.

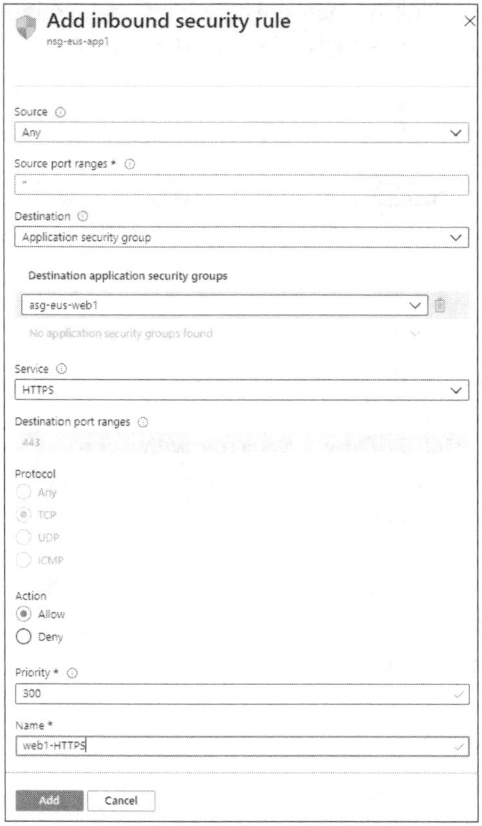

FIGURE 4-17 Add inbound security rule

Interpret and validate NSG flow logs

NSG flow logs are a monitoring tool that is built into NSGs to assist with monitoring network traffic for validation, compliance, and intrusion detection. With NSG flow logs, you capture the network traffic and store the logs in an Azure storage account. When using a general-purpose v2 storage account, you can also maintain retention and automatically delete logs up to one year after they are created.

Flow logs capture network traffic at layer 4 for both inbound and outbound traffic. Captured information includes both allow and denied traffic, as well as throughput information in the bytes and packets per flow. The information saved by flow logs includes, but is not limited to:

- Timestamp
- Source and destination IP address
- Source and destination port number
- Protocol
- Traffic direction
- NSG decision

- Flow state
- Packets
- Bytes

The flow logs save this information in JSON format in the storage account that you specify. To create an NSG flow log, follow these steps:

1. Sign in to the Azure portal at *https://portal.azure.com*.

2. In the search bar, search for and select **Network security groups**.

3. On the Network security groups page, select the previously created NSG.

4. On the NSG, click the **NSG flow logs** blade.

5. On the NSG flow logs blade, click **Create**.

6. In the Subscription dropdown menu, select the subscription to place the flow log in.

7. In the Flow Log Name field, provide a name for the flow log. For example, enter **flow-nsg-app1**.

8. Leave the remaining fields set to their default values and click **Review + create**. Figure 4-18 displays the completed configuration.

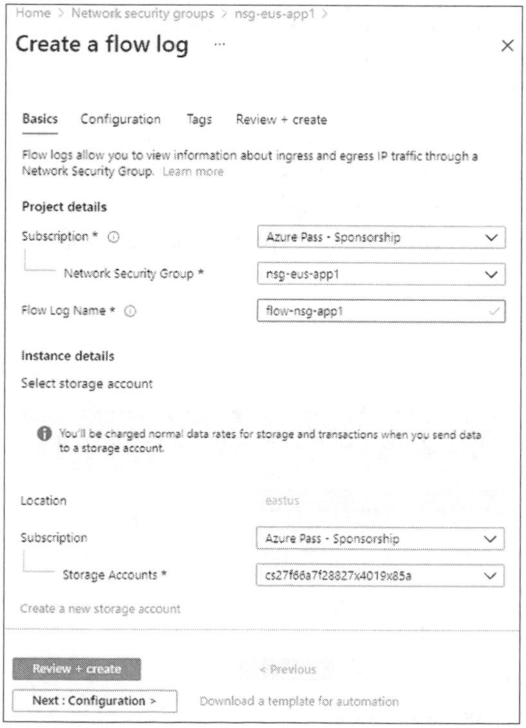

FIGURE 4-18 Create a flow log

9. Click **Create**.

After you complete these steps, you'll need to ensure that you have traffic generated to the resources that the NSG is allowing or blocking traffic to. This could be as simple as accessing a sample website on a VM in the virtual network.

After you generate traffic, the NSG flow log will appear in the storage account that you used during the configuration. The storage account will have a blob container named *insights-log-networksecuritygroupflowevent* and then a tree of sub-containers that reference the subscription, resource provider, NSG, date, and MAC address. The following location is the full path of the sample in the storage account.

```
Location: insights-logs-networksecuritygroupflowevent / resourceId= / SUBSCRIPTIONS /
7F66A7F2-8827-4019-85AA-167B8E3D219F / RESOURCEGROUPS / NETWORKING / PROVIDERS /
MICROSOFT.NETWORK / NETWORKSECURITYGROUPS / NSG-EUS-APP1 / y=2021 / m=11 / d=26 /
h=04 / m=00 / macAddress=002842262CD2
```

Inside this location is a PT1H.json file that contains the traffic flow for the date, time, and MAC address of the request. A sample portion of the JSON file is displayed below.

```
{"records":[{"time":"2021-11-26T04:24:06.9762336Z","systemId":"c55b1f21-c587-4ed3-baf5-
ed8ddf971399","macAddress":"002248266FC9","category":"NetworkSecurityGroupFlowEvent",
"resourceId":"/SUBSCRIPTIONS/7F66A7F2-8827-4019-85AA-167B8E3D219F /RESOURCEGROUPS/
NETWORKING/PROVIDERS/MICROSOFT.NETWORK/NETWORKSECURITYGROUPS/NSG-EUS-APP1",
"operationName":"NetworkSecurityGroupFlowEvents","properties":{"Version":2,
"flows":[{"rule":"DefaultRule_AllowInternetOutBound","flows":[{"mac":"002842262CD2",
"flowTuples":["1637900636,10.0.2.4,52.239.247.228,41926,443,T,O,A,B,,,,",
"1637900641,10.0.2.4,52.239.247.228,41926,443,T,O,A,E,8,1508,13,12663"]}]},
```

When you have a production amount of traffic through the NSG, opening and reading the flow logs on your own would be very challenging. Instead, you can associate the flow log with Traffic Analytics as part of a Log Analytics workspace to be able to search and visualize the data that is captured. Alternatively, you can capture this data with other third-party log ingestion tools, such as Splunk.

Verify IP flow

A useful troubleshooting tool with NSGs is the IP flow verify tool that is a part of Network Watcher. Network Watcher is a collection of monitoring and troubleshooting tools for your virtual network and resources; more of its tools are discussed in skill section 4.4.

IP flow verify enables you to select the NIC of a virtual machine and then test the IP connection to a remote IP address. This connection test can be inbound or outbound, using TCP or UDP and any port combination that you specify.

To test the IP flow to a virtual machine, follow these steps:

1. Sign in to the Azure portal at *https://portal.azure.com*.

2. In the search bar, search for and select **Network Watcher**.

3. From Network Watcher, click the **IP flow verify** blade.

4. Depending on the number of VMs that you have, a VM might automatically be selected. Otherwise, configure the dropdown menus to select a virtual machine and network interface.

5. Ensure that the Protocol field is set to **TCP** and the Direction field is set to **Inbound**.

6. The Local IP address field should have been filled automatically when you selected the NIC. For example, it might say **10.0.2.4**. In the Local port field, enter the port number that you allowed in the NSG rule. For example, enter **443**.

7. In the Remote IP address field, provide a public IP address. For example, enter **8.8.8.8**.

8. In the Remote port field, specify a random remote port. For example, enter **50000**.

9. Click **Check**. If you allowed 443 inbound from any source (remote) IP address, then the result should return as "Access allowed" with the name of the NSG and rule that is allowing this access. Figure 4-19 displays the successful configuration.

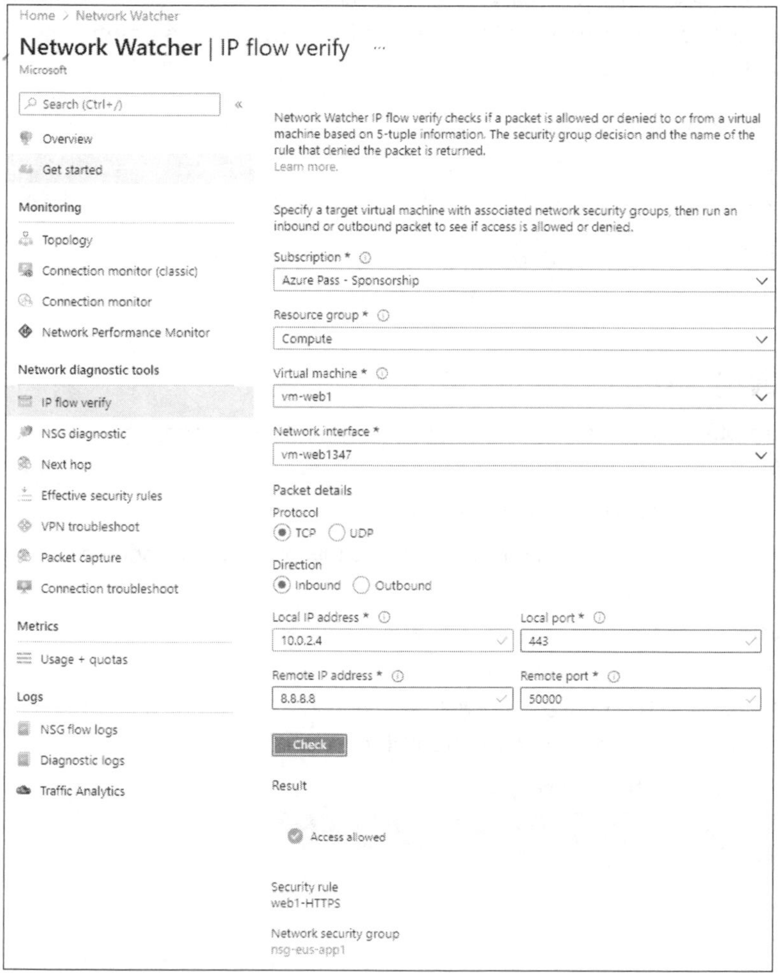

FIGURE 4-19 IP flow verify

Note that the IP flow verify and NSG rules only check to verify that the virtual network and NSGs are not blocking the traffic. The VM would still need any software firewall to accept connections on the specified port number and need the service to be configured on the VM.

Skill 4.3: Implement a Web Application Firewall (WAF) deployment

Web Application Firewall policies are a combination of managed rule sets and custom rules that you can apply across multiple devices. There are different policies sets for Azure Front Door, Application Gateway, and Azure CDN.

If you compare this section to the objective domain, there is some overlap between the Azure Front Door and Azure Application Gateway services that were discussed in Chapter 3. For the configuration of those services, refer back to those sections. This skill section focuses on creating and associating a Web Application Firewall (WAF) policy, which includes whether the policy is in Detection or Prevention mode.

> **This skill covers how to:**
> - Implement a WAF policy
> - Associate a WAF policy

Implement a WAF policy

A WAF policy can help protect your resources from SQL injection, cross-site scripting, and other malicious attacks.

You can create a WAF policy for the following resources:

- **Azure Front Door.** This is the global Front Door service that will protect resources in all regions where Front Door is used.
- **Azure Application Gateway.** This is a regional service and requires an application gateway in each region that you deploy in.
- **Azure CDN (Preview).** This is for a content delivery network. As of this writing, this feature is in preview, and it is not covered in this skill section.

Each policy that you create has the following properties:

- Policy mode
- Managed rules

- Policy settings
- Custom rules
- Associations

Configure Detection or Prevention mode

Regardless of which resource you create the policy for, the policy mode allows you to set the policy in either *Detection* or *Prevention* mode. The names are explicit in what they provide. Detection mode detects any possible malicious activity, but it does not take additional steps to block that activity. The resource will need diagnostic logs enabled, where the activity will be logged and available for you to report on. Prevention mode blocks the activity and connection when it is detected.

Azure Front Door rule sets

A WAF policy with Azure Front Door provides a pre-configured set of common rules from the Open Web Application Security Project (OWASP) categories and rule groups. These rule groups include:

- Protocol-attack
- Local File Include (LFI)
- Remote File Include (RFI)
- Remote Code Execution (RCE)
- PHP
- Cross-site scripting (XSS)
- SQL Injection
- Session fixation
- Java protection

For Azure Front Door WAF policies, there are three default rule sets that you can configure:

- DefaultRuleSet_preview-0.1
- DefaultRuleSet_1.0
- Microsoft_DefaultRuleSet_1.1

In addition to the default rules provided by Microsoft and OWASP, you can create custom rules that look for a match based on the following conditions:

- Geo-location
- IP address
- Size
- String

If traffic matches what you configure, then you can choose an action to take on the traffic. The available actions are:

- Allow traffic
- Deny traffic
- Log traffic only
- Redirect traffic

Azure Application Gateway rule sets

The WAF policies for application gateways are similar to those for Front Door, but they have different managed rule sets and slightly different configuration options for custom rules. The available managed rule sets for an application gateway are:

- Microsoft_BotManagerRuleSet_0.1
- OWASP_2.2.9
- OWASP_3.0
- OWASP_3.1
- OWASP_3.2

You can select one or more of these rule sets to be included in the WAF policy for application gateways. If you need to create custom rules for an application gateway, the options are slightly different:

- IP address
- Number
- String
- Geo-location

The action to take when traffic matches a condition are also slightly different for an application gateway, as the option to redirect does not exist. The available actions are:

- Allow traffic
- Deny traffic
- Log traffic only

To create a WAF policy for an Azure Front door, follow these steps:

1. Sign in to the Azure portal at *https://portal.azure.com*.
2. In the search bar, search for and select **Web Application Firewall policies**.
3. On the WAF policies page, click **Create**.
4. On the Basics tab, in the Policy for dropdown menu, select Global WAF (Front Door).

5. In the Front door SKU dropdown, select the appropriate SKU for the type of front door resource that you have deployed. For this example, leave the default, **Front Door**.

6. In the Policy name field, provide a name for the policy. For example, enter **wafapp1**.

7. For the Policy state and Policy mode fields, leave the default values of **Enabled** and **Detection**.

8. Click **Next: Managed rules**. Figure 4-20 displays the completed Basics tab.

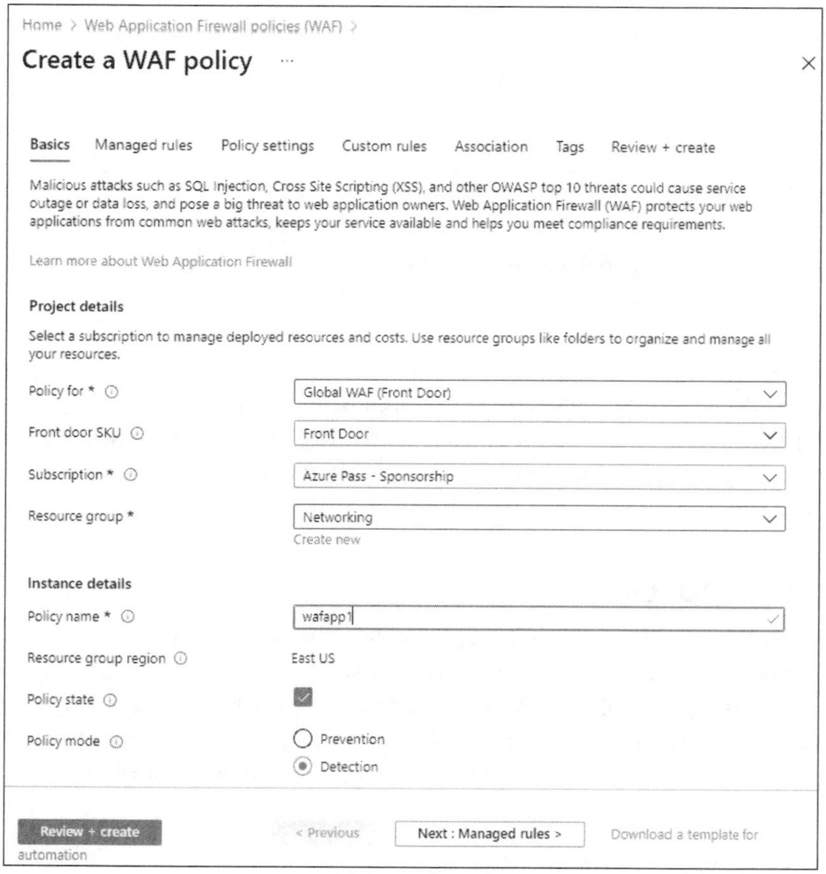

Home > Web Application Firewall policies (WAF) >

Create a WAF policy ···

Basics   Managed rules   Policy settings   Custom rules   Association   Tags   Review + create

Malicious attacks such as SQL Injection, Cross Site Scripting (XSS), and other OWASP top 10 threats could cause service outage or data loss, and pose a big threat to web application owners. Web Application Firewall (WAF) protects your web applications from common web attacks, keeps your service available and helps you meet compliance requirements.

Learn more about Web Application Firewall

Project details

Select a subscription to manage deployed resources and costs. Use resource groups like folders to organize and manage all your resources.

Policy for *   Global WAF (Front Door)
Front door SKU   Front Door
Subscription *   Azure Pass - Sponsorship
Resource group *   Networking
                      Create new

Instance details

Policy name *   wafapp1
Resource group region   East US
Policy state
Policy mode   ○ Prevention
                 ● Detection

Review + create   < Previous   Next : Managed rules >   Download a template for automation

FIGURE 4-20 WAF policy basics

9. On the Managed rules tab, in the Default rule set field, select **Microsoft_DefaultRuleSet_1.1**.

10. Click **Review + create**. Figure 4-21 displays the relevant portion of the Managed rules tab.

11. Click **Create**.

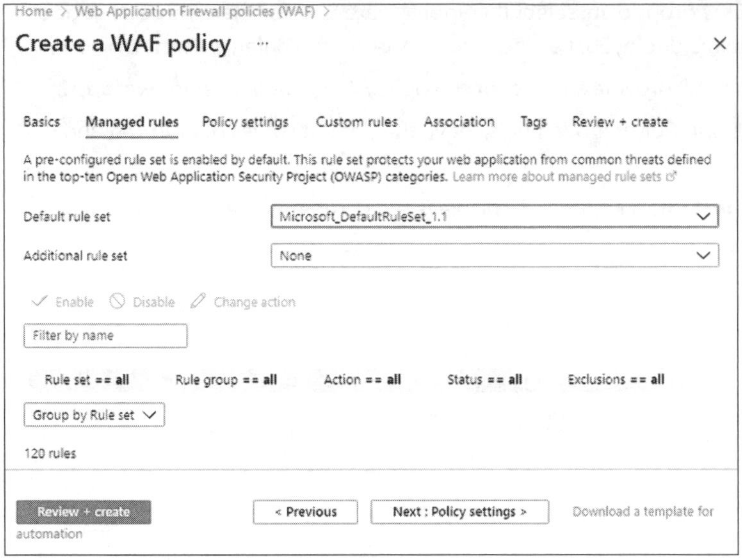

FIGURE 4-21 WAF policy managed rules

As the walkthrough demonstrates, the Azure portal will allow you to create a WAF policy without associating it to a resource. This is similar behavior to NSGs, NICs, and other resources demonstrated. Associating the WAF policy with the resource, in this case Front Door, is covered in the next section.

Associate a WAF policy

In order for the rules that you configure in the policy to apply to the resource, you need to associate the policy with the resource. You can reuse a policy across multiple resources if you would like the same rule set to be applied. This can be especially useful when you are using application gateways and you have multiple regions deployed. Instead of managing each application gateway individually, you can create a shared policy that is used across all regions.

To associate an existing WAF policy with a resource, follow these steps:

1. Sign in to the Azure portal at *https://portal.azure.com*.
2. In the search bar, search for and select **Web Application Firewall policies**.
3. On the WAF policies page, select the previously created policy.
4. On the policy page, click the **Associations** blade.
5. On the Associations blade, click **Add frontend host**.
6. On the Add frontend host page, in the Frontdoor dropdown menu, select the Azure Front Door that you previously deployed. For example, select **contosoapp1**.
7. In the Frontend host dropdown menu, select the host configured in the front door. For example, select **contosoapp1.azurefd.net**.

8. Click **Add**. Figure 4-22 displays the completed configuration.

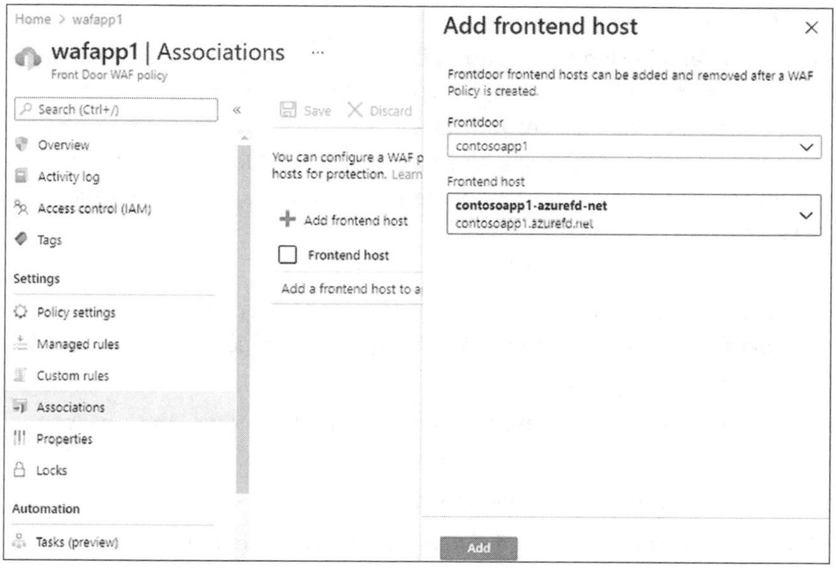

FIGURE 4-22 Add frontend host

Skill 4.4: Monitor networks

Azure has several built-in tools that allow you to monitor and alert on the metrics, logs, and IP flows that are important for your overall network. This could be for auditing reasons, security, or compliance with industry or other regulation. Network Watcher is one of the primary tools in Azure that provides a variety of tools to monitor the environment. This skill section outlines and provides walkthroughs for some of those tools.

This skill covers how to:

- Configure network health alerts and logging by using Azure Monitor
- Create and configure a Connection Monitor instance
- Configure and use Traffic Analytics
- Enable and configure diagnostic logging
- Configure Azure Network Watcher

Configure network health alerts and logging by using Azure Monitor

Azure Monitor is the default and "included" monitoring system with Azure services. Compare this to Azure Log Analytics and Azure Sentinel, which are also Azure monitoring services but are not necessarily "included' with the services you deploy. These other services require additional configuration and money to configure and use. However, Azure Monitor as a monitoring tool is free, with the associated costs being a storage account for long-term storage and on-going metric analysis for alert.

The type of resource that you are monitoring determines the type of metrics that are available to look at. For example, virtual machine metrics are different from app service metrics. For virtual machines specifically, there are additional guest diagnostics that you can enable to obtain more information for Azure Monitor.

For each metric, you can create an alert based on conditions for the metric. Alerts have three components:

- **Scope.** The Azure resource that you wish to monitor and evaluate.
- **Condition.** What should be evaluated with the metric to trigger the action.
- **Action.** The notification or automation to take when the condition is met.

When you are configuring the condition, there are options to configure for the operator and the data the evaluation is compared against. The built-in operators are:

- Greater than
- Greater than or equal to
- Less than
- Less than or equal to

Then depending on the type of metric that you selected, you would configure the condition with one of these aggregation types:

- Average
- Count
- Maximum
- Minimum
- Total

A common metric to monitor for virtual machines might be whether the *Percentage CPU* metric has an *Average* that is *Greater than* 75%. But for how long might the average need to be higher than 75% for the alert to trigger? That is where the aggregation granularity and frequency of evaluation come in. You can set the granularity from 1 minute to 24 hours, with the frequency (or resolution) from every minute to every hour.

After you decide the condition for an alert, you configure the actions to either notify or perform some type of automation when the alert is triggered. There are many built-in options for alerts:

- Notifications
  - Email Azure Resource Manager role
  - Email address
  - SMS message
  - Push notification
  - Voice message
- Actions
  - Automation runbook
  - Azure Function
  - Event Hub
  - ITSM connector
  - Logic App
  - Secure Webhook
  - Webhook

To create an alert based on the Percentage CPU metric for a virtual machine that sends an email, follow these steps:

1. Sign in to the Azure portal at *https://portal.azure.com*.
2. In the search bar, search for and select **Virtual machines**.
3. On the list of VMs, select an existing VM.
4. On the VM, click the **Alerts** blade.
5. On the Alerts blade, click **Create**, and then click **Alert rule**.
6. Note that Scope is already set to the VM because that is where we created the rule from. In the Conditions section, click **Add condition**.
7. In the Select a signal field, search for and select **Percentage CPU**.
8. Note that Operator defaults to **Greater than** and Aggregation to **Average**. In the **Threshold value** field, enter **75**.
9. Verify that the Aggregation granularity is set to **5 minutes** and that the frequency of evaluation is set to **Every 1 minute**.
10. Click **Done**. Figure 4-23 displays the completed configuration.

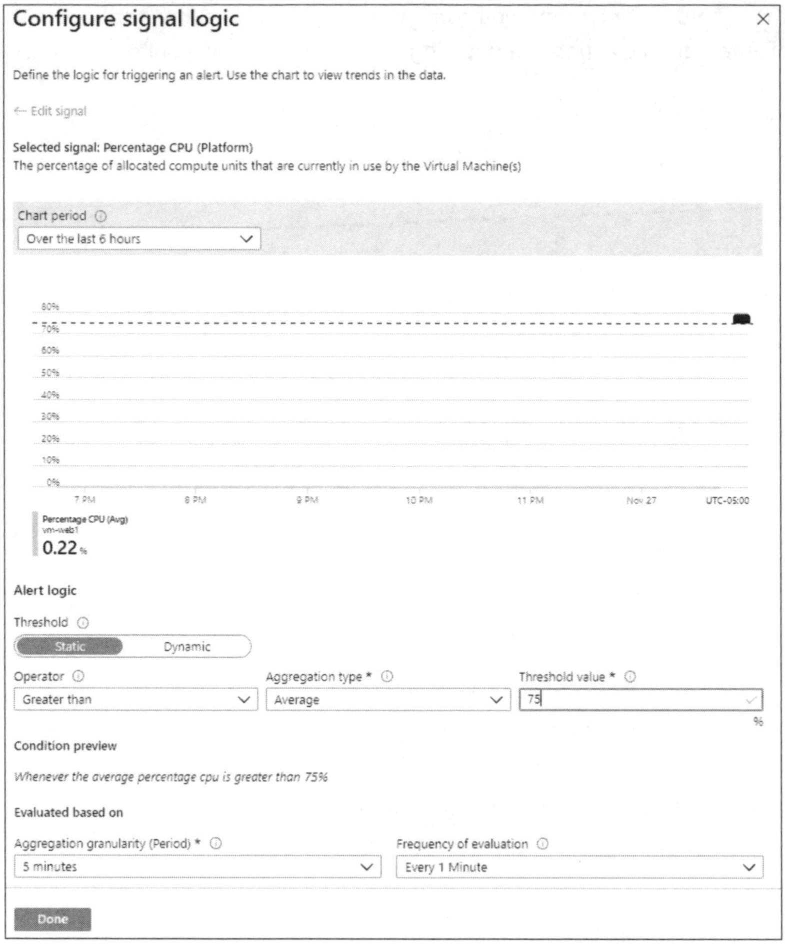

FIGURE 4-23 Configure signal logic

11. After clicking Done, you are returned to the Create alert rule page. In the Actions section, click **Add action group**.

12. On the Add action groups page, click **Create action group**.

13. On the Basics tab of the action group, in the Action group name field, provide a name for the group. For example, enter **email-vms**. Leave all other fields at their default values.

14. Click **Next: Notifications**. Figure 4-24 displays the completed Basics tab.

15. In the Notification type dropdown menu, select **Email/SMS message/Push/Voice**.

16. In the Email/SMS message/Push/Voice flyout, select the checkbox next to **Email**.

17. In the Email field, provide an email address. For example, enter **az700examref@outlook.com**.

18. Click **OK**. Figure 4-25 displays the completed configuration.

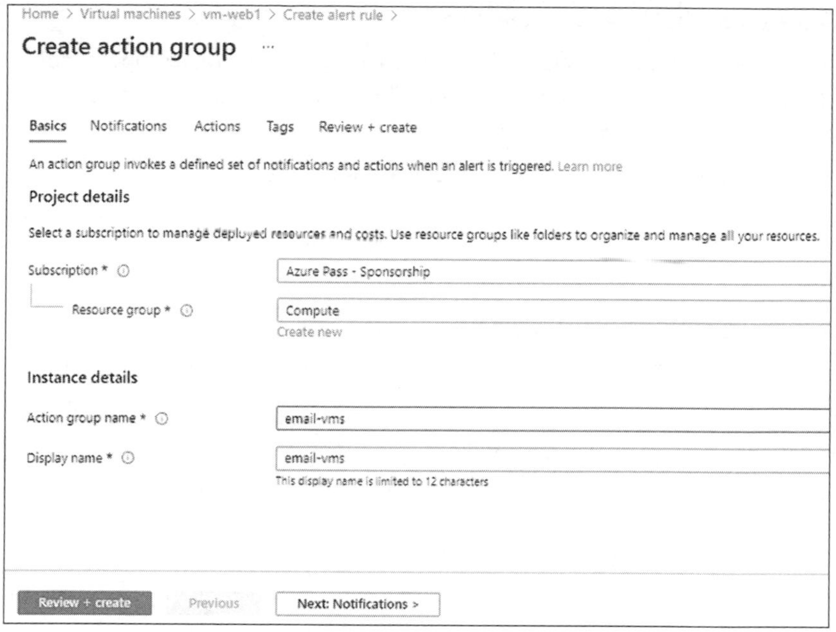

FIGURE 4-24 Create action group basics

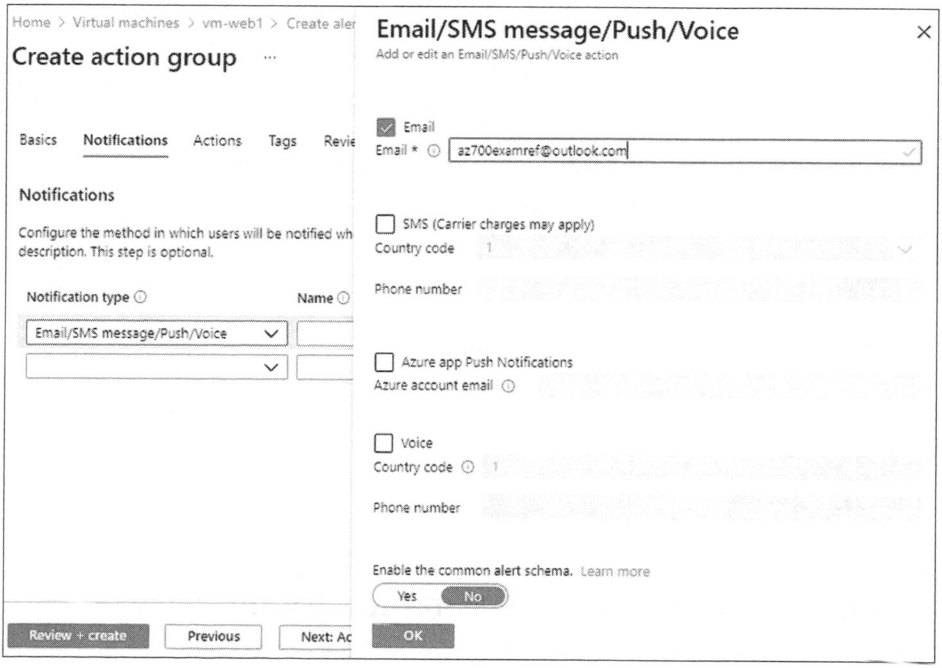

FIGURE 4-25 Action group email settings

19. In the Name field, name the Notification **Email admin**.

20. Click **Review + create**, and then click **Create**.

21. You will be returned to the Create alert rule page, where now you have a scope, condition, and action configured. In the Alert rule name field, provide a name for the alert rule. For example, enter **VM-email-admin**.

22. Click **Create alert rule**. Figure 4-26 displays the final configuration.

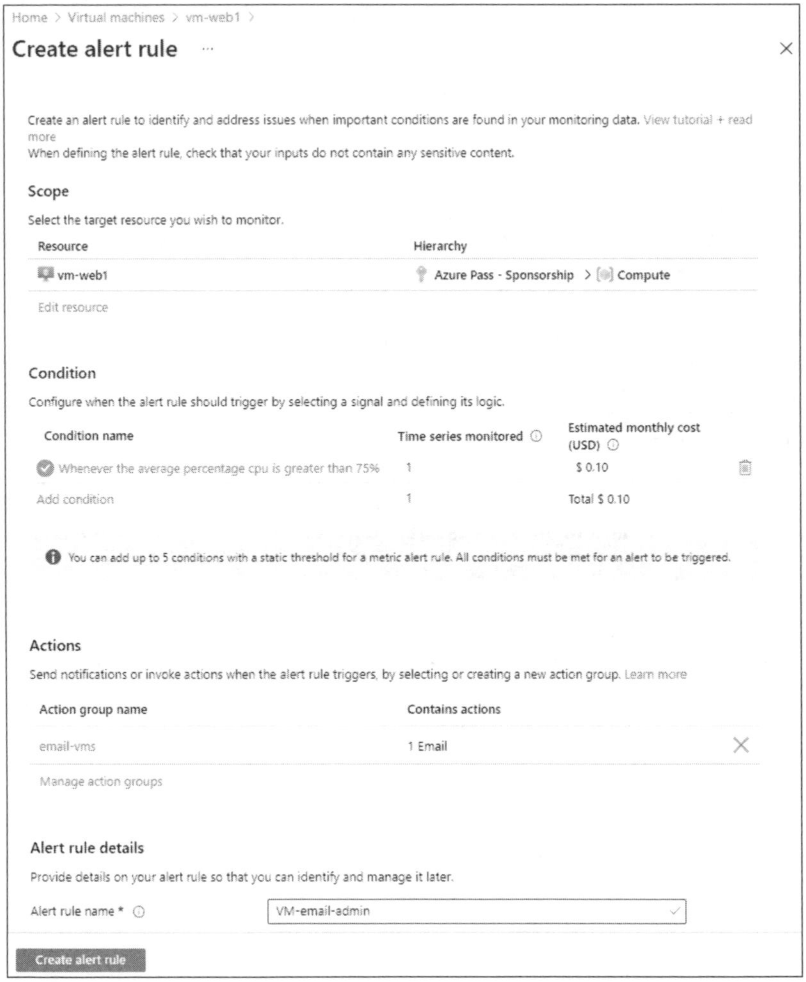

FIGURE 4-26 Create alert rule

Create and configure a Connection Monitor instance

Another tool in Network Watcher is Connection Monitor, which enables you to monitor the connectivity in a hybrid network environment. Connection Monitor sends data to a Log Analytics workspace.

Connection Monitor uses test groups to define the Azure and external resources to monitor connectivity for. The test group has a test configuration that specifies how these resources should be able to connect. You can also optionally enable alerts for the connection using the same alert process outlined in the previous section.

To create a Connection Monitor instance, follow these steps:

1. Sign in to the Azure portal at *https://portal.azure.com*.

2. In the search bar, search for and select **Network Watcher**.

3. From Network Watcher, click the **Connection monitor** blade. Do not use the *Connection monitor (classic)* blade.

4. On the Connection monitor blade, click **Create**.

5. On the Basics tab of the Create Connection Monitor page, provide a name for the monitor. For example, enter **App1Monitoring**.

6. Leave the remaining fields at their default value and click **Next: Test groups**. Figure 4-27 displays the completed Basics tab.

FIGURE 4-27 Create Connection Monitor Basics

7. In the Test group name field, provide a name for the group. For example, enter **AppGroup1**.

8. In the Sources field, click **Add sources**.

9. On the Add Sources page, select the checkbox next to the virtual network that you previously created. Note that the VMs in the virtual network must have the Network Watcher extension added.

10. Click **Add endpoints**. Figure 4-28 displays the Add Sources configuration.

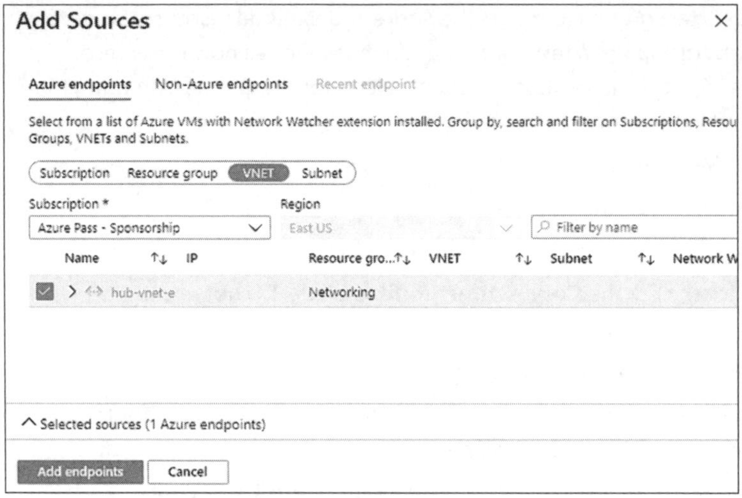

FIGURE 4-28 Connection Monitor add sources

11. You will be returned to the Add test group details page. Click **Add Test configuration**.

12. In the Test configuration name field, provide a name for the test. For example, enter **app1-http-test**.

13. Leave the remaining values at default, and click **Add Test configuration**.

14. You will be returned to the Add test group details page. Click **Add destinations**.

15. On the Add Destinations page, click the **External Addresses** tab.

16. On the External Addresses page, select the checkbox next to an Office 365 option and then click **Add endpoints**. Figure 4-29 displays the completed configuration.

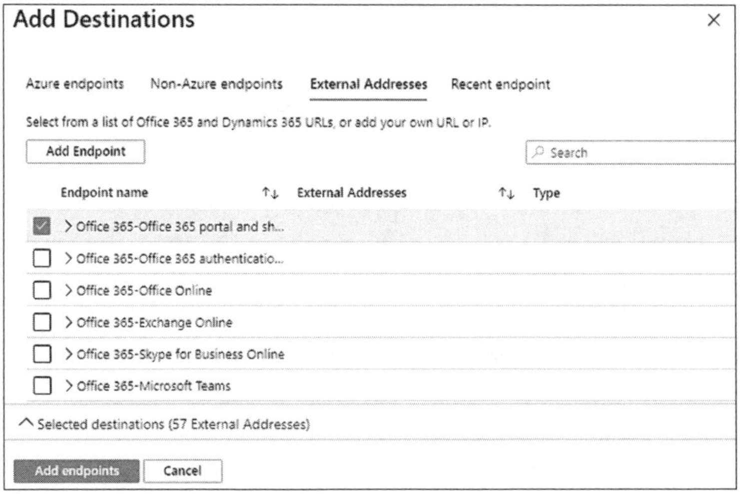

FIGURE 4-29 Connection Monitor Add Destinations

17. You will be returned to the Add test group details page. Review and confirm the settings, and then click **Add Test Group**. Figure 4-30 displays the final configuration.

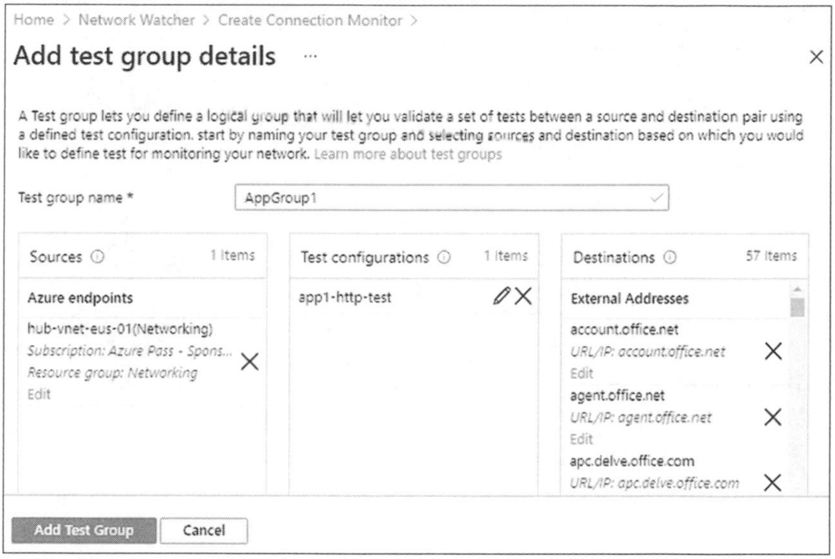

FIGURE 4-30 Add test group details

18. Click **Review + create**, and then click **Create**.

Configure and use Traffic Analytics

Network Watcher also contains a tool named Traffic Analytics, which allows you to analyze the NSG flow logs for multiple Azure regions, virtual networks, and subnets using one tool. This tool assists with maintaining compliance and auditing the environment's network traffic. For more information on NSG flow logs, refer back to skill section 4.2.

To configure Traffic Analytics with an NSG that is already configured for flow logs, follow these steps:

1. Sign in to the Azure portal at *https://portal.azure.com*.

2. In the search bar, search for and select **Network Watcher**.

3. From Network Watcher, click the **Traffic Analytics** blade. Figure 4-31 displays the data that has been collected by the flow log and visualized in Traffic Analytics.

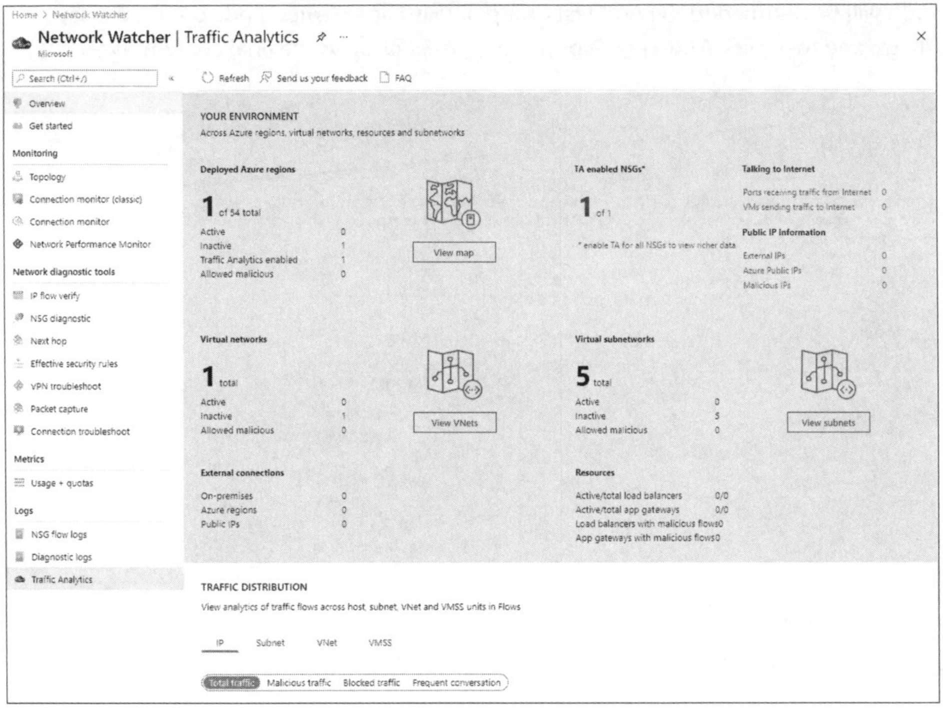

FIGURE 4-31 Traffic Analytics

Enable and configure diagnostic logging

There are a few resources in Azure that you can collect additional information from if you enable diagnostic logging. This must be enabled because you must have a repository configured to save the data, meaning there is a cost associated with enabling the log. For NSG diagnostic settings, the supported destinations include:

- Log Analytics workspace
- Azure Storage account
- Event Hub
- Third-party solution

For NSG logging, you can enable *allLogs*, or select between two categories: *NetworkSecurityGroupEvent* and *NetworkSecurityGroupRuleCounter*.

To configure diagnostic settings for an NSG, follow these steps:

1. Sign in to the Azure portal at *https://portal.azure.com*.
2. In the search bar, search for and select **Network security groups**.
3. On the Network security groups page, select the NSG that you previously created: **nsg-eus-app1**.
4. On the NSG, click the **Diagnostic settings** blade.

5. On the Diagnostic setting page, click **Add diagnostic setting**.

6. In the Diagnostic setting name field, provide a name for the configuration. For example, enter **nsg-app1-alllogs**.

7. In the Logs section, select the checkbox next to **allLogs**.

8. In the Destination details section, select the checkbox next to **Archive to a storage account**.

9. In the Subscription and Storage account dropdown menus, select an appropriate storage account.

10. Click **Save**. Figure 4-32 displays the completed configuration.

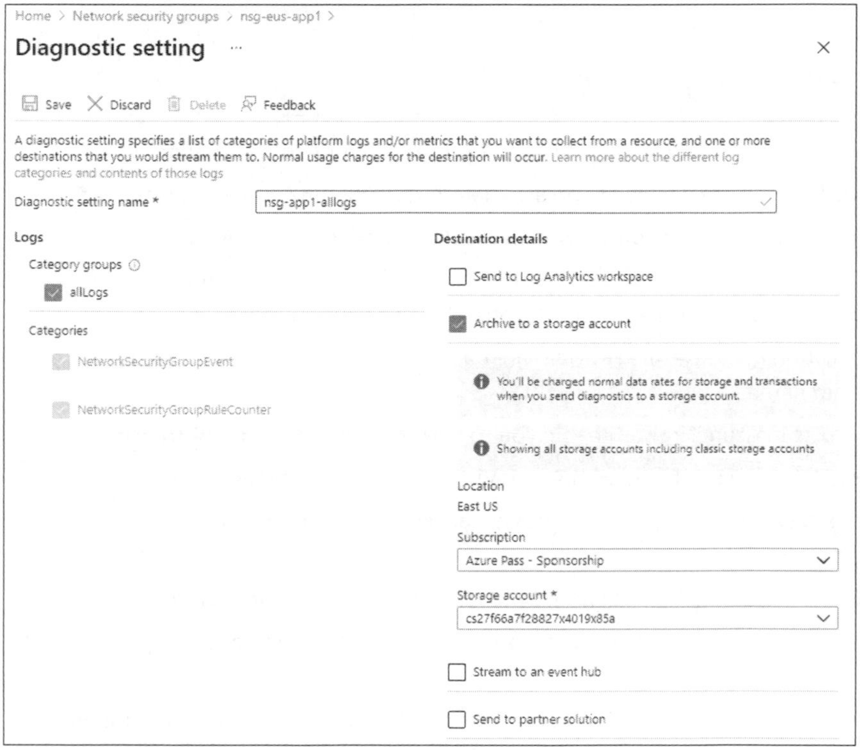

FIGURE 4-32 NSG diagnostic settings

Configure Azure Network Watcher

Network Watcher is a collection of tools that you can use to troubleshoot and monitor the resources that you have deployed across your subscriptions. There is not much to configure for Network Watcher, as each tool operates independently.

The other tools that were not mentioned specifically in the objective list for the exam include:

- **Topology.** A network map of the resources that you have deployed in a subscription.

- **NSG diagnostic.** Provides a way to test NSGs in a traffic flow to determine which NSG might be allowing or blocking traffic unexpectedly.
- **Next hop.** Verifies the next hop route from an IP address when using user-defined routes.
- **Effective security rules.** Displays the end result of NSG rules when multiple NSGs might be configured or various priority rules have been defined.
- **VPN troubleshoot.** A troubleshooting tool for virtual network gateways and establishing VPN connections.
- **Packet capture.** A packet capture tool that saves packet trace information to a .CAP file that you can download and analyze offline.

Chapter summary

- Azure Firewalls provide layer 3 to layer 7 protection for Azure virtual networks.
- Azure Firewalls are deployed and associated with a single Azure virtual network.
- Azure Firewalls are configured with network, application, and NAT rules.
- Network rules in Azure Firewalls are based on packet header information such as source and destination IP address, protocol, and port number.
- Application rules in Azure Firewalls are based on service tags or fully qualified domain names.
- NAT rules in Azure Firewall enable you to perform network and port translation.
- Firewalls can be combined with Azure Virtual WAN to create secure hubs.
- Network security groups (NSGs) provide packet filtering based on packet header information.
- NSGs can be associated with both subnets and network interface cards.
- Application security groups act as a group for network interfaces to simplify NSG rules.
- NSG rules define whether a packet should be allowed or denied, either inbound or outbound from the resource it is associated with.
- NSG priority is critical in designing rules with various levels of restrictions.
- NSG flow logs capture the traffic flow and decisions made by an NSG in a storage account.
- The IP flow tool in Network Watcher helps you ensure that IP traffic can communicate through NSGs.
- WAF policies can be used with Azure Front Door, Azure Application Gateway, and Azure CDN.
- WAF policies provide managed and custom rule sets for protecting resources.
- WAF managed rule sets are based on predefined OWASP rules.

- Azure Monitor displays metrics for the resources that you have deployed.

- The metrics captured with Azure Monitor can be used to create an alert rule.

- Alert rules have scopes, conditions, and action groups.

- Alert conditions measure the metric that is being monitored for it to be triggered.

- Action groups are the notifications or actions taken when an alert is triggered.

- Connection Monitor uses a test configuration to monitor connectivity between resources.

- Traffic Analytics is used in combination with NSG flow logs to visualize and summarize the data that has been gathered.

- NSG diagnostic logs capture additional information on the NSG and are stored in Log Analytics, Azure Storage Accounts, Event Hub, or third-party providers.

- Network Watcher is a collection of network monitoring and troubleshooting tools that can be used in your Azure environment.

Thought experiment

In this thought experiment, demonstrate your skills and knowledge of the topics covered in this chapter. You can find the answers in the section that follows.

Contoso has a three-tier application that consists of a web tier, an API tier, and a database tier. Contoso also has a virtual network with a subnet dedicated for each tier of the application. The virtual network also has subnets for management and a virtual network gateway. The gateway is a site-to-site VPN to their on-premises datacenter. All of these resources are currently deployed in one Azure region. The organization plans to deploy to a second region in the near future and needs to be able to replicate the current environment with the least amount of administrative overhead.

The web tier of the application accepts HTTPS requests and runs on a virtual machine scale set. The API tier accepts connections from the web tier and then communicates with the database. The organization needs to ensure that the subnet traffic is restricted to only what is required by the application and that any other combination is denied. The management network should be the only network that can communicate with the other subnets. Outbound traffic must have stateful packet inspection when leaving the network.

The organization has a compliance requirement to be able to identify connections and filtering that occur at the web tier. The data that is captured must be able to be retained for one year.

With the above information, answer these questions for Contoso:

1. What service should be deployed to protect the outbound traffic of the virtual machines?

2. What service should be deployed to protect inbound HTTPS traffic, and how should it be configured?

3. What should be used to restrict traffic for each subnet, and how should it be configured?

4. What should be used to meet the compliance requirement?

5. What should be used to minimize the deployment overhead in the second Azure region?

Thought experiment answers

This section contains the solution to the thought experiment. Each answer explains why the answer choice is correct.

1. What service should be deployed to protect the outbound traffic of the virtual machines?

   An Azure Firewall should be deployed with the virtual network. When you associate a firewall with a virtual network, then all the outbound traffic from the network will be traversed through the firewall.

2. What service should be deployed to protect inbound HTTPS traffic, and how should it be configured?

   The inbound HTTPS traffic should have an application gateway with OWASP rules enabled.

3. What should be used to restrict traffic for each subnet, and how should it be configured?

   Filtering network traffic at the subnet level is performed by network security groups. The network security groups should have at least two inbound rules for each subnet: one inbound for the appropriate connection and one for the management subnet. For example, the API tier should only allow connections from the web tier. The database tier should only accept connections from the API tier.

4. What should be used to meet the compliance requirement?

   The compliance requirement of monitoring the web traffic and retaining data for one year can be accomplished by using NSG flow logs. The flow logs can be stored in Azure Storage Accounts with retention policies configured.

5. What should be used to minimize the deployment overhead in the second Azure region?

   You should use a WAF policy to configure the application gateway rule sets. This will minimize the administrative overhead of deploying an application gateway in the second region.

CHAPTER 5

Design and implement private access to Azure services

Most of the services in Azure are public endpoints and publicly accessible by default. For some security requirements or routing efficiency concerns, that is not always necessarily what an organization wants for its services. For example, most organizations do not want Azure SQL databases to be accessible over the internet.

This chapter introduces Private Link, which enables you to publish your own applications and make them accessible privately. Then private endpoints can be used to consume those services as well as Azure's services.

Service endpoints introduce how to optimize any possible routing inefficiencies that site-to-site VPNs or ExpressRoute might introduce. Service tags can be used with network security groups and Azure Firewall to filter specific Azure services.

Finally, we look at integrating platform as a service (PaaS) services with virtual networks for App Services, Kubernetes, and App Service Environments.

Skills in this chapter:

- Skill 5.1: Design and implement Azure Private Link service and private endpoints
- Skill 5.2: Design and implement service endpoints
- Skill 5.3: Configure VNet integration for dedicated platform as a service (PaaS) services

Skill 5.1: Design and implement Azure Private Link service and private endpoints

Azure Private Link is the broader name for two components: Private Link services and private endpoints. It can be easy to confuse the two services, but they are the two components of a Consumer and Provider service. Private endpoints are the consumer side, which connects to Azure services or published applications. The Azure services or applications that you publish are the Provider side, by using an Azure Private Link service.

Using Private Link ensures that all communication from the end-client connects to the service by using private IP addresses through a virtual network. This can then be integrated with DNS and combined with virtual networks or ExpressRoute.

Create a Private Link service

Azure Private Link services allow private access to your application by using private connectivity over the Microsoft network. To use Private Link services, your application must be running behind an Azure Load Balancer Standard SKU. The Private Link service uses a Service Provider and Service Consumer workflow.

When you create a Private Link service, Azure will assign a globally unique name, called an *alias,* for your service. You can share the alias or resource URI of your application with your customers for them to connect to privately. When a customer attempts to connect to the application for the first time, the service provider can accept or reject the request.

The overall steps for completing both sides of the Private Link service include:

1. Create and configure your application using an Azure Load Balancer Standard SKU.
2. Create the Private Link service and associate it with the frontend IP address of the load balancer.
3. Share the generated alias of the Private Link service with your customers.
4. As customers configure their private endpoints, accept or reject the connection requests.

As the provider, the Private Link service, load balancer, and virtual network must all be in the same Azure region. However, the consumers of the service can access the service from any Azure region using the Microsoft network.

To create a Private Link service, follow these steps:

1. Sign in to the Azure portal at *https://portal.azure.com*.
2. In the search bar, search for and select **Private Link**.
3. From the Private Link center, click the **Private link services** blade.
4. On the Private link services blade, click **Add**.
5. Select the desired subscription and resource group to deploy the service in.
6. In the Name field, provide a name for the service. For example, enter **pls-eus-app1**.

7. In the Region dropdown menu, select the desired Azure region. This must be the same region as the load balancer and virtual network you plan to associate the service with. For example, select **East US**.

8. Click **Next: Outbound settings**. Figure 5-1 displays the completed Basics tab.

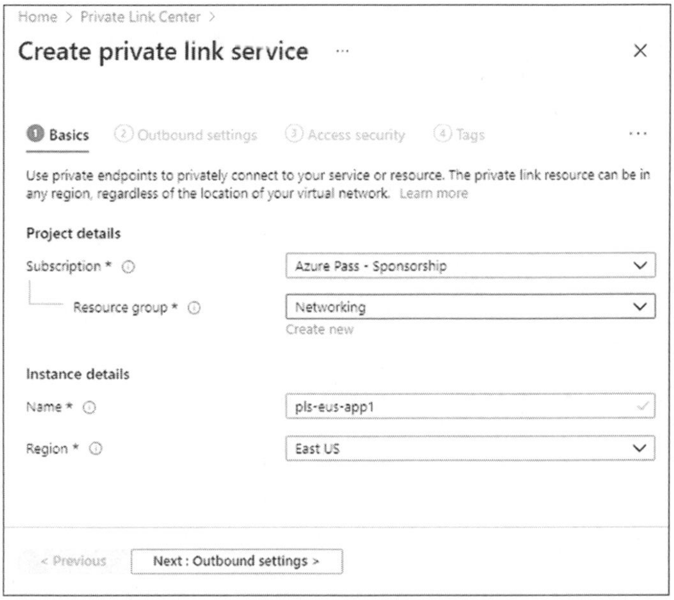

FIGURE 5-1 Private Link service basics

9. In the Load balancer dropdown menu, select the load balancer that is used with your application. For example, select **lb-eus-app1**.

10. In the Load balancer frontend IP address dropdown menu, select the frontend IP address that is used with your application. For example, select **pip-lb-app1**.

11. In the Source NAT subnet dropdown menu, select the subnet where your application resides. For example, select **hub-vnet-eus-01/app1**.

12. Leave the remaining fields set to their defaults and click **Next: Access security**. Figure 5-2 displays the completed Outbound settings tab.

13. In the Who can request access to your service field, select the desired access security level. For example, select **Anyone with your alias**.

14. Click **Next: Tags.** Figure 5-3 displays the Access security tab.

Create private link service ···

✓ Basics   ② **Outbound settings**   ③ Access security   ④ Tags   ⑤ Review + create

A private link service enables private connections to a standard load balancer and the virtual machines behind it. Select the standard load balancer, the virtual network, and subnet containing the virtual machines. Private IP addresses will be allocated from the selected subnet. Learn more

Load balancer * ⓘ	lb-eus-app1 ⌄
Load balancer frontend IP address * ⓘ	20.119.68.47 (pip-lb-app1) ⌄
Source NAT Virtual network ⓘ	hub-vnet-eus-01 (required) ⌄
Source NAT subnet * ⓘ	hub-vnet-eus-01/app1 (10.0.2.0/24) ⌄
Enable TCP proxy V2	◯ Yes ◉ No

Private IP address settings

Configure the allocation method and IP address for each NAT IP. Increase the number of NAT IPs to compensate for higher outbound traffic. You can have up to 8 NAT IPs. Dynamic allocation will manage the allocation process for you. Static allocation will require you to specify a public IP address. Learn more

Allocation	Private IP address	Primary	
Dynamic Static			🗑
Dynamic Static		☐	

< Previous   Next : Access security >

FIGURE 5-2 Private Link service outbound settings

Create private link service ···

✓ Basics   ✓ Outbound settings   ③ **Access security**   ④ Tags   ⑤ Review + create

Determine how your private link service will be consumed by consumers without existing permissions. You can expose it using a short friendly name, and auto-approve connections from trusted subscribers. If you already have permissions to the subscription that hosts this private link service, no action is required on this page. Learn more

Visibility

The visibility setting determines who can request access to your private link service.

- **Role-based access control only**: This private link service will only be available to individuals with role-based access control permissions within your directory. (Most restrictive)
- **Restricted by subscription**: Any user with access to specific subscriptions (that you'll add below) can request access to your service, even across directories.
- **Anyone with your alias**: Anyone with your private link service alias can request access to your service. (Least restrictive)

Who can request access to your service?   ◯ Role-based access control only
   ◯ Restricted by subscription
   ◉ Anyone with your alias

Auto-approval

Select subscriptions to auto-approve from your visible subscriptions. Your private link services will be visible to all subscriptions. Learn more

Add subscriptions

Subscription

< Previous   Next : Tags >

FIGURE 5-3 Private Link service access security

15. Click **Next: Review + create**, and then click **Create**.

Note that on the Access security screen you have three options to choose from:

- Role-based access control only
- Restricted by subscription
- Anyone with your alias

The default and most restrictive option is *Role-based access control only*. This requires that anyone connecting to the service already have permission defined through RBAC to connect to your service. Selecting *Restricted by subscription* or *Anyone with your alias* allows others to request access to your service, but it does not automatically approve them by default. You can configure specific subscriptions to auto-approve requests from.

Plan and create private endpoints

Private endpoints are the consumer side of the Private Link scenario and support client connections from a subnet to a number of Azure services or a service that has been published through Private Link services.

For example, you can configure private endpoints on a subnet that contains virtual machines that need access to an Azure storage account. By default, storage accounts are accessed by using public IP addresses. With private endpoints, you can configure the storage account to be accessible by using a private IP address on the same virtual network as your VMs. This ensures private connectivity from the VMs to the service that you configure by using private, non-routable IP addresses. This can be a required configuration in many high-security or compliance environments.

To create a private endpoint for a PaaS service such as a storage account, follow these steps:

1. Sign in to the Azure portal at *https://portal.azure.com*.
2. In the search bar, search for and select **Private Link**.
3. From the Private Link center, click the **Private endpoints** blade.
4. On the Private endpoints blade, click **Add**.
5. Select the desired subscription and resource group to deploy the service in.
6. In the Name field, provide a name for the service. For example, enter **ple-eus-storage**.
7. In the Region dropdown menu, select the desired Azure region. This must be the same region as the load balancer and virtual network you plan to associate the service with. For example, select **East US**.
8. Click **Next: Resource.** Figure 5-4 displays the completed Basics tab.

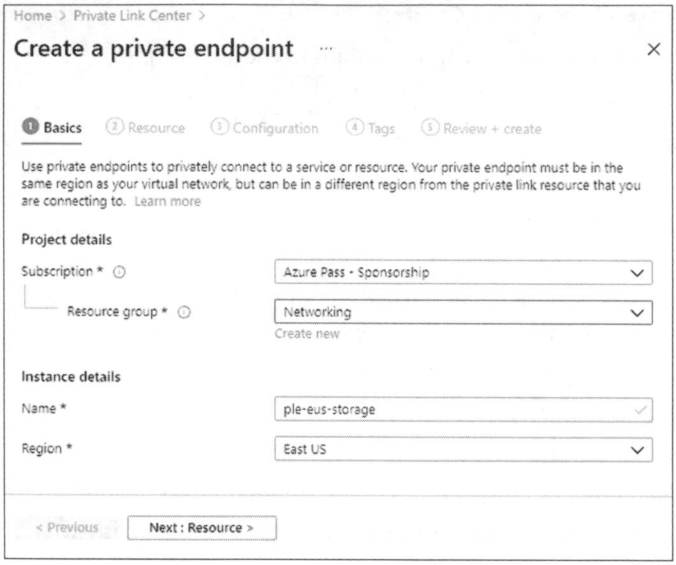

FIGURE 5-4 Private endpoint basics

9. In the Connection method field, ensure that the default, **Connect to an Azure resource in my directory**, is selected.

10. In the Subscription dropdown, ensure that your subscription is selected.

11. In the Resource type dropdown, select an Azure resource to connect to. For example, select **Microsoft.Storage/storageAccounts**.

12. In the Resource dropdown menu, select the Azure resource deployed in your subscription. For example, select the storage account named **az700app1**.

13. In the Target sub-resource dropdown menu, select the type of storage used for your app. For example, select **blob**.

14. Click **Next: Configuration**. Figure 5-5 displays the completed Resource tab.

15. In the Virtual network dropdown menu, select the virtual network where you will connect to the resources. For example, select **hub-vnet-eus-01**.

16. In the Subnet dropdown menu, select the subnet that has the address range where you want the address assigned to the resource. For example, select **hub-vnet-eus-01/app1**.

17. In the Private DNS integration section, leave the default settings and click **Next: Tags**. Figure 5-6 displays the completed Configuration tab.

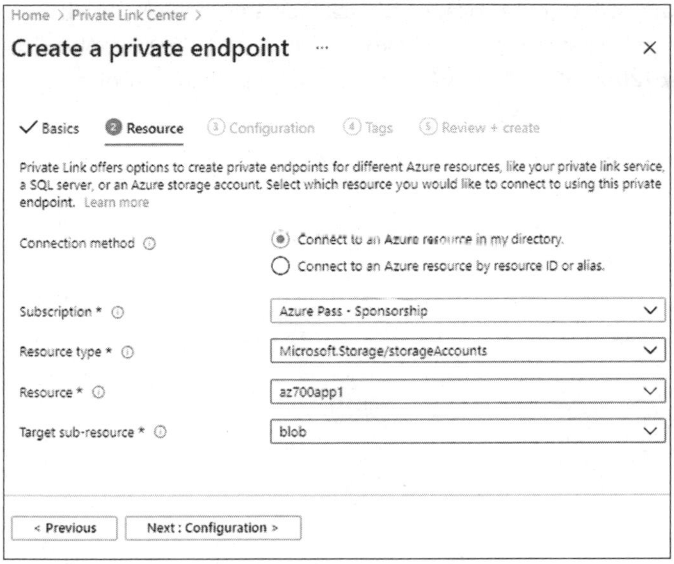

FIGURE 5-5 Private endpoint resource

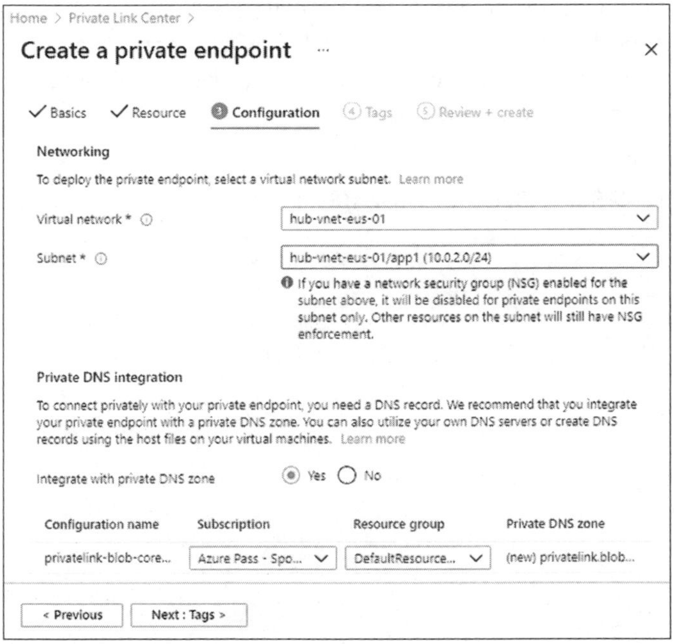

FIGURE 5-6 Private endpoint configuration

18. Click **Next: Review + create**, and then click **Create**.

19. After the deployment completes, click **Go to resource**.

20. On the Overview tab of the new resource, locate and click the name in the Network interface field. The NIC name will start with the name of the endpoint. For example, click **ple-eus-storage.nic.bab72045-96c3-43ec-b2ea-faaeff062c5a**. Figure 5-7 displays the relevant portion of the Overview blade.

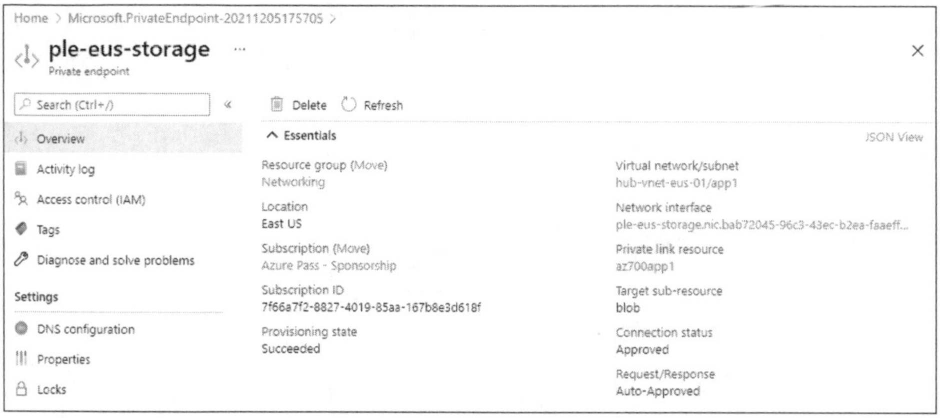

FIGURE 5-7 Private endpoint overview

21. On the Overview blade of the network interface, locate the Private IP address field. This is the IP address that is assigned to the NIC associated with the private endpoint, and how you can connect to the storage account from the same virtual network. Figure 5-8 displays the relevant portion of the NIC overview blade.

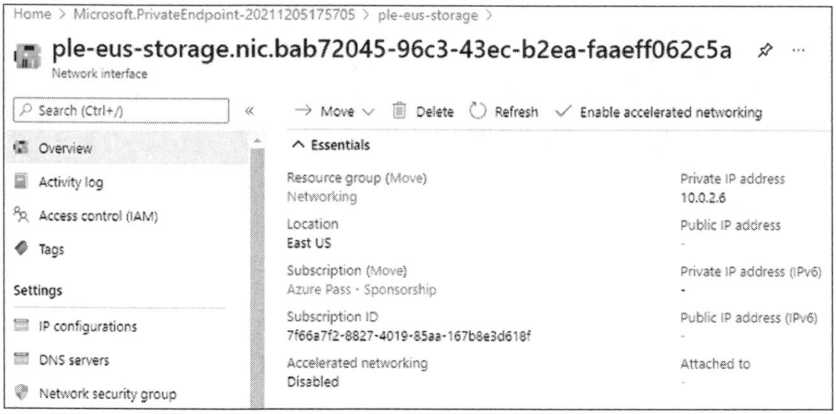

FIGURE 5-8 NIC overview

By completing these steps, you have added a private endpoint for a storage account named az700app1 and associated with the app1 subnet of the virtual network. The address range of the app1 subnet is 10.0.2.0/24, and the private endpoint is assigned an address from this range: 10.0.2.6.

With the default security in a virtual network, any resource in any of the subnets in the hub-vnet-eus-01 virtual network would be able to communicate with the storage account using the private IP address of the endpoint.

Integrate Private Link with DNS

A critical component of Private Link is DNS. Using the example from the previous section, when you create an endpoint and associate it with a subnet, that endpoint has a NIC with a private IP address. The reason this is critical is the way that Azure PaaS services work by default: with public IP addresses. Using the same storage account as in the prior section, this is the result when trying to access the blob storage of the account. For this test we'll ping the blob service:

```
ping az700app1.blob.core.windows.net
```

```
Pinging blob.blz22prdstr06a.store.core.windows.net [52.239.169.132] with 32 bytes of
data:
```

The results of the ping are not what is relevant. What the ping command reveals is that the DNS name that was tested, *az700app1.blob.core.windows.net*, translates to another name, *blob.blz22prdstr06a.store.core.windows.net*, which then resolves to a public IP address: *52.239.169.132*.

If the private endpoint has been configured and has the IP address 10.0.2.6, why isn't the private IP address returned? When you create a private endpoint, the default configuration also creates a Private DNS zone. For the storage account example, the DNS zone is named privatelink.blob.core.windows.net, and the zone has an A record that resolves to the private IP address of the NIC. This Private DNS zone gets associated with the virtual network that you configured.

Anytime that you attempt to resolve the DNS of the blob storage outside of the virtual network, it still resolves to the public IP address. Only when you resolve the name from inside the virtual network, because of the Private DNS zone associated, will the private IP address be returned. If we run the same ping test from the vm-web01 machine that is in the virtual network, these are the results:

```
ping az700app1.blob.core.windows.net
```

```
Pinging az700app1.privatelink.blob.core.windows.net [10.0.2.6] with 32 bytes of data:
```

Note that not only is the translated name different to represent the private link, but it returns the private IP address that is assigned to the storage account: 10.0.2.6.

Integrate a Private Link service with on-premises clients

Based on the information presented in the last section, the private IP address that is assigned to a service with a Private Link endpoint is only returned if the DNS request occurs within the virtual network. Therefore, the only way to integrate with on-premises clients, or even clients that are in other subscriptions, is with a DNS forwarder in the additional environment and a DNS server in the virtual network.

The DNS server in the virtual network should accept forwarded DNS requests and then use the Azure DNS server, 168.63.129.16, as its DNS server. In any location that needs to use the private IP address, such as on-premises, a DNS server needs to be configured as a conditional forwarder for the DNS names of the services you'll use in Azure. For example, the on-premises forwarder should be configured for the FQDN *blob.core.windows.net*.

The network flow of an on-premises request would follow these steps:

1. An on-premises client makes a request to the on-premises DNS server for az700app1. blob.core.windows.net.

2. The on-premises DNS server, configured with a conditional forwarder for blob.core. windows.net, forwards the request to a DNS server in the virtual network.

3. The DNS server in the virtual network is configured with Azure DNS, 168.63.129.16, and forwards the request.

4. Azure DNS responds with the private address configured with the private endpoint, 10.0.2.6.

5. The client connects directly to the Azure resource using the private IP address. Figure 5-9 outlines these five steps taken to resolve DNS from on-premises.

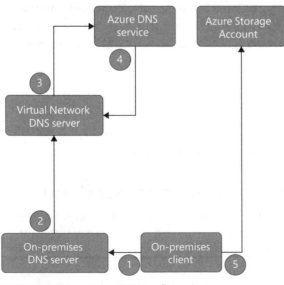

FIGURE 5-9 On-premises DNS configuration

Skill 5.2: Design and implement service endpoints

Service endpoints allow you to optimize the routing to Azure services, especially in the event that you have configured user-defined routes that might impact how a virtual machine accesses a service. Service endpoints are associated with subnets within a virtual network to give you granular control over the routing possibilities. Service endpoints can also have policies to restrict specific resources even further and can be used in combination with network security groups, Azure Firewall, and service tags to provide a fine-grain level of access control.

This skill covers how to:

- Create service endpoints
- Configure service endpoint policies
- Configure service tags

Create service endpoints

Service endpoints, not to be confused with private endpoints, are used to optimize the routing between your virtual network and Azure PaaS services such as storage, databases, app services, and more. This is particularly useful when you have configured user-defined routes that first route internet-bound traffic through a network virtual appliance or on-premises. An added benefit of service endpoints is that the resources in the virtual network do not need a public IP address to be able to access the Azure PaaS services.

Take an example of a single-region deployment in East US that has:

- Virtual machines
- Storage accounts
- Azure SQL Databases
- Azure Key Vault
- ExpressRoute

If the ExpressRoute connection has a user-defined route to send all traffic that is destined for the internet through the ExpressRoute connection, that would include traffic to the public endpoints of the listed Azure services. This means that traffic from a VM to an Azure SQL Database would traverse the ExpressRoute network and then go over the public internet from the on-premises location back to the East US public endpoint.

This configuration not only adds unnecessary latency for the database connection but then sends it over the public internet. Service endpoints prioritize the routing from the virtual network to the Azure service using the Microsoft network backbone. This also eliminates the need for any public IP address or network address translation (NAT) to be performed on the source subnet. Any traffic from the VMs to the Azure SQL Database in this example will show a source IP address of the private address of the VM.

To create a service endpoint for an existing subnet, follow these steps:

1. Sign in to the Azure portal at *https://portal.azure.com.*

2. In the search bar, search for and select **Virtual networks**.

3. In the list of virtual networks, select a previously deployed network. For example, select **hub-vnet-eus-01**.

4. From the virtual network, click the **Subnets** blade.

5. On the Subnets page, select the subnet to create a service endpoint on. For example, select **app1**.

6. In the Service Endpoints section of the subnet, click the dropdown menu and select the checkbox next to the desired service. For example, select **Microsoft.Sql**.

7. Click **Save**. Figure 5-10 displays the completed configuration.

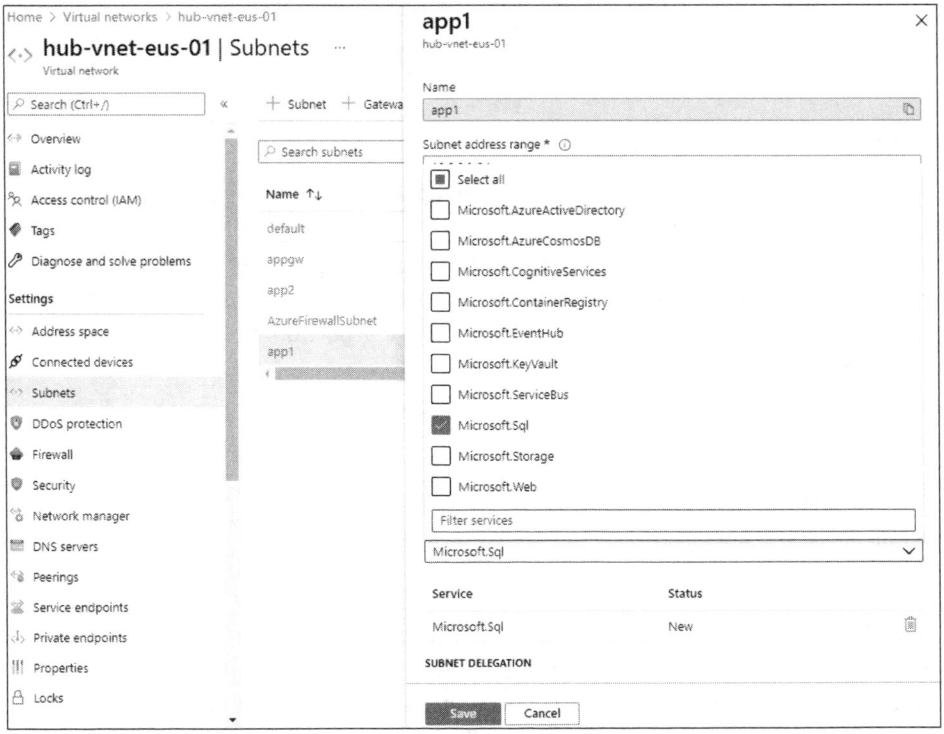

FIGURE 5-10 Create service endpoint

By completing the configuration, any traffic from the app1 subnet that is destined for an Azure SQL Database will have optimized routing from the virtual network to the service. Additionally, the source IP address field will be from the 10.0.2.0/24 range.

When making the configuration change on an existing subnet, ensure that no critical services are running during the change. A new route with the address prefixes of the service with a next hop type of *VirtualNetworkServiceEndpoint* is created, and any existing connections might be disconnected.

EXAM TIP

It can be easy to confuse service endpoints and private endpoints. Be sure to read the scenarios specifically and choose the appropriate service for what is provided.

Configure service endpoint policies

Creating a service endpoint only changes the routing from the virtual network to the destination service. By default, it does not perform any IP filtering or access control from the network to the service. Service endpoint policies allow you to configure granular access control to specific service resources. Combine these policies with network security groups to ensure that only the specific resources in a subnet can access specific PaaS resources.

When you create a policy, you specify a definition that contains the destination resource of the service. The policy allows only the traffic to the specified services; access to all other resources for that service will be denied.

As of this writing, only the Microsoft.Storage resource provider is available to configure service endpoint policies. You can optionally configure resource aliases, which are currently limited to:

- /services/Azure
- /services/Azure/Batch
- /services/Azure/DataFactory
- /services/Azure/MachineLearning
- /services/Azure/ManagedInstance
- /services/Azure/WebAPI

To create a service endpoint policy, follow these steps:

1. Sign in to the Azure portal at *https://portal.azure.com*.
2. In the search bar, search for and select **Service endpoint policy**.
3. On the Service endpoint policies page, click **Create**.
4. Select the desired subscription and resource group to deploy the service in.
5. In the Name field, provide a name for the policy. For example, enter enter **sep-eus-policy1**.
6. In the Region dropdown menu, select the desired Azure region. This must be the same region as the load balancer and virtual network you plan to associate the service with. For example, select **East US**.

7. Click **Next: Policy definitions**. Figure 5-11 displays the completed Basics tab.

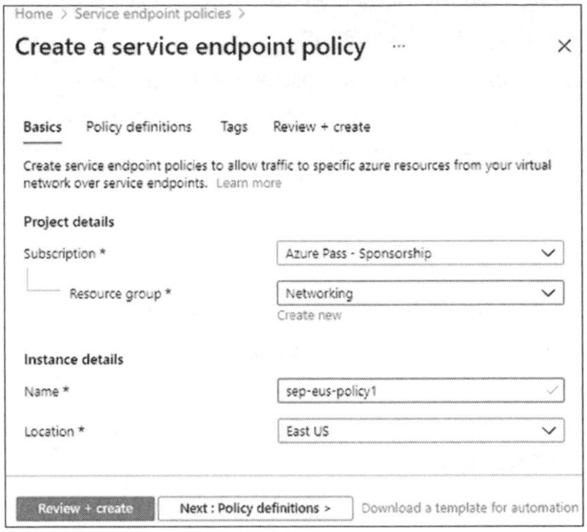

FIGURE 5-11 Create service endpoint policy basics

8. On the Policy definitions tab, click **Add a resource**.

9. In the Add a resource pane, complete the form with these settings to allow access to only one previously created Azure storage account, az700app1.

   - Service: **Microsoft.Storage**
   - Scope: **Single account**
   - Subscription: **Your subscription**
   - Resource group: **App1**
   - Resource: **az700app1**

10. Click **Add**. Figure 5-12 displays the completed Add a resource pane.

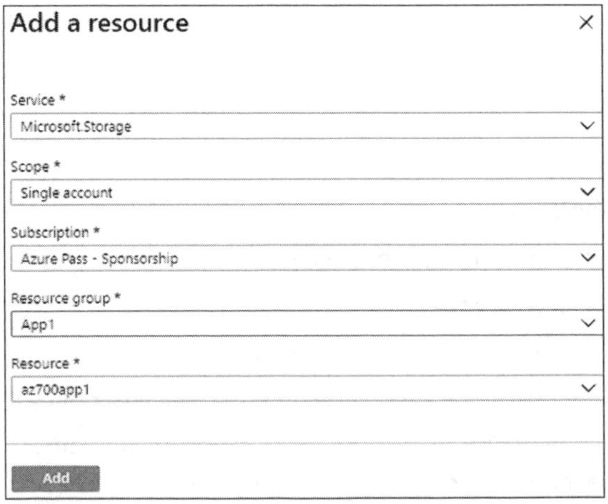

FIGURE 5-12 Service endpoint policy add a resource

11. Click **Review + Create**, and then click **Create**.

12. After the resource deploys, click **Go to resource**.

13. On the newly created policy, click the **Associated subnets** blade.

14. On the Associated subnets blade, click **Edit subnet association**. Figure 5-13 displays the new policy and menu option.

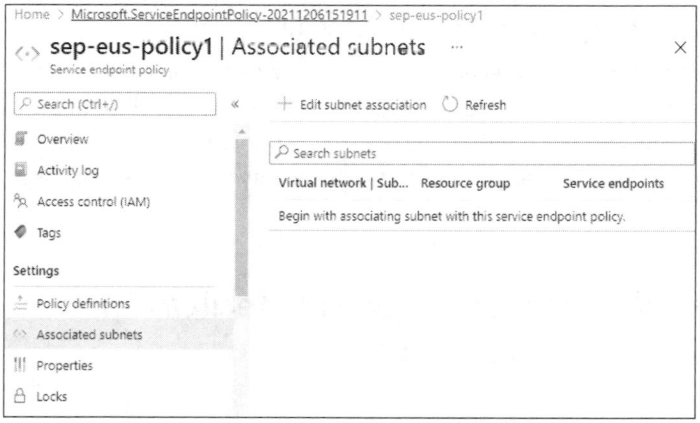

FIGURE 5-13 Service endpoint policy associated subnets

15. In the Virtual network dropdown menu, select the virtual network that contains a subnet with a service endpoint defined. For example, select **hub-vnet-eus-01**.

16. The subnet with a service endpoint that was previously configured will be displayed. Select the **checkbox** next to the subnet name.

17. Click **Apply**. Figure 5-14 displays the completed configuration.

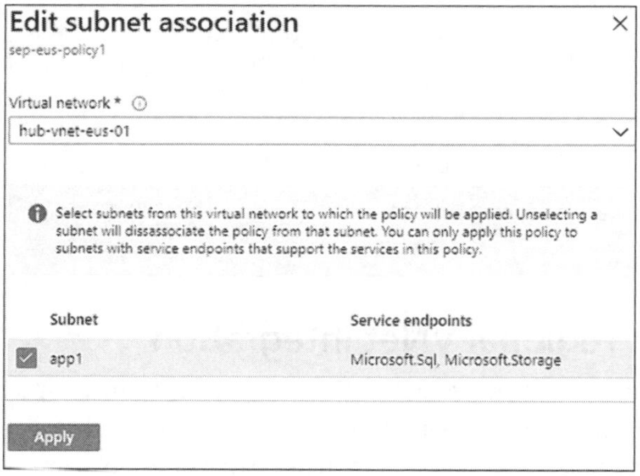

FIGURE 5-14 Service endpoint policy edit association

Configure service tags

The name of the objective listed on the exam is "configure service tags"; however, service tags themselves are not configurable by Azure administrators. Service tags represent the group of dozens, if not hundreds, of IP addresses that could be used to access a given Azure service in either one region or the global Azure infrastructure. For example, for storage accounts there is a Storage service tag that represents any IP address associated with Azure. Or there is Storage. EastUS, which represents only the storage IP addresses for the East US region.

Service tags can be used with both network security groups and Azure Firewall to filter and restrict traffic to and from specific resources in specific regions. This is useful in environments that have compliance regulations in certain countries, or data sovereignty requirements based on the application's deployment location. Configuring a network security group was discussed in Chapter 4, skill section 4.2.

Skill 5.3: Configure VNet integration for dedicated platform as a service (PaaS) services

A virtual network is typically associated with infrastructure and IaaS resources such as virtual machines. However, because virtual networks can also be the center point for VPNs, ExpressRoute, peered connections, and more, it can be important to integrate PaaS services with virtual networks.

Azure App Services are one key PaaS service that provides integration directly with virtual networks. With VNet integration, you can allow outbound communication from an App Service to other resources that are connected to the virtual network. Similar scenarios are also true with Azure Kubernetes Service (AKS) and App Service Environment (ASE).

This skill covers how to:

- Configure App Service for regional VNet integration
- Configure Azure Kubernetes Service (AKS) for regional VNet integration
- Configure clients to access App Service Environment

Configure App Service for regional VNet integration

Virtual network integration, or VNet integration, provides outbound connectivity from an App Service to the virtual network that you configure. Note that this is the reverse direction that a private endpoint provides. When you configure VNet integration on its own, it does not allow inbound communication to an App Service through the virtual network.

Configuring VNet integration is supported on Basic, Standard, Premium, Premium v2, and Premium v3 App Service SKUs. App Service Environments are deployed directly into a virtual network and do not need additional configuration to integrate into a virtual network.

By configuring VNet integration, the code running in an App Service has network connectivity to the resources in the virtual network. For regional VNet integration, there must be a dedicated subnet in the virtual network to integrate with. The subnet does not need a specific name, but it does require the subnet to be a minimum size depending on the number of scale instances the App Service Plan might use. Table 5-1 outlines the available addresses and maximum scale instances.

TABLE 5-1 VNet integration subnet requirements

Subnet size	Maximum available addresses	Maximum scale instances
/28	11	5
/27	27	13
/26	59	29

By default, when you enable VNet integration, a Route All setting is enabled. When Route All is enabled, all traffic leaving an App Service is subject to the NSGs and UDRs that are associated with the integrated subnet. Combine this setting with either service or private endpoints, and you can configure private communication from an App Service to a bulk of Azure PaaS services.

To integrate an existing App Service instance to a virtual network, follow these steps:

1. Sign in to the Azure portal at *https://portal.azure.com*.
2. In the search bar, search for and select **App Services**.
3. On the App Services page, click the **Networking** blade.
4. On the Networking blade, in the Outbound Traffic section, click **VNet integration**. Figure 5-15 displays the Networking blade.

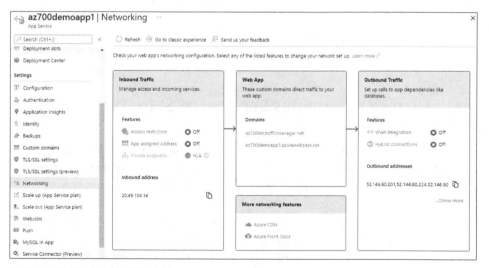

FIGURE 5-15 App Service Networking

5. On the VNet Integration page, click **Add VNet**.

6. In the Virtual network dropdown menu, select the name of a virtual network to associate with the App Service. For example, select **hub-vnet-eus-01**.

7. In the Subnet field, select **Create New Subnet**.

8. In the Subnet Name field, provide a name for the new subnet. For example, enter **ASIntegration**.

9. In the Virtual Network Address Block dropdown menu, select the appropriate address space to add the subnet to. For example, select **10.0.0.0/16**.

10. In the Subnet Address Block field, provide a new IP range for the subnet that is available in the existing address space. For example, specify **10.0.5.0/24**.

11. Click **OK**. Figure 5-16 displays the completed configuration.

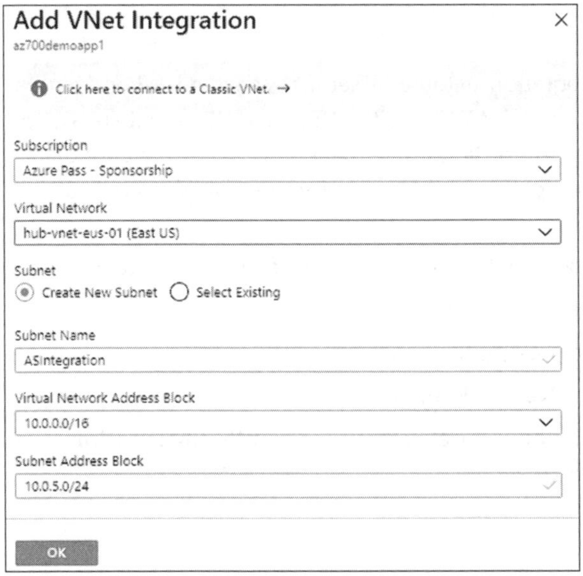

FIGURE 5-16 Add VNet Integration

Configure Azure Kubernetes Service (AKS) for regional VNet integration

Unlike with App Service, there is no specific menu or configuration option for integrating a virtual network with Azure Kubernetes Service (AKS). This could be open to interpretation to mean either deploying a private AKS cluster or using the *kubenet* networking option when deploying the cluster.

With private AKS clusters, the control plane (API) of the cluster has a private internal IP address that is used for network traffic between the API server and the node pools. With AKS, the control plane and API server are managed for you. You can configure communication between these two services by using Azure Private Link. A private AKS cluster also uses a private DNS zone. The agent nodes have A records created in the private zone that resolves to their private IP address.

NEED MORE REVIEW? **AZURE KUBERNETES SERVICE PRIVATE CLUSTERS**

For more information on AKS private clusters, visit *https://docs.microsoft.com/en-us/azure/ aks/private-clusters.*

When you deploy an AKS cluster using kubenet, the nodes receive an IP address on the virtual network. Any additional pods cannot communicate with each other directly, and require additional routing and IP forwarding for cross-pod connectivity. These UDRs and the IP forwarding are maintained and configured by the AKS service. However, you can deploy a load balancing solution with a custom route table for custom management.

NEED MORE REVIEW? **AZURE KUBERNETES SERVICE VIRTUAL NETWORKS**

For more information on AKS virtual network concepts, visit *https://docs.microsoft.com/en-us/ azure/aks/concepts-network#azure-virtual-networks.*

Configure clients to access App Service Environment

As of this writing, there are three versions of App Service Environment (ASE). For this section, we will focus only on ASEv3, the latest version available. App Service Environments are typically used when the scale requirements are more than 30 individual instances, or when there are other security requirements for a single-tenant system or isolated network hosting.

When you deploy an app into an ASE that uses a single subnet, the app uses the inbound address that is assigned to the ASE. If the ASE has an internal virtual IP (VIP), then the inbound address will be the VIP for all apps that are deployed. Finally, if the ASE has an external VIP, then the inbound address to the app will be the public IP and registered in public DNS.

The number of addresses that you need in an ASE will vary depending on how many instances and traffic the apps will have. The recommended size for an ASE is a /24 CIDR address prefix—for example, 10.0.5.0/24. The minimum address space of an ASE is a /27 address prefix. If you choose to deploy a smaller subnet, it is possible that the addresses in the subnet will be exhausted and the ASE will not scale.

When you configure an ASE, there are a few network components to define:

- **ASE virtual network.** The virtual network the ASE is deployed to.
- **ASE subnet.** The subnet that the ASE is deployed to.
- **Domain suffix.** The domain suffix used by the apps in the ASE.
- **Virtual IP.** Either an internal or an external virtual IP address.

- **Inbound address.** The VIP that you choose and how inbound connectivity is established.
- **Default outbound address.** The IP address used when the ASE makes any outbound connections.

For the ASE to accept inbound connections, any NSG should accept traffic on both ports 80 and 443 for the web traffic. You can also open ports 4022, 4024, and 4026 for Visual Studio remote debugging traffic, and port 8172 for the Web Deploy service.

If you plan to use your own DNS for clients to connect to the ASE, then a zone for the ASE must be created using the asename.appserviceenvironment.net domain. You can use both public and private DNS zones depending on where the clients will be connecting from.

Chapter summary

- Private Link has two components: private services and private endpoints.
- Private services allow you to publish your own application as a provider for other subscriptions to access the application from as a consumer.
- Private endpoints are the consumer side of Private Link and establish the virtual NIC that connects to a private service.
- For Azure services, DNS is a critical component of Private Link. Externally, services still resolve with public IP addresses. Only the virtual network from which the private endpoint is configured returns a private IP address.
- To configure hybrid environments with private endpoints, you must configure additional DNS services with conditional forwarding.
- Service endpoints provide optimized routing to Azure PaaS services but still use a public IP address for the service.
- Service endpoints do not require public IP addresses to be on the Azure resources that you deploy and manage.
- Service endpoint policies allow you to configure granular access restrictions for service endpoints.
- Service tags represent the address prefixes that are used by Azure for a given service.
- Service tags can be a global tag or defined by service per region.
- App Service supports both private endpoints and VNet integration. Private endpoints support inbound connections to App Service. VNet integration supports outbound connections from App Service.
- VNet integration requires a dedicated subnet on the virtual network it will be associated with.

- AKS can be integrated with virtual networks through a private cluster or with kubenet.
- ASEv3 are associated with a virtual network and can be deployed to a single subnet.
- The recommended subnet size for ASE integration is a /24 address range.
- The minimum subnet size for ASE integration is a /27 address range.
- The NSG for the subnet the ASE uses should accept both 80 and 443 traffic.
- Other ports can be open for Visual Studio debugging traffic (4022, 4024, 4026) and Web Deploy traffic (8172).
- ASE uses the appserviceenvironment.net domain for DNS.

Thought experiment

In this thought experiment, demonstrate your skills and knowledge of the topics covered in this chapter. You can find the answers in the section that follows.

An organization has an application that it intends to sell to its customers. It expects its customers to access the service from their own subscriptions. Some of the organization's customers have a requirement to access the service by using private IP addresses. Part of the application for the organization will use Azure SQL Databases. The organization also wants to use a private IP address range to communicate from its services to the database.

Additionally, the organization has a high-secure virtual network with financial trading compliance requirements. One of the requirements is that all traffic must flow through a firewall. Currently, the organization is sending all traffic from the dedicated virtual network to its on-premises firewall. Network traffic in the high-secure environment must not go over the public internet when accessing Azure services. Additionally, the services will be deployed in only two Azure regions. Traffic attempting to reach Azure services in other regions must be blocked.

Finally, the organization has decided to use App Service Environments for one of its applications. It needs to plan how to configure Web Deploy and Visual Studio remote debugging with the app. The app should grow to over 30 instances and must be able to scale without network limits.

1. How should the organization publish access to its application?
2. How should the organization access the Azure SQL Database service?
3. How can the organization meet the compliance goals in the high-secure environment?
4. What can the organization use to block traffic to other Azure regions?
5. What should the organization do to use Web Deploy and Visual Studio remote debugging?
6. What size subnet should the ASE be deployed to?

Thought experiment answers

This section contains the solution to the thought experiment. Each answer explains why the answer choice is correct.

1. How should the organization publish access to its application?

    The organization should consider using Azure Private Link services to publish the application. This will allow its customers to create private endpoints and connect to the application using private IP addresses.

2. How should the organization access the Azure SQL Database service?

    The organization should use a private endpoint to access the Azure SQL Database instance. This will allow the organization to create a virtual NIC in the subnet it wants to configure and allow private IP addresses to be used to access the database.

3. How can the organization meet the compliance goals in the high-secure environment?

    To meet the compliance requirements, the organization should consider using service endpoints. This will optimize the network traffic for Azure services and ensure that they do not go over the public internet.

4. What can the organization use to block traffic to other Azure regions?

    The organization can use service tags with network security groups to block traffic to regions that are not being used.

5. What should the organization do to use Web Deploy and Visual Studio remote debugging?

    The NSG that is associated with the subnet that the ASE is deployed in should have the following ports open: 4022, 4024, 4026, and 8172.

6. What size subnet should the ASE be deployed to?

    To provide the maximum amount of scale, the subnet should provide a /24 address range.

Index

A

O-P

Q-R

Plug into learning at

MicrosoftPressStore.com

The Microsoft Press Store by Pearson offers:

- Free U.S. shipping

- Buy an eBook, get three formats – Includes PDF, EPUB, and MOBI to use with your computer, tablet, and mobile devices

- Print & eBook Best Value Packs

- eBook Deal of the Week – Save up to 50% on featured title

- Newsletter – Be the first to hear about new releases, announcements, special offers, and more

- Register your book – Find companion files, errata, and product updates, plus receive a special coupon* to save on your next purchase

Hear about it first.

Since 1984, Microsoft Press has helped IT professionals, developers, and home office users advance their technical skills and knowledge with books and learning resources.

Sign up today to deliver exclusive offers directly to your inbox.

- New products and announcements

- Free sample chapters

- Special promotions and discounts

- ... and more!

MicrosoftPressStore.com/newsletters